*Routledge Revivals*

# Textual Communication

First published in 1991, *Textual Communication* examines the character and development of the novel from Richardson to Nabokov in relation to the printing and publishing industry.

The book blends literary theory with a historical analysis of communication, carrying the debate on the novel beyond the pioneering work of Booth and Genette, while responding to and taking issue with the writings of Foucault, Baudrillard, McLuhan, and Barthes. It analyses the structures of the industry which manufactured and marketed novels to show how novelists solved the communication problems that they faced in the eighteenth, nineteenth, and twentieth centuries. It also pinpoints critical moments in the history of the novel when new narrative strategies appeared, and places them in the context of the communication environment in which the texts were produced.

Using Lacan's theory of the divided subject, the book defines textual communication as a form of interaction in which two divided subjects, the author and the reader, try to communicate with each other under or against the law of the book market, censorship, literary conventions, and language.

# Textual Communication

A Print-Based Theory of the Novel

By Maurice Couturier

First published in 1991
by Routledge

This edition first published in 2021 by Routledge
2 Park Square, Milton Park, Abingdon, Oxon, OX14 4RN
and by Routledge
605 Third Avenue, New York, NY 10017

*Routledge is an imprint of the Taylor & Francis Group, an informa business*

© 1991 Maurice Couturier

All rights reserved. No part of this book may be reprinted or reproduced or utilised in any form or by any electronic, mechanical, or other means, now known or hereafter invented, including photocopying and recording, or in any information storage or retrieval system, without permission in writing from the publishers.

**Publisher's Note**
The publisher has gone to great lengths to ensure the quality of this reprint but points out that some imperfections in the original copies may be apparent.

**Disclaimer**
The publisher has made every effort to trace copyright holders and welcomes correspondence from those they have been unable to contact.

A Library of Congress record exists under LCCN: 90008268

ISBN 13: 978-0-367-74325-3 (hbk)
ISBN 13: 978-1-003-15714-4 (ebk)

Book DOI: 10.4324/9781003157144

# Textual Communication

## A print-based theory of the novel

Maurice Couturier

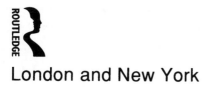

London and New York

First published 1991
by Routledge
11 New Fetter Lane, London EC4P 4EE

Simultaneously published in the USA and Canada
by Routledge
a division of Routledge, Chapman and Hall, Inc.
29 West 35th Street, New York, NY 10001

© 1991 Maurice Couturier

Typeset in 10/12pt Bembo by
Ponting–Green Publishing Services, London

Printed in Great Britain by
T J Press (Padstow) Ltd, Padstow, Cornwall

All rights reserved. No part of this book may be reprinted
or reproduced or utilized in any form or by any electronic,
mechanical, or other means, now known or hereafter
invented, including photocopying and recording, or in any
information storage or retrieval system, without permission
in writing from the publishers.

**British Library Cataloguing in Publication Data**

Couturier, Maurice
 Textual communication: a print-based theory of the
 novel.
 1. Fiction. Forms: Novels – Critical studies
 I. Title
 809.3

**Library of Congress Cataloging in Publication Data**

Couturier, Maurice
 Textual communication: a print-based theory of the novel /
 Maurice Couturier.
  p. cm.
 Includes bibliographical references.
 1. Fiction–History and criticism–Theory, etc. 2. Fiction–20th
 century–History and criticism–Theory, etc. 3. Fiction–Publishing.
 I. Title.
 PN3331.C68  1991
 809.3–dc20    90-8268

ISBN 0–415–03920–7

# Contents

|  | Introduction | vii |
|---|---|---|
| 1 | **The printing industry** | 1 |
|  | *The early history of the printing industry* | 1 |
|  | *The eighteenth-century bookseller* | 15 |
|  | *The law* | 23 |
|  | *England* | 23 |
|  | *France* | 32 |
|  | *The author* | 36 |
|  | *The public* | 42 |
|  | *Conclusion* | 47 |
| 2 | **The bookhood of the novel** | 52 |
|  | *The object* | 52 |
|  | *Presentation* | 52 |
|  | *Title-page* | 56 |
|  | *Advertisements and dedications* | 66 |
|  | *Prefaces* | 70 |
|  | *Tristram Shandy: An anatomy of the printed book* | 87 |
|  | *Conclusion* | 91 |
| 3 | **The many births of the novel** | 93 |
|  | *Introduction: The New Rhetoric* | 93 |
|  | *Mock epics* | 97 |
|  | *The picaresque novel* | 110 |
|  | *The epistolary novel* | 124 |
|  | *Conclusion: Novel vs romance* | 138 |
| 4 | **The modernist novel** | 145 |
|  | *The environment* | 145 |
|  | *The market* | 145 |
|  | *The law* | 152 |

|   | | |
|---|---|---|
| | Twin-voiced openings | 158 |
| | The protagonist's 'I' | 172 |
| | The dialogue | 172 |
| | The interior monologue | 177 |
| | Free indirect speech revisited | 180 |
| | Conclusion: Telling and showing | 189 |
| 5 | **The postmodernist novel** | 193 |
| | The environment | 194 |
| | The market | 194 |
| | The law | 201 |
| | Voiceless openings | 206 |
| | The black box | 215 |
| | Conclusion: Textual communication | 225 |
| | Epilogue: Is the author really dead? | 231 |
| | Bibliography | 236 |
| | Index | 244 |

# Introduction

One of the first literary critics to have sensed the role of print in the rise of the modern novel is Ian Watt. In his now famous book published in 1957, he wrote:

> The literary importance of the new medium is difficult to analyze . . . It was not until the rise of journalism that a new form of writing arose which was wholly dependent on printed performance, and the novel is perhaps the only literary genre which is essentially connected with the medium of print: it is therefore very appropriate that our first novelist should have been a printer himself.
> (Watt 1967: 196)

Watt had the right intuition, but he did not exploit it to elaborate his theory of the novel. He had other preoccupations, of course; he wanted to study the social and political environment in which the eighteenth-century novel appeared. Yet this book certainly paved the way for communication-oriented approaches to the modern novel.

Five years after the publication of *The Rise of the Novel*, Marshall McLuhan published his controversial *Gutenberg Galaxy* in which he analysed some of the most important changes brought about by the invention and development of print. He showed how print turned the public into a patron, and suggested that it encouraged the development of 'equitone prose' and eventually that of the fixed point of view (McLuhan 1962: 273–5). One of his disciples, Walter Ong, later made a stronger claim on the subject in *Orality and Literacy*:

The print world gave birth to the novel, which eventually made the definitive break with episodic structure, though the novel may not always have been so tightly organized in climactic form as many plays. The novelist was engaged more specifically with a text and less with auditors, imagined or real (for printed prose romances were often written to be read aloud).

(Ong 1982: 148–9)

Following McLuhan's suggestion, Ong tried to show how print promoted the unity of plot and the unity of point of view in the modern novel. The theory is not sufficiently grounded in the study of actual novels, but it is largely correct. The modern novel does belong to the 'Gutenberg Galaxy': the word 'novel' is almost synonymous with printed literature, just as the French word 'romance' was originally synonymous with literature written in the vernacular, as we will see later.

Neither communication theorists nor literary critics have so far exploited this important intuition that the novel owes its existence, originality, and development to the new medium. Since Proust's rejection of Sainte-Beuve's historical and biographical approach to writing and criticism, since I. A. Richards and New Criticism, since Russian Formalism, the modern critics have tried to objectify the text which, until then, had usually been studied from the author's angle. They have often been encouraged to do so where the novel is concerned by the fact that the textual strategies have become so elaborate that the author now seems to have totally faded out of his books. By constituting the novel into a semiotic object, the critics have been able to study it more scientifically, from the Other's angle as it were, without being hindered by the author's intentions. Wayne C. Booth's *The Rhetoric of Fiction* (1961) was an important stage in this respect, though it remained largely author-oriented as the title suggests. It was Gérard Genette's *Figures III*, published in 1972, which more or less concluded this semiotic stage in this century-long evolution. This book, which has undeniably been one of the most useful, pedagogically, in the last generation, presents an elaborate analysis of an objectivized *Remembrance of Things Past*, yet it reads, at times, like a *Contre Proust*.

It is because the structuralists and poststructuralists

consistently refused to raise the question of the author that this objectification, this near fetishization of the text has taken place. Foucault, himself a structuralist, sensed decades before anyone that the critics would have to adopt a new stance some day if they wanted to attain a new legitimacy. In his article 'What is an Author?' originally written in 1969, he said:

> Perhaps it is time to study discourses not only in terms of their expressive value or formal transformations, but according to their modes of existence. The modes of circulation, valorization, attribution, and appropriation of discourses vary with each culture and are modified within each. The manner in which they are articulated according to social relationships can be more readily understood, I believe, in the activity of the author-function and in its modifications, than in the themes or concepts that discourses set in motion.
>
> (Foucault 1980:158)

Foucault was interested in discourses, not in fetishized texts or idealized institutions. In his books on prisons, psychiatric hospitals, and sex, he always insisted on studying the 'modes of existence' of the discourses produced around those institutions and topics.

The present book is an attempt to study the rise and development of the modern novel in reference to its 'modes of existence' and particularly to print. Starting from Watt's and McLuhan's intuitions, I have tried to analyse the structures of the industry which manufactured and marketed the novels in order to show how the novelist, through his narrative strategies, managed to solve the communication problems he had to face in each period, that is, roughly, in the eighteenth century, in the late nineteenth and early twentieth centuries, and finally in the last thirty-five years.

I have no intention of rewriting the history of the publishing industry, nor that of the novel. Many important historians and critics, on whose authority I rely heavily here, have already done that. I am concerned only with the most critical moments in the history of the novel when new narrative strategies appeared; I want to show the connection between the changes in the communication environment and the main shifts in the rhetoric of the novelistic text. More space is going to be devoted to textual analysis than to history proper; but, instead of analysing the narrative strategies semiotically, I will study them in terms of communication and interaction. This comparatively new approach, if it needs a name, could be labelled 'textual communication' criticism.

As almost everybody agrees, now, McLuhan exaggerated the logic of the media and underestimated the responsibility of the communicating subjects. Bateson, Goffman, Watzlawick, and their colleagues, at almost the same time, were developing their theory of interaction which is concerned both with the communication system and the involvement of the subjects. The pragmaticians, Grice, Strawson, Austin, or Searle, on the other hand, who were sometimes unaware of the work being done in the field of psychology by Bateson and his disciples in and around Palo Alto, developed theories of verbal communication which are very close, in many respects, to those of the Palo Alto circle. Yet what was lacking in all those approaches was a coherent theory of the subject which often made it difficult to explore such boundary but vital phenomena as the unsaid and the unconscious in verbal and non-verbal communication.

This was the reason why Lacan arrogantly rejected all these theories. He was slightly unfair, for these theories do not necessarily contradict his own but sometimes complement it. Yet it is true that the subject posited by McLuhan, Bateson, and Austin, for instance, is the Cartesian subject of knowledge, whereas Lacan's subject is the split subject of the unconscious and desire labouring under the law of the Other. I will make use of Lacan's theory in my attempt to define textual communication as a form of interaction in which two divided subjects, the author and the reader, try to communicate with each other under or against the law of the book market, censorship, literary conventions, and the language (the Lacanian 'Other'), while seemingly addressing idealized images of themselves.

More space will be devoted to the eighteenth century than to the other two periods, the modernist and the postmodernist. The first chapter is almost entirely historical: it gives a general presentation of the book market in eighteenth-century England and France, and tries to describe the double bind in which the novelist was caught from the start. The second describes the various aspects of the novel as a book: its format, its title-page, with particular emphasis on the problem of anonymity, the dedications, and the prefaces; it ends with a brief study of *Tristram Shandy* as an anatomy of the printed book. The third chapter deals with the many births of the modern novel in the eighteenth century according to the three modes of literary discourse, the lyrical, the dramatic, and the epic.

The fourth chapter, on the modernist novel, begins with a brief description of the new environment in which the modernist novelist had to work, with emphasis on censorship; it then shows how the modernist novelist, who was acutely aware of the law of the Other, tried to disentangle his 'I' from those of his narrators and protagonists in order to promote the showing effect of his texts. This chapter pays particular attention to so-called 'free indirect speech' which Ann Banfield calls 'represented speech and thought'. The last chapter, which is about the postmodernist novel, also opens with a description of the new environment; it goes on with an investigation of the many strategies used by the postmodernist novelist in his attempt to become the ultimate law-giver and to imprison his reader in the black box of the book. The conclusion offers a critical reading of Foucault's article on the author-function and reassesses the myth of the death of the author.

This book has a history of its own, like the novels it analyses. Its literary foundations were laid years ago in a 700-page dissertation on Nabokov's novels which addressed some of the subjects developed here, as well as in many subsequent publications on postmodernist fiction, Barthelme in particular. Its communication foundations were pedagogical and interdisciplinary: six years ago, my colleagues at the University of Nice and I created a department called 'Art, Communication, Languages' to promote the study not only of verbal and non-verbal communication but also of the arts which constitute sophisticated forms of communication. Among many other things, we started a creative writing programme, a comparatively new thing in France. Many of the subjects addressed here were first discussed with them as well as with my colleagues at the research centre which I chair within the English Department, the CRELA. I take this opportunity to thank them warmly.

I would also like to express my deep gratitude to my wife,

who has helped me articulate some of my ideas in a day-to-day dialogue, and to Janice Price who, all these years, has patiently guided me and supported me morally by showing her faith in the book.

Nice and Los Angeles, April 1989

# Chapter 1

# The printing industry

With the invention of the printing press in the fifteenth century, the structure of the book trade changed completely. The church, whose role in that trade had been important through its many authors, rewriters, translators, and copyists, was gradually supplanted by the industry which, in turn, tried to appropriate the texts it published. But the rapid growth of this new trade soon induced the legislator to intervene, either for political or for economic reasons; not unfrequently, it managed to use the members of the industry as its agents to enforce its many laws and regulations. The new technology, along with the growing complicity between the state and the industry, and the rise of a genuine market, created a new environment and promoted a new form of communication between author and reader.

## THE EARLY HISTORY OF THE PRINTING INDUSTRY

As M. T. Clanchy, Lucien Febvre, Henri-Jean Martin, and other historians have explained, the publication of a religious book or a literary work before Gutenberg did not necessarily imply, as it does now, reproducing it in hundreds or thousands of copies and distributing it to prospective customers around the country. Clanchy chronicles how the troubadour Jaufre Rudel, Lord of Blaye, sent a poem to the Comte de Marche *c*.1150 ' "without a parchment document" (*senes breu de parguamina*) by the mouth of the jongleur, Filhol. The jongleur is thus being used as a kind of living letter' (Clanchy 1988: 143). Many of the longer texts were likewise published orally. Clanchy cites the example of Gerald of Wales who published his *Topography of Ireland* c.1188 'by reading it at Oxford to different audiences on three successive days' (148). This was the easiest and the cheapest way for the author to make his text known to a large public, without surrendering his rights upon it. The author 'published' his written text by reading publicly, each new reading constituting, as it were, a new edition. The reader, in this case, was not the audience but the author himself; the listeners, who memorized what they could, knew all the time that the 'Real Text', as Pynchon would have phrased it (Pynchon 1975: 520–1), existed somewhere in the writer's hand (or hands).

This method of publication gradually disappeared as the spoken word became less reliable and valuable than the written and printed word. For the author, this development was only a mixed blessing, as Febvre and Martin explain:

> It was absolutely impossible for them to preserve any kind of copyright on their works, unless they jealously kept for themselves the text they had composed or adapted. But if they had acted like this, they would have been unable to gratify that sense of pride which any creator seeks by making himself known to the largest public possible.
>
> (Febvre and Martin 1971: 29; my translation)

This text is worth studying. It describes the paradoxical situation in which the author will increasingly find himself as manuscript and printed literature develops: he will seek to be famous and admired, and will need therefore to publicize his text; at the same time, he will refuse to surrender his rights in it, knowing that it will start to be plundered and misinterpreted from the moment it is no longer supported by his presence and his voice.

Even before printing was invented, a number of texts started to be published in comparatively large quantity. At first, most of the copies were made in and for the monasteries, but when the universities started to appear and expand, it became necessary to copy more and more texts, and in larger and larger quantities. This gave birth to a technique called the *pecia* (meaning a signature or section of a book): the stationer who owned an *exemplar*, that is, a copy of the text, divided it into as many sections as it contained and rented them out to different customers or copyists. This way many copies could be made at the same time. The work would be done by professional copyists, such as the monk Lydgate who copied texts in English for the public until his death in 1466. Such a technique did not allow the wide circulation of texts that we know now, yet Febvre and Martin cite the case of the *Voyage de Jean de Mandeville* completed in 1356 and of which 250 manuscript copies have reached us in different languages (1971: 22–36).

The medieval fiction-writer was more rarely a creator than a rewriter. His activity did not differ much, at first, from that of the more traditional (that is, oral) storyteller who memorized a number of narratives and recited them from castle to castle or from village to village, editing them in the process. He would take a story which circulated orally and write it down, usually adding a great deal of his own, either accidentally or deliberately. Famous works such as *La Chanson de Roland*, *La Châtelaine de Vergi*, *Aucassin et Nicolette*, *La Farce de Maître Pathelin*, or the troubadour novel *Flamenca* as we know them now are often the written versions of older narratives which had circulated orally until a clerk or a scribe decided or was asked to write them down.

In some rare cases, the name of the scribe has come down to us. For example, the story of Amadis de Gaule, which was known in Spain and Portugal as early as the fourteenth century, was written down in thick volumes by Garcia Rodriguez de Montalvo at the turn of the sixteenth century. The first printed edition of that famous romance came out in Saragossa in 1508. It is Montalvo's work which the curate and the barber discover, among other romances of chivalry, in Don Quixote's library (chapter VI of *Don Quixote*). More than sixty editions were published in Spanish during the sixteenth century, plus a large number in French, Italian, English, German, and Dutch (Febvre and Martin 1971: 398).

Should Montalvo be considered as the author of *Amadis de Gaule*? The word *auteur* appeared in French in the twelfth century from the Latin *auctor*, itself derived from the verb *augere*, meaning 'to increase, to enlarge'. According to the Littré dictionary, Froissart was the first writer to call himself an *auteur* in the fifteenth century. In the seventeenth century, Furetière related the word *auteur* to the Greek *autor*, and he explained that an author was not only an increaser but a '*créateur*' (Viala 1985: 285). The word appeared in English around the fourteenth century with the spelling '*auctor*' derived from the confusion, in medieval Latin, between *auctor* and *actor*. The word did not apply only to writers but to all kinds of creators or inventors. Chaucer called Christ 'the auctour of matrimony' in 1386 (*OED*). The Latin root *augere* was soon forgotten both in French and in English. In Johnson's *Dictionary*, there are four definitions, none of them related to the Latin root: 'The first beginner or mover of any thing', 'the Efficient; he that effects or produces any thing', 'The first writer of any thing', and 'A writer in general' (Johnson 1755: 'Author').

In the accepted sense, Montalvo cannot be called the author of *Amadis de Gaule*. His name would probably never have reached us if he had not also been governor of Medina del Campo; it is associated with the book not only because he transcribed and added to the old story but because he had the money and influence to have the book printed and marketed.

For, in those days, the rights to a book derived more from one's ability to market it than from one's capacity to write it. The ordinary author of a written text (be it a romance or a work of history or theology) had no way of claiming his rights or of protecting them durably. His status was often that of a menial working for the church, as Lough explains:

> Many medieval writers were tonsured 'clerks' and therefore in a position to hold livings in the Church without necessarily being ordained priests. No doubt some of the authors of anonymous works came into this category, as well as certain of those who are little more than names to us; it has been suggested, for instance, that Chrétien was perhaps a canon at Troyes.
>
> (Lough 1978: 24)

The situation will continue in France after the invention of printing: Ronsard, Baïf, and Du Bellay all had livings or church titles. Antoine Héroët, Pontus de Tyard, and Amyot were bishops. They did not define themselves primarily as authors but as members of the institution which either hired their quills or left them enough spare time to practise their 'hobby'. In many cases, they did not claim to have any more rights in their works than has a mason in the house he has been hired to build.

When an author worked independently of the church and was patronized by a nobleman or a member of the royal family, he usually found it much easier to claim his rights in his works, especially through the dedication. Many medieval works were dedicated to the King, a member of his family, a *seigneur* or even municipal authorities who gave the author some money in return. Lough cites the example of Guillaume de Machaut who received 300 *écus* from Amédé VI, Comte de Savoie, for a poem dedicated to him, and also that of Arnoul Gréban who received ten *écus d'or* in 1452, 'for a copy of his *Mystéres de la Passion*' (1978: 24). This was apparently the only payment the author ever received for his work which, from that moment, fell into the hands of the copyists and booksellers who were not required to give him additional money. As we shall see, the practice will continue long after the invention of printing. Members of the church often sought patronage, though they had other sources of income. Ronsard dedicated some of his works to the Regent, Cathérine de Médicis; he was even patronized by foreign sovereigns: his *Elégies, Mascarades and Bergerie*, published in 1565, was dedicated to Queen Elizabeth of England (Lough 1978: 53).

Not enough attention has been paid to those dedications which, in most cases, are not even reprinted in our modern editions. The author usually begins by paying tribute to the dedicatee and by declaring himself his obedient servant; he thanks him for accepting the poem or the book, without ever mentioning, however, that he is usually being paid (or expects to be paid) for lavishing such compliments upon the exalted person or institution he is dedicating his work to. However, the dedication was not only a way of thanking the dedicatee for his generosity. In those days when so many works were published anonymously, a dedication ensured that the name of the author would henceforth be associated with that of the dedicatee. The latter, who was usually responsible for having the work copied and distributed among his friends, always made sure that the dedication was reproduced in each copy since it contributed so much to his prestige. This guaranteed that the author's name would not be skipped by the copyist who was often too prone to put his own instead.

At the same time, the dedicatee, who was usually a political or religious figure of high rank, indirectly pledged that the work was commendable. Boccaccio begs Andreina Acciajuoli to have his *De claris mulieribus* dedicated to him for the following reason: 'If you consider it worth your while to encourage my book to produce itself in public [*procedendi in publicum*], once it is broadcast [*emissus*] under your patronage, it will be spared, I think, all malignant insults' (Febvre and Martin 1971: 30; my translation).

The invention of print did not change the author's plight substantially, at first. Rabelais, who was a monk and a doctor, did not apparently seek or find any patron for his first two books. *Pantagruel* and *Gargantua* were published in Lyons by Claude Nourry and François Just respectively, the first in 1532 and the second in 1534 or 1535. The author, who then lived in that city, did not sign his books but offered them to the public under the anagrammatic pseudonym of 'M. Alcofibras, Abstracteur de Quinte Essence' (Rabelais 1973: 33). The booksellers obviously financed the publication of these books and probably never gave any money to Rabelais who at that time supported himself as a doctor.

*Pantagruel* has almost the same presentation and format as that of the chapbooks which we will examine later. It opens with a 'Prologue de l'auteur' which reads like a farcical prescription to the reader advising him to take the book as a medicine. As for *Gargantua*, it begins with an address to the reader which constitutes an apology of laughter ('Better is it to write about laughter than tears,/ For laughter is the privilege of man'; 37; my translation); this address in verse is followed by a 'Prologue de l'auteur' which takes up more or less the same argument as that of the earlier book.

When the *Tiers Livre* came out in 1456 *chez* the Parisian bookseller Christian Wechel, it carried the name of the author on the title page, as well as his titles 'Docteur en Médecine' and 'Calloïer des isles Hières' (Monk of the isles of Hières). The publication of this new book was a great deal more official than that of the earlier ones. Before the usual 'Prologue de l'auteur', there is a dedication to 'the spirit of the Queen of Navarre', which suggests that the said queen either granted her protection or gave some money to Rabelais. For the first time, too, the king's privilege, signed by Cardinal Du Thier, is printed in full. This privilege states that Rabelais will retain the sole right to have this book and his previous ones printed by whichever printer he wishes for a period of ten years 'so that he may cover the expenses necessary to the opening of the said printing' (360–1; my translation). Though it is signed by a churchman, this privilege has nothing to do with an imprimatur; it states the legal rights of the author but never mentions the content and value of the book. The *Tiers Livre* was in fact immediately censored by the Sorbonne.

The status of Rabelais as an author had obviously changed between the first two books and the third. It was no longer the bookseller who was taking the risk of publishing the book but the author himself who had obtained the patronage of the Queen of Navarre and a privilege from the King of France. Now, he could sign his work and claim his legal rights in it. A century before, he would have needed no such privilege to have the book copied; the invention and development of printing was clearly beginning to change the nature of the book trade as well as the status of the author.

Cervantes belongs unambiguously to the new typographic era which Walter Ong opposes to the earlier chirographic one (Ong 1982). The first edition of *Don Quixote*, published in 1605, contained many preambles. The first text is a 'Certificate of Price' signed by Juan Gallo de Andrada, 'scrivener of the Chamber of our master the King', stipulating that the book be sold at 'two-hundred-ninety maravedis and a half' (a price solely based on the cost of paper, by the way), and requesting that the said certificate 'be placed in the front of the book' (Cervantes 1949: 7). Then comes a 'Certificate of Errata' in which the Licentiate Francisco Murcia de la Llana certifies that this book is the exact copy of the original. The certificate is immediately followed by the 'Royal Privilege' which not only guarantees the rights of the author for a period of ten years, but also notifies him to submit it to the scrivener of the chamber each time he has it printed, 'this by way of seeing that the said printing conforms to the original' as well as of fixing the price of each volume (8). The printer who will take it upon himself to print the book (after getting the author's permission, we presume, though the privilege does not specify) will also be subjected to the same rules. This is indeed a strange document: while it seems to grant a privilege to the author, it also brings him and the printers under the law of the king as far as the price and content of the book are concerned. We find here the first signs of that official censorship which will develop on a large scale with the growth of the printing industry.

The privilege is immediately followed by the dedication to the patron, the Duke of Béjar, then by the prologue addressed to the 'idling reader', and again by a number of prefatory poems. All this in spite of the fact that, in his prologue, Cervantes expresses the wish 'to bring the tale unadulterated and unadorned, stripped of the usual prologue and the endless string of sonnets, epigrams, and eulogies such as are commonly found at the beginning of books' (11). The latter remark poses an interesting problem which we will take up again in the next chapters: where does the novel really begin? Should some of the preambles, or all of them, be excluded from the text proper, and on what grounds?

The economy of the book trade and the status of the author had obviously changed a great deal from Gerald of Wales to Cervantes. At the turn of the seventeenth century, the printing industry, which had played such a decisive part in broadcasting the ideas of the Reformation, was developing so quickly that the political and religious authorities were trying to bring it under control, either for economic or for moral reasons. At the same time, the author was beginning to be officially recognized. He knew now that his name would for ever be attached to his work if it appeared in the first edition. This recognition was as much due to the royal privilege which granted him a status (while cramping his freedom), as to the patronage of the grandee whose generosity was acknowledged in the dedication. In the next centuries, many books (and many novels, especially) would still be published anonymously, but not for the same reasons as during the chirographic era.

The standard procedure which we have just described for the serious works published in the late sixteenth and early seventeenth centuries was obviously becoming a handicap to the development of the printing industry. The authorities had become very touchy after all the political and religious strife which had followed the Reformation. It was probably because censorship was beginning to develop on a large scale that a number of printers and booksellers invented a new formula, the chapbook in England, the *bibliothèque bleue* in France, or the *pliego de cordel* in Spain, to make the most of the economic resources of printing without any restrictions.

Neither Margaret Spufford nor Roger Chartier, the authors of the most recent books on the subject, has suggested that the formula was developed as a reaction against the growing concentration of the book trade in or around the capitals, and the increasing censorship encouraged by this concentration. There are at least two reasons to believe that this was the case. The first one is that the authors and printers of chapbooks apparently never sought a royal privilege when the formula began to appear; they would start to do so in the eighteenth century, as we shall see. The second reason is that the books were not marketed in the usual way by urban booksellers but peddled by *porte-balles* or *colporteurs* in France, and by chapmen in England who sold their goods around the country. Here is the inventory, made in 1690, of the hampers of a Kent chapman, John Cunningham:

> His hampers were full of textiles to be made up presumably by the purchasers at home, scotch cloth, over a hundred yards of holland in six different qualities, flaxen cloth, blue linen, striped dimity, narrow muslin, wide muslin, and his only made-up goods, muslin neck cloths at 9d each, and three shirts. Amongst all this cloth, the appraisers listed one Bible and 'some other books' at a total value of 3s.
> 
> (Spufford 1981: 121)

The appraisers did not consider it worth their while to itemize the 'other books' which, with the Bible, were worth only 3s out of a total of £26 2s 11d. The chapbooks were cheap goods which the chapman peddled around the country with his more valuable fabrics. They were not meant for urban readers but for rural ones who could not find any reading material because they lived too far from a big city. The chapman, whose activities were not always too reputable, was a convenient intermediary to market such unofficial or even underground publications.

In France, this mode of peddling had started in the cities in the sixteenth century with the so-called '*canard*' ('duck' – a word which in modern French commonly designates the daily newspaper). The *canard* was a little booklet, marketed by urban pedlars, and narrating famous events, either real or fantastic. Among the 517 editions known to have been published between 1530 and 1630 in France, eighty-nine narrate executions, eighty-six apparitions in the sky, sixty-two possessions by the devil, forty-five miracles, thirty-seven inundations, and thirty-two earthquakes (Chartier 1987: 109).

Spufford, who does not distinguish between the urban and the rural market, would probably include the *canard* among the chapbooks since the number of pages is for her such an important criterion. In her study of the collection of small books made by Samuel Pepys between 1682 and 1687, she counts as chapbooks only the 193 printed items containing less than seventy-two pages on the grounds that the bigger books would have cost over 6d, a price which, presumably, would have been too high for a chapman to sell them (1981: 130).

Chartier does not consider size to be a proper criterion: he gives the example of *bibliothèque bleue* in-quartos which contain one or two hundred pages (Chartier 1987: 111). He founds his definition on other criteria: the blue colour and poor quality of the cover and paper, the sloppy quality of the print due to the use of old fonts (and old woods for the pictures), the corpus and the location of the printers. Though a great number of French chapbooks were published in Lyons, Rouen, Caen, Rennes, and other cities, many of them were printed in Troyes, near Paris, by a little group of printers, the Oudots especially (Chartier 1987: 110–11). The rise of that dynasty was not only due to the proximity of Paris with its book-hungry university, but also to the fact that Troyes had always been a big European centre for the paper trade (Febvre and Martin 1971: 52–3). When one considers that an ordinary in-octavo of 240 pages, printed in 1,000 copies on good-quality paper, cost approximately 190 French pounds around 1644, and that the paper itself cost 100 pounds, one will easily understand why the key to the development of such a popular formula as the *bibliothèque bleue* was not so much the proximity of a big university town as the availability of cheap paper (Febvre and Martin 1971: 171).

In the corpus of works published as chapbooks or in the *bibliothèque bleue*, fiction occupied a limited place, at first. Though no reliable statistics on the trade in seventeenth-century England and France are available, it seems that a majority of them were religious books and craft books presenting the skill required in a given profession. There were also books of entertainment. Over a third of the items in Pepys's collection was made up of 'small merry books', namely: 'jestbooks and burlesques, the courtship and lovers' dialogues, and the secular songs' (Spufford 1981: 156). The only 'novels' in the collection were: *Patient Griselda*, the story of a model wife which dates back to the Middle Ages, a twenty-four-page quarto selling at 3d, Robert Greene's *Dorastus and Fawnia*, Quarles's *Argalus and Parthenia*, the idyllic story of a shepherd's life, and *Antonius and Aurelia*, a 3d quarto (156). Many romances of chivalry, published as chapbooks, are absent from the collection, for example *Amadis of Gaule* and *Paladine of England* published in 1588 by Anthony Munday, who was a draper's son apprenticed to the stationer and printer John Alde and 'therefore in close touch with the market' as Margaret Spufford notes, or again *Palmerin in England* which appeared between 1581 and 1594, or *Don Bellianis of Greece* published in 1598, and many others (233).

By the eighteenth century, however, it seems that this publishing formula gave more and more room to books of entertainment and works of fiction. Chartier presents the inventory of a famous Troyes printer's stock, that of Etienne Garnier, which was made in 1789, more than two centuries after the birth of the *bibliothèque bleue*. Out of the stock of 443,069 books belonging to the *bibliothèque bleue*, 42.7 per cent were religious books, 28.8 per cent were books of fiction and 26.8 per cent books of apprenticeship (craft books, abecedaria, mathematics manuals, and so forth). But Chartier immediately corrects these figures by comparing them to the number of editions as computed by A. Morin in 1974: now the books of fiction come first, with 41.4 per cent of the editions, followed by the books of instruction (books of apprenticeship among others) with 28.3 per cent of the total, and the religious books with 28.1 per cent (Chartier 1987: 249). These figures show that the religious books were always printed in larger quantity than the books of fiction, but also that the latter represented almost half of the editions, in the eighteenth century at least. By then, the expression *bibliothèque bleue* had come to designate 'recreational books' (*livres récréatifs*), as a sentence at the end of the catalogue published by Nicolas Oudot's widow suggests: 'We also expand the *Bibliothèque bleue* both by seeking ancient stories and by new little stories [*Historiettes*]' (Chartier 1987: 265; my translation). The sentence is ill-balanced in French, too: those who rediscovered the ancient stories were obviously not the same persons as those who wrote the *Historiettes*. This passage makes it clear that the publisher's role was a great deal more important than that of the authors in that flourishing trade.

Most of the chapbooks, like the romances of chivalry, the Robin Hood chapbooks, or the various versions of King Arthur's story, were published anonymously. These stories belonged to the oral tradition before they were put into writing. Rarely have the names of the amanuenses who wrote down those texts or abridged books already written come down to us; Grub Street apparently hosted so many needy scribes or garreteers that the printer who hired them did not have to give their names on title-pages (Collins 1973: 26–8).

There are rare cases when a legend of the kind cherished by the oral tradition developed anonymously through chapbooks, such as the Guilleri saga in France. Philippe Guilleri and his younger brother Mathurin Guilleri were two highwaymen of the Robin Hood type who robbed the wealthy travellers of Poitou at the beginning of the seventeenth century. Mathurin was arrested and executed in 1606, and Philippe in 1608. In 1609, two sixteen-page booklets narrating the story of the elder Guilleri were published, one in Poitiers, the other in Paris. Chartier calls these books *occasionnels* ('occasionals'), a vague term which could as well designate a *canard*. These booklets, which were reissued a number of times in the seventeenth century, spread the legend of the Guilleris in rural France. The first *Bibliothèque bleue* edition of the story was published by Jean Oudot's widow in 1718 and was entitled *Histoire de la vie, grandes voleries et subtilités de Guilleri et de ses compagnons et de leur fin lamentable et malheureuse*; it carried an official authorization given in 1716. We notice, by the way, that Chartier is implicitly restricting the use of the label *bibliothèque bleue* to the cheap books published in Troyes or by someone related to a Troyes dynasty like that of the Oudots, since he refuses to apply the label to the seventeenth-century *occasionnels*. Both the *occasionnels* and the works published in the *bibliothèque bleue* were anonymous; but they were not so in order to protect the authors since, obviously, they contained nothing objectionable morally or politically, but because the publishers considered themselves the sole owners of the text. This is confirmed by the fact that the eighteenth-century publisher sought and was granted an official authorization (Chartier 1987: 331–3).

This case is instructive in many respects: it shows, first, that the very concept of *bibliothèque bleue* and that of chapbook was ill-defined, second, that the typographic age sometimes developed its legends in ways not dissimilar to those of the oral age, and third, that the boundary between official and underground publication was thin, as will be, from the start, the boundary between serious and popular fiction. Also, it suggests that a new kind of anonymity was beginning to develop, the Grub Street kind. The rights to this popular story were tacitly shared by the public, who had made of Guilleri a kind of French Robin Hood, and by the printers, who had paid a scribe to write down the story, and had printed it. The publishing formula was therefore meant to remove all the obstacles between the merchant and his customers, namely the author himself and the law, though the latter had apparently become more difficult to by-pass by the beginning of the eighteenth century.

There is no evidence, however, that any of those books would have been censored even in the seventeenth century if they had been officially published, for censorship was comparatively tolerant in those days when religion was not being attacked. When Quevedo's picaresque novel, *Historia de la vida del Buscón* (1626), was published in French in 1633, by the Parisian bookseller Billaine, it was not censored. The translator's name, de la Geneste, appeared in the address to the reader. The story joined the corpus of the *bibliothèque bleue* in 1657 when Nicolas II Oudot published *L'Aventurier Buscón*; Quevedo's name was given in the title, but that of the translator had now disappeared. For good reasons, of course: whereas the first edition of the *bibliothèque bleue* version was based on La Geneste's translation, as were to be all the following ones, the text had now been so severely shortened (it still had 160 pages) and bowdlerized that it was barely La Geneste's work any more. It still contained many sexual and scatological passages, but they were considerably toned down.

Taking into consideration that the book was going to be read by a large public of mostly rural and uneducated people, the printer had imposed a severe censorship on the text without ever being asked to do so. The fortunes of this book give additional evidence of the changes which were taking place in the French book trade at the turn of the seventeenth century. When the *bibliothèque bleue* version was reissued by Jean Oudot in 1730, it was prefaced by an authorization given in 1705 and a privilege granted in 1728 (Chartier 1987: 302–19). Its career, which had started more or less clandestinely, was developing openly with the official approval of the censors, a clear indication that anonymity had nothing to do with censorship at that time but very much with the printer's or bookseller's desire to keep all the rights in the book he was marketing.

The Guilleri and Buscón sagas give evidence of the fact that, even in France where the book trade was kept under strict surveillance, the booksellers were gradually discovering the law of the market. They realized that, in order to increase their profits and exploit the possibilities offered by the new technology, they had to keep as close as possible to their customers – even by supplanting the author – and also to refrain from transgressing the written or tacit laws regulating censorship. They were more than willing to bowdlerize their texts if, in return, they could reach a larger public and remain unhampered by the censors who usually lived in the capital.

The historians of the modern novel have never paid much attention to the growth, until the eighteenth and early nineteenth century, of this publishing formula. It would be unfair to claim that the modern novel owes its rise to it. Fiction was already present among the incunabula (books printed before 1500) in which the literary works (classical, medieval, or contemporary) represented more than 30 per cent of the books published, as against 45 per cent for religious books, 10 per cent for law books and 10 per cent for scientific books (Febvre and Martin 1971: 351). Some eighty medieval romances were printed before 1550; the most successful ones were: *Les Quatre fils Aymon* (eighteen editions before 1536), *Fierabras* (with almost as many editions), and *Pierre de Provence* (with nineteen editions before 1536; Febvre and Martin 1971: 396). As for Rabelais's *Pantagruel*, it went through over fifty editions, and his collected works over thirty, before 1600 (Lough 1978: 59). But, in the absence of truly reliable figures, it is not possible to prove that, from the fifteenth until the eighteenth century, books of entertainment (and among them books of fiction) gained considerable ground over the religious books (Bibles, *livres d'heures*, saints' lives, etc.) if one excludes the chapbooks and *bibliothèque bleue* titles from our computation. The latter probably contributed more than any other publishing formula to the birth of the fiction trade which, nowadays, has taken on such extraordinary proportions with the development of the paperback.

A double market had therefore appeared almost instantly at the beginning of the typographic era. First, an official market for serious books, or books written by serious or acknowledged writers like Rabelais; its chief target was usually the wealthy and educated who could afford to pay for good-quality paper. Second, a nearly underground market for usually shorter books written by hack writers hired by business-minded printers and booksellers; this market was run by the urban and rural pedlars who sold their goods to the manual workers, craftsmen, and peasants who could read but had little money to spend on luxuries. This double market also marked the birth of a double literary standard: the more popular works were usually snubbed by the more educated people but, in the long run, they provided the more serious books with a larger audience. The chapbooks and *bibliothèque bleue* titles probably paved the way for the modern novel as a popular genre.

## THE EIGHTEENTH-CENTURY BOOKSELLER

The book trade, which had expanded steadily until the end of the seventeenth century in Europe, acquired a new momentum in the eighteenth century. Marjorie Plant, who wrote the first reliable history of the English book trade, shows how fast the trade grew between the end of the seventeenth and the beginning of the nineteenth century:

> Pamphlets and reprints apart, the yearly average of under a hundred new books which had remained fairly constant from 1666 to 1756 had risen for the period 1792–1802 to 372, and for the next twenty-five years to about 580, but it

is doubtful whether the total number of volumes had risen in the same proportion.

(Plant 1965: 434)

Judging from these figures, the number of new books published at the end of the eighteenth century was more than three times higher than a century before. In France, 1,000 volumes were being published every year around 1700 as against 380 a century before (Viala 1985: 143).

Such figures are a little misleading, however. They fail to take into account the number of copies printed each time. Whereas it is not uncommon now to print as many as 50,000 copies at a time, in the eighteenth century, most books were printed in runs of less than 2,000 copies (Febvre and Martin 1971: 308–13). Yet the print orders were increasing for literary works, as Lane indicates:

It had taken two years for Milton's *Paradise Lost* (1667) to sell thirteen hundred copies, but Fielding's *Joseph Andrews* (1742) sold sixty-five hundred copies in just over a year and Richardson's *Sir Charles Grandison* (1754) the same number in less than half that time.

(Lane 1982: 2)

The pamphlets and reprints excluded from Plant's figures, and which, we presume, also comprised the occasionals and chapbooks mentioned earlier, represented much bigger sales, of course. Watt lists, among the eighteenth-century pamphlets with the biggest sales, 'Swift's *Conduct of the Allies* (1711), with a sale of 11,000 copies, and Price's *Observations on the Nature of Civil Liberty* (1776), with a sale of 60,000 in a few months' (Watt 1967: 36). He also mentions that the 'highest figure recorded for a single work, that of 105,000, was for Bishop Sherlock's 1750 *Letter from the Lord Bishop of London to the Clergy and People of London on the Occasion of the Late Earthquake*' (36).

The data still remain too fragmentary to reconstruct a complete picture of the book trade in the eighteenth century. Yet they clearly show how fast, after the end of the seventeenth century in England, a primitive craft, printing, and a rudimentary trade, bookselling, developed into a full-scale industry.

The chief agent in this evolution was the publisher, who, in

1700, was usually called a bookseller. Terry Belanger defines the term in the following way: 'In 1700... the word *bookseller* usually signified a person engaged in either, or both, the wholesale and retail aspects of the book trade, whereas the *publisher* usually meant what we would today call a *distributor* or *jobber*' (Belanger 1982: 8). The person who published books in those days was less frequently a printer than a century before, though he often remained very close to the printing industry. According to Plant, London counted, in 1700, '188 persons calling themselves booksellers (or publishers), 42 who were printers, and only 25 who were both printer and publisher. There were still 7 acting as both bookseller and binder, as distinct from 4 who were full-time binders' (Plant 1965: 64). Fifty years later, there were eighty-six persons described as 'booksellers and publishers', forty-two 'booksellers', twenty-eight 'printers', fifteen 'printer-publishers' (65). These figures probably do not mean that the book trade was flourishing less in 1700 in London than fifty years later but that the publishing and printing trade was getting more concentrated and being run more professionally.

The printing industry and the book trade were also developing in the provinces. At the beginning of the eighteenth century, there were fifty-five 'publishers' in the provinces; whether they had the same status as the London booksellers, Marjorie Plant does not say. Half a century later, there were 'about 120 in the confused category of booksellers and publishers, of whom a few were also printers' (64–5). These figures seem to suggest that the titles given to or claimed by the professionals involved in the publishing trade were interchangeable as the profession gradually shifted from a print-oriented structure to a market-oriented one.

The development of the publishing trade in the provinces was encouraged by at least two factors. The first was the construction, often by French Huguenots, of paper mills; there were 100 of them in 1696. Yet England was far from producing as much paper as France (whose population, let us not forget, was much higher than that of England) in the first half of the eighteenth century. According to Febvre and Martin, 300,000 reams were manufactured in England in 1722, as against almost three times as many in France less than a century before (Febvre and Martin 1971: 55–60). The second factor which encouraged the growth of publishing in the provinces was the decision taken in 1695 to drop the restrictions imposed by the law of 1615 on the number of printers (twenty-two in London, plus those allowed in the university towns of Oxford and Cambridge). Those restrictions were originally meant to curb the role of foreign printers whose share of the market had always been important. In 1725, there were printers in Manchester, Birmingham, Liverpool, Bristol, Cirencester, Exeter, Worcester, Norwich, Canterbury, Tunbridge Wells, York, Newcastle, and Nottingham (Febvre and Martin 1971: 274). But England lagged behind France here too, despite the fact that in the latter country censorship laws and an edict passed by Colbert in 1666 to limit the number of printing-works were beginning to cripple the industry. According to the census of 1701, there were fifty-one printing-works in Paris, twenty-nine in Lyons, twenty-nine in Rouen, twelve in Bordeaux, twelve in Caen, eleven in Troyes, eleven in Toulouse, eight in Rennes, and eight in Strasburg (Lough 1978: 11).

The bookseller was no longer a craftsman but often an enlightened businessman. He needed a great deal of money to finance the printing and distribution of the books he published, to buy the copyrights which would become very costly in the course of the century, and sometimes also to hire garreteers to write, abridge, or translate for him.

Often, he made little money on the first edition of a book. Here is the budget for Johnson's *Idler* published in two volumes in 1761. The total expenses for the 1,500 copies printed were £115 16s 6d, advertising accounting for £20 0s 6d, a high percentage of the total cost, printing for £41 13s, and paper for £52 3s. Paper still represented almost half of the total as it did in seventeenth-century France. The book made a profit of £126 3s 6d, one-third of which went to the publisher, Newbery, and the rest to the author. Newbery was not a retailer; he sold the sets in lots of 100, a common practice in those days. Considering that each lot was sold for £16 (a little more than 3s a set) and that each set was then sold for 5s sewed and 6s bound by the retailer, the latter still made a handsome profit of about 2s per set, depending on the cost of transportation (Plant 1965: 235).

The figures for a novel such as Smollett's *Humphrey Clinker*, published in 1770, are comparable. Here, the author received a down-payment, called 'copy money', of £210; printing and paper for 2,000 copies cost £155 15s 6d, and advertising £15 10s. The entire edition sold at £24 per 100, which gave a profit of only £46 6s 4d to each of the two publishers (Plant's name for them), Benjamin Collins and William Johnston. This comparatively small profit was partly due to the fact that the 'copy money' was so high. With the second edition, which brought no additional payment to the author, the publishers made a total profit of £240 12s; considering that the printing and advertising costs must have been more or less the same as for the first edition, this constitutes a 140 per cent profit (Plant 1965: 236).

The history of the retail trade still remains to be written. Usually, the bookseller was also a retailer. He sold the books he published, plus many others he had received from other booksellers with whom he had an agreement. A retailer could not build up his stock like a modern book dealer, but he already had ways to keep up with the book trade. In France, he could consult such catalogues as *Bibliographia Gallicana* or *Bibliographia Parisiana*, published between 1643 and 1653 (Martin 1988: 258), or such periodical publications as the *Journal des savants* (it started in 1665), and in England the *Philosophical Transactions*, published by the Royal Society of London after 1668, or such literary reviews as the *Monthly Review* started by Griffith in 1749 and the *Critical Review* started by Smollett in 1756 (Febvre and Martin 1971: 333; Collins 1973: 241). The booksellers bartered books all over Europe, having little choice, in most cases, as to the kind of books they received once they had signed a contract with another bookseller.

Books were often transported by boat or by cart, and were placed inside barrels to keep them dry. To lower the weight of the goods and also the price of transportation (which was comparatively high), the books were often shipped unbound (Febvre and Martin 1971: 315–16). The penny post, which had been established in London in 1680, gradually provided a cheaper and more efficient mode of transportation after 1720 (Watt 1967: 189). No payment was involved when booksellers were bartering books of equal value; otherwise, they had to use letters of exchange which were settled triangularly and at often long intervals (Febvre and Martin 1971: 317–18). This naturally created some problems in times of war.

Despite all these difficulties, the English booksellers fared extremely well during the eighteenth century. They published an increasing number of books which they sold at lower and lower prices. Whereas at the beginning of the century, an ordinary octavo volume would sell for 5s or 6s (Plant 1965: 245–7), at the end of the century it would sell for around 3s. With the Napoleonic wars, prices went up again, and reached the half-guinea mark around 1820 (Sutherland 1976: 11).

After 1750, booksellers also started to run circulating libraries or *cabinets de lecture* from their shops, lending books to customers who paid a monthly subscription (Lough 1978: 248; Chartier 1987: 192). Also, they made a great deal of money from copyrights which they often traded for very high prices (Collins 1973: 42–3; Belanger 1982: 13).

Many booksellers rose to prominence, such as Jacob Tonson, or Bernard Lintot who published Pope, or again William Taylor who published *Robinson Crusoe*. Yet the two leading names, where the novel is concerned, are those of Robert Dodsley and Andrew Millar. Dodsley started his career as a poet when he was still a footman. He was backed by Defoe and Pope, who helped him get some of his works published. In 1735 (he was then thirty-two), the year when his 'Toy-Shop' was staged, he became a bookseller. Johnson came to him with his poem 'London', saying that it had been written by one of his friends. Dodsley later asked Johnson to write his dictionary. Among the authors published by Dodsley, one finds Pope, Young, Goldsmith, Sterne, and Gray (Mumby 1967: 227–35).

Millar is the best-known bookseller of his day with Dodsley. He published the works of Fielding as well as those of Thomson. Collins recounts how he promoted *Amelia*. Fearing that he might not be fully repaid for the £1,000 he had given the author, he advertised that 'to satisfy the earnest Demand of the Publick, this Work has been printed at four Presses; but the Proprietor notwithstanding finds it impossible to get them bound in Time, without spoiling the Beauty of the Impression, and therefore will sell them sew'd at Half-a-Guinea'. Also, he told the booksellers at a sale held just before the publication of *Amelia* that he could not sell them this last work of Fielding's with the usual discount because the demand was going to be too high. The ruse worked, and Millar quickly sold out all the copies printed (Collins 1973: 44–5). He also played an important part in building up a taste for popular historical books by publishing the works of Robertson and Hume (Mumby 1967: 235).

There were some important publishers in the provinces too, such as William Hutton in Birmingham, John Hinxman, who published the first edition of *Tristram Shandy* when he was still at York but who later returned to London, Thomas Gent, also of York, and the Foulis Press founded in Glasgow in 1741 (Mumby 1967: 244–7).

This comparative concentration of the book trade in the hands of a small number of booksellers was partly the result of the profession having started to organize itself very early, not only in England but everywhere in Europe (except in Holland). One century after the invention of printing, corporations of printers and booksellers had appeared in many cities: one was founded in Venice in 1548, one in London in 1557, the Stationers' Company, and one in Paris in 1570 (Febvre and Martin 1971: 208). Officially, the corporation was meant to help protect the rights of the printers and booksellers. Here are a number of situations in which it could intervene:

> Should a forbidden book be offered for sale? The government would immediately ask the syndic [of the corporation] to start an inquest and to discover the names of the culprits. Should a local bookseller complain that one of his books had been pirated by a bookseller elsewhere? The corporation would intervene. Should a privilege be improperly granted to a bookseller? Those who had reasons to complain would come and expose their grievances before the assembly of the corporation.
> 
> (Febvre and Martin 1971:208; my translation)

The corporations often represented the leading members of the profession who wanted to defend themselves against the competition on the one hand and the guilds of *compagnons* or jobbers on the other (Febvre and Martin 1971: 207).

The Stationers' Company (the name probably reflects the fact that the booksellers had adopted a stationary point or booth in the streets) was descended from the Brotherhood of Manuscript Producers, formed in 1357, and from the Brotherhood of the Craft of Writers of Text-Letters, known as the 'Limners', which was chartered by the Lord Mayor in 1405 (Wittenberg 1978: 9–10). It was chartered by Philip and Mary in 1557 for the evident purpose of preventing the propagation of the Protestant Reformation; the Company was granted the monopoly of printing for the whole kingdom, and the master and wardens of the society 'were empowered to search, seize, and burn all prohibited books, and to imprison any person found exercising the art of printing without authority' (Wittenberg 1978:12). The Company, like its continental sisters, was mainly meant to curb sedition within the industry. It was not very wealthy; after the Great Fire of London, which destroyed the Hall and charter, and after the incursions of L'Estrange, the censor (more anon), it lost a great deal of its power.

To make up for this loss of influence, a number of wholesalers formed an association – between 1690 and 1719 says Belanger (1982: 13–14) and in 1719 says Collins (1973: 18–19) – named the Conger, a term which may be derived from 'congeries' or 'conger eel'. It bought large parts of the editions produced by its members and other London wholesalers. The books were then divided among themselves and stored in their warehouses. This association and the New Conger formed by another group in 1734 later joined forces and founded the Chapter, named after the Chapter Coffee-House where its members met (Collins 1973: 18–19).

The profession, which had apparently lost some of its rights by the Licensing Act of 1709, was becoming better and better organized. Before the parliamentary debate of 1774 concerning the protection of authors' rights, a campaign developed against its monopoly. Collins quotes an argument published then against the London booksellers:

> A few persons, who call themselves booksellers, about the number of twenty-five, have kept the monopoly of books and copies in their own hands, to the entire exclusion of all others but more especially the printers, whom they have always held it a rule never to let become purchasers of copy.
>
> (1973: 16–17)

This diatribe confirms that the book trade had grown more and more concentrated in the course of the century. It also shows that the trade was now market- rather than print-based, the printers complaining of the ill-treatment they were receiving from the booksellers. As we will see, the state often found it convenient to encourage such a concentration, which made it considerably easier to enforce censorship; the booksellers and publishers were all too ready to oblige since they needed protection, particularly against piracy.

## THE LAW

### England

In her marvellous book *The Printing Press as an Agent of Change* (1979), Elizabeth Eisenstein has shown the seminal function of the new technology on the development of science and philosophy, as well as on the rise of the Reformation. Though the church and the state had sometimes encouraged the industry at first, they soon discovered that it had to be kept under control as it could broadcast heretic and seditious ideas with unprecedented speed. In the present section, we will see how these two institutions brought their authority to bear on the book trade, helping substantially to change the relationship between publisher, author, and reader.

The law did not develop its control at the expense of the profession, but often with its complicity. A printer or bookseller who had financed the publication of a new book always needed protection against those who tried to reissue it or make fraudulent copies of it. The first complaint of piracy in England was apparently made by one Wynkyn de Worde in 1533, who sought protection for a treatise on grammar and obtained a 'privilege' for the second edition (Wittenberg 1978: 7). To guarantee their rights, the booksellers tended more and more to seek such privileges and to plead for stricter licensing laws to regulate the trade. The state was only too glad to oblige: while granting its protection, it could implement more rigorous censorship laws. This tacit complicity between state and profession explains why it is virtually impossible to study censorship legislation and copyright legislation separately. There was a trade-off between the two parties, each getting what they needed most in the arrangement.

In England, the licensing system was first established by a

decree of the Star Chamber issued in 1538 forbidding printers to print any book in English 'Onles vpon examination made by some of his gracis privie counsayle, or other suche as his highnes shall apoynte, they shall have lycense to do' (Thomas 1969: 9). Those were troubled times, and the state needed to control whatever material got published in the kingdom. Less than a generation later, with the incorporation of the Statiooners' Company (1557), the state partly surrendered its censoring rights to the book trade which, as we saw above, was granted the right to police the market to a large extent. Books still had to be licensed before publication. When the power of the Company was confirmed in 1559, a list of the authorities empowered to grant such licences was published: the Archbishops of Canterbury and York, the Bishop of London and Vice-Chancellors of Oxford and Cambridge Universities. The list was revised by the 'Decree of Starre-Chamber Concerning Printing' of 1637 which stipulated that all the books printed be licensed, authorized, and 'entered into the Registers Book of the Company of Stationers' and that all printed matter bear the imprint and address of the publisher, plus the name of the author (Wittenberg 1978: 15). The state did not totally surrender its control over the profession, however; the licensing law stipulated that people publishing Catholic and Puritan literature could be sentenced to death. Some Puritans were sent to the Tower of London, pilloried, and heavily fined for publishing seditious books. William Prynne was one of them: in 1637, he lost the stumps of his ears (he having already lost his ears in 1634), and his face was branded on both sides with the letters 'S.L.' for 'seditious libeller' (Thomas 1969: 9–30).

During the Civil War, the Parliament issued twenty-seven licences to various bodies, such as schoolmasters, ministers of religion, and doctors. The order of January 1642 contained the first definition of the right of the author:

> It is ordered that the the Master and the Wardens of the Company of Stationers shall be required to take especial Order, that the Printers doe neither print, nor reprint any thing without the name and consent of the Author: And that if any Printer shall notwithstanding print or reprint any thing without the consent and name of the Author, that he

shall then be proceeded against, as both Printer and Author thereof, and their names to be certified to this House.
(Wittenberg 1978: 17)

Yet these orders did little to improve the situation of the author although they substantially increased the power of the Company. Milton ignored them and, in 1643, published *The Doctrine and Discipline of Divorce* unlicensed and unregistered; the Stationers' Company complained to the House of Commons about the tract but nothing came of it. The following year, Milton published *Areopagitica: A Speech of John Milton's for the Liberty of Unlicensed Printing to the Parliament of England* in which he attacked the licensing system and begged Parliament to drop its rulings of the previous year; the tract was so successful that the Company could do nothing against it (Wittenberg 1978: 19).

With the Restoration, there was a great deal of pressure to implement stricter regulations and to curb the power of the Stationers' Company, which eventually led to the Licensing Act of 1662. The Act largely ignored the interests of the Company; it stipulated that all books should be licensed by the proper authority, law books by the Lord Chancellor, the Lord Keeper, or the Lord Chief Justice, history by the Secretary of State, heraldry by the Earl Marshal or King of Arms, and all others by the Archbishop of Canterbury and the Bishop of London. Besides, Sir Roger L'Estrange was appointed as surveyor of the printed presses and Censor of the Press (Plant 1965: 144–5). A clause confirmed that the consent of the owner was required before a book could be published, but it did not say if the owner was necessarily the author (Wittenberg 1978: 21).

The following year, L'Estrange published his 'Considerations and Proposals in order to the Regulation of the Press' which stated his chief objectives. It concluded with an interesting statement about the conflicts within the profession:

> To conclude, both printers and stationers, under colour of offering a service to the publique, do effectually but design one upon another. The printers would beat down the bookselling trade by managing the press as themselves please, and by working upon their own copies. The stationers, on the other side, they would subject the printers to be absolutely

their slaves; which they have effected in a large measure already, by so encreasing the number, that the one half must either play the knave or starve.

(Mumby 1967: 57–8)

This text shows unambiguously that the state drew a great deal of its power from the conflicts within the profession and the industry. Availing himself of this strife and of the state of shock in which the country found itself after the Civil War, L'Estrange imposed a ruthless law. A few months after his appointment, he had John Twyn arrested and executed for printing a pamphlet entitled 'A Treatise on the Execution of Justice' described as 'seditious, scandalous, and poisonous', (Mumby 1967: 159). Lists of licensed books were published in the *Term Catalogue* which continued to appear until 1711, that is even after the Licensing Act fell into disuse in 1695 (Thomas 1969: 13–15). L'Estrange's régime had crippling effects on the printing profession: it brought the number of printers at work in London down from sixty to twenty (Mumby 1967: 157).

The Licensing Act was not only meant to prevent the publication of seditious books, however, but also that of obscene literature in general. It required that books should contain nothing 'contrary to good life or good manners' (Thomas 1969: 13), a phrase which seems to echo the French description of obscene literature as 'contraire aux bonnes mœurs'. Though a number of abortive attempts had been made, as early as 1580, to ban obscene literature, it was only after 1662 that censorship began against this kind of literature. Thomas cites a number of booksellers who were convicted for publishing licentious books. In 1677 the bookseller who had imported the Latin and French edition of *L'Escole des filles* from Amsterdam had his shop closed down for a few hours. Pepys managed to read the book 'for information sake'; after he had done so, he 'burned it, that it might not be among my books to my shame' (Thomas 1969: 27). In 1683, John Wickens was sentenced to pay a fine of 40s, a small punishment, for publishing *The Whore's Rhetorick*; the following February the book was again listed in the *Term Catalogue*. The penalty was higher (£20) for Crayle and Streater in 1690 after they had brought out *Sodom: or, The Quintessence of Debauchery*.

However, few booksellers stayed in prison very long, and none was executed, as far as we know, for bringing out licentious books. And even when, in 1692, the first Society for the Reformation of Manners was founded, it did not claim to suppress indecent literature, a clear indication that such literature was not yet considered as dangerous by the public at large (Thomas 1969: 22–28).

It is not known how many of the convictions mentioned above were the result of accusations made by members of the publishing and printing profession, but when one reads the arguments listed by John Locke in 1695 and which the House of Commons had asked him to write when it decided not to renew the Licensing Act, one realizes that the members of the Stationers' Company were very active when it came to protecting their rights. Locke accuses them of using censorship to ban 'innocent and useful Books' so that they might later authorize 'what belongs to, and is the Labour and Right of, others', for publication by 'themselves and their Friends' (Thomas 1969: 28–9). Obviously, L'Estrange had failed to deprive the Company of its authority; wittingly or unwittingly, he had allowed the law to serve the petty interests of some friends or influential members of the profession. After this unhappy experience, which showed the perverse effects of censorship, the state decided to stop interfering with the profession for a while.

The London booksellers were not very happy with this absence of legislation, however. They applied to Parliament for a new Licensing Act, first in 1703, a second time in 1706, and finally, with success, in 1709, on the grounds that their own by-laws could not adequately protect them against one another. This was a very controversial issue. Defoe joined the debate with his *Essay on the Regulation of the Press* and Matthew Tindal with his *Reasons against Restraining the Press*, both published in 1704. Tradition has it that Swift himself drafted the original bill (Mumby 1967: 195).

The state's chief objective in passing this new Act (officially entitled 'An Act for the encouragement of Learning, by vesting the copies of printed books in the authors or purchasers of such copies, during the times therein mentioned') was not, as in 1662, to ban the publication of seditious texts, or even of licentious literature, but to regulate the trade by defining literary property more strictly. Authors and publishers 'were given the copyright of books already printed for a period of twenty-one years, dating from April 10, 1710, and no longer' (Mumby 1967: 195); the copyrights on new books were now the sole property of the author for a period of fourteen years, and they were automatically renewed for another fourteen years should the author still be living. Before publication, all copies were to be entered in the Register of the Stationers' Company, a concession to the profession which could thereby keep the trade under control (Plant 1965: 118; Mumby 1967: 195) This Act officially marked the end of perpetual copyrights, though booksellers and publishers continued to act throughout most of the century as if they still held such rights once they had published a book. So did Millar, for instance, who had bought the rights in Thomson's *Seasons* published in 1726–30, and who sued Taylor for reprinting the work in 1763, after the author's twenty-eight years had expired; the court was divided but eventually decided in favour of Millar (Mackinnon 1988: 1118).

Naturally, the new Act protected the booksellers against piracy. It stipulated in its first section, which also defined copyright, that a 'bookseller could now procure the destruction of all pirated copies and a fine of one penny on each pirated sheet, of which fine, however, the bookseller had only half, the Crown having the rest' (Collins 1973: 55). It was not so much a question, for the publisher, of recouping his losses, since half of the money went to the Crown, as of getting the official protection of the law. Few booksellers sought to inflict such penalties; yet the Act was deemed efficient enough despite the fact that piracy continued to thrive for a century.

The Act did not apply in Ireland, where piracy was practised on a large scale. Richardson tried to publish *Sir Charles Grandison* there, but the text was pirated and published in part by three publishers before he could himself bring it out. Three pirated editions of half of the novel were published in Dublin before a single one appeared in London. Richardson attacked the Irish publishers in a pamphlet:

> It has been customary for the *Irish* Booksellers to make a Scramble among themselves who should first intitle himself to the Reprinting of a new *English Book* and happy was he, who could get his agents in England to send him a copy of a

supposed saleable Piece, as soon as it was printed and ready to be published.

(Collins 1973: 63)

The situation was not to change substantially until 1801 when the copyright laws were extended to that country (Mumby 1967: 195).

The members of the profession obviously realized, after a while, that they had paid too high a price to get protection against each other and against piracy. The Act had substantially increased the rights of the authors without totally guaranteeing those of the booksellers. In the middle of the century, the debate on literary property was reopened. William Warburton, in his *Letter from an Author to a Member of Parliament, concerning Literary Property* (1747) tried to prove 'a Work of the *Mind* to be susceptible of Property, like that of the *Hand*' (Warburton 1747: 9); an anonymous pamphlet published in 1762 insisted that 'if an author cannot maintain an exclusive right to his copy, the powers of genius must languish, and few will have an opportunity of producing those excellent talents with which nature hath enriched them' (Anon 1762: 43). By that time, Warburton had come to adopt a different attitude on the subject; he was now against literary property as vested in the authors on the grounds that the latter had no rights in their ideas and that 'If their Works were to become a Property, they might be taken in Execution for debt' (Warburton 1762: 34).

The conflicts between authors and booksellers, or between different booksellers who wanted to publish books written by authors now dead, gradually induced the profession to beg Parliament to bend the copyright law in its favour. In 1774, a bill (of which there is no copy left) was introduced to revive perpetual copyright; the bill was passed by the House of Commons but rejected by the House of Lords; this put an end to the booksellers' hope of ever regaining perpetual copyright (Collins 1973: 103). The author's rights were implicitly confirmed against those of the booksellers. After the Copyright Act of 1842, which extended the author's rights to forty-two years, the literary property was stated on contracts. This new Act, though it maintained the obligation to register each new publication at Stationers' Hall, tended 'further to shift the law's protection from printer and publisher (for whom copyright legislation was originally devised) to the author, to whom it gave longer possession', as Sutherland points out (1976: 94–5).

The state was clearly trying to bring the expanding market and industry under control, fearing that it might become a state within the state if nothing was done to stop it. The rulings on copyright played a more important role, in that respect, than the rulings on censorship. Only exceptionally were the state's interventions caused by the publication of political libels, though a nineteen-year-old printer, John Matthews, was arrested in London in 1719 for having a libel in favour of the pretender in his pocket. Although he did not know the author he was convicted and hanged (Thomas 1969: 41).

The state also tried to suppress licentious literature, but with only moderate success on the whole. When Edmund Curll (1675–1747), who had published volumes on venereal diseases, hermaphrodites, impotence, and sodomy, brought out in 1718 *A Treatise of the Use of Flogging in Venereal Affairs* and then, in 1724, a new edition of *Venus in the Cloister*, he was arrested and judged, but the court had difficulty in producing a precedent. The case was concluded in 1728 when Curll was found guilty, fined twenty-five marks for each of the books, and pilloried. This case remained a leading precedent in English law until the Obscene Publication Act of 1959 (Thomas 1969: 78–83).

English justice was comparatively ill-armed for the pursuing of dirty books of one kind or another. This absence of legal instruments, which bears witness to the comparative spirit of tolerance in the country at that time, partly explains the ease with which the novel developed in England compared with France. The attitude of the law towards licentious books around the middle of the eighteenth century is well illustrated by the publishing history of *Fanny Hill*, originally entitled *Memoirs of a Woman of Pleasure*, which was published anonymously in 1749, the same year as *Tom Jones*. The publisher, Ralph Griffiths, did not insert his name on the title-page, but instead put that of a printer on the Strand, G. Fenton, of whom nothing else is known; he probably never existed

(Quennell 1963: vii). Hardly had the book been published when the Secretary of State issued a warrant for the arrest of the author, printer, and publisher; they were soon released 'on a recognizance of £100' (Wagner 1985: 14). Cleland then prepared an abridged and bowdlerized version, entitled *Memoirs of Fanny Hill*, which was published in 1750; author, printer, and publisher were again arrested, but no legal action seems to have been taken against them. The President of the Privy Council even arranged for Cleland to receive a pension of £100 per annum. Of the later editions, only those that had retained the sodomitical passage in volume II were censored or caused the arrest of their publishers (Wagner 1985: 14). The novel acquired a bad name mostly because of the illustrations which soon began to accompany the text. Henry Spencer Ashbee lists twenty English editions of the novel between 1749 and 1845 alone (Wagner 1985: 16).

This tolerance is the more surprising as the development of education as well as that of printing and publishing made it so much easier for women to read romances and novels. In the past, most of the licentious texts were meant for an all-male public, few women being able to read, probably, or to have access to such literature. Now, we find the heroine of Fielding's *Shamela* reading *Venus in the Cloister*. Pamela is herself an inveterate reader, and her virtue has obviously suffered from over-exposure to all kinds of books. The Catholic church, which censored only a few English novels in the eighteenth century, listed *Pamela* in its *Index Librorum Prohibitorum*, sensing, decades before the English Establishment, the 'bad influence' such literature could have on the weaker sex. A century later, Thackeray was to describe Richardson as an author to make 'pretty little maidens blush' in *The Virginians* (Thomas 1969: 90). Richardson's purpose was totally different, of course; when, in July 1754, the *World* wrote on the moral danger of 'putting Romances into the hands of young Ladies', he joined Johnson and Hawkesworth in criticizing Swift as well as Fielding (Thomas 1969: 88).

One of the most severe indictments of the novel in the century was an essay written by Vicesimus Knox in 1778, and entitled 'On Novel Reading'. It contrasted the novel and the romance in the following way:

> If it be true, that the present age is more corrupt than the preceding, the great multiplication of Novels has probably contributed to its degeneracy. Fifty years ago there was scarcely a Novel in the kingdom. Romances, indeed, abounded; but they, it is supposed, were rather favourable to virtue.
>
> (Williams 1970: 304)

Knox also criticized Sterne and the 'languishing and affectedly sentimental compositions' formed on the pattern he had set, on the grounds that they 'tend to give the mind a degree of weakness, which renders it unable to resist the slightest impulse of libidinous passion' (Williams 1970: 306). His judgement was right, of course, given the circumstances. The romance, which belonged to the oral, pre-typographic age, was basically more moral and conservative, contributing as it often did to the development of a political and moral consensus, than the novel, which was not only the most distinguished but also one of the most subversive products of the typographic age.

**France**

In France, the law was a great deal less tolerant. There never was the kind of complicity between the state and the publishing profession that we have found in England, and neither was there the sort of trade-off that we have described. This can largely be explained by the fact that in France, where the religious struggles had been a great deal more bitter and violent, there was a much greater complicity between the Crown and the church.

It was the printers and booksellers, here again, who first induced the Crown to meddle with their trade. It had been a common practice, since the end of the fifteenth century, for them to seek a privilege from the authorities (the King, the *prévôt* of Paris, or the Parliament of Paris) whenever they wanted to bring out a new book, if only to prevent other printers or publishers from bringing out the same work. Their pleas led Francis I to issue a declaration in 1537 instituting the *dépôt légal* whereby a copy of every printed book had to be sent to the library of the château at Blois (Lough 1978: 39). Another royal edict of 1563 required that, before one could publish a book, one had to get permission from the Chancellor who, henceforth, became the sole person to grant printing privileges in the country (Febvre and Martin 1971: 340). The *Ordonnance de Moulins* of 1566 confirmed the authority of the Chancellor and stipulated that the privilege be inserted in the book, along with the name and address of the printer 'and this under penalty of losing their possessions and of being inflicted corporal punishment' (Lough 1978: 40; my translation).

Obviously, the King had very little concern for the welfare of the profession in all those decisions. He was above all trying to increase his political and moral authority and to curb the circulation of seditious or heretical literature in the country, using the church or the university as a screen. For instance, an edict had been passed in 1521 instituting preliminary examination of theological works by the university; but it was the secular arm, eventually, which punished the nonconforming booksellers and authors: the humanist Louis de Bergwin was burnt at the stake in 1529 for heresy; the writer and printer Etienne Dolet was hanged and burnt in Paris in 1546 for 'blasphemy, sedition, exhibition of prohibited and cursed books' (Lough 1978: 40).

The King had no more consideration for the authors than he did for the profession, so nothing was done for almost two centuries to define literary property. The printer or bookseller usually did not bother to ask the author's permission to publish a book, once he had secured a privilege from the Chancellor. The bookseller Ribou, who had procured a copy of Molière's *Les Précisieuses ridicules*, got a privilege forbidding the author to print the play which he had published without Molière's permission. Molière had enough influence at the Court to have the privilege revoked, but no edict or law really existed in the country to protect him and his fellow writers against such grabbing practices (Febvre and Martin 1971: 237; Viala 1985: 85–122).

Censorship developed on a grand scale in the seventeenth century. A poet, Etienne Durand, was executed in Paris in 1618 for composing a satire against Louis XIII and the Duke of Luynes. The *Code Michaux* of 1629 made it compulsory to submit all manuscripts to a censor appointed by the Chancellor; there were as many as fifty-six censors during the

1699–1704 period; Fontenelle was one of them (Lough 1978: 76–8). The new censorship laws were directed more against libellous and heretical books than against licentious books, which continued to be published in France throughout the century. Among the most notorious titles, one finds Michel Millot's *L'Escole des filles*, published in Paris in 1655, Nicholas Chorier's *L'Académie des dames*, first published in Latin in 1660 and then in French in 1680, and Jean Barrin's *Vénus dans le cloître*, published in France in 1683 (Thomas 1969: 19). All three books ran into some difficulties but continued to circulate. Yet, Claude Le Petit was sent to the stake in 1662 for his *Bordel des Muses* (Lough 1978: 76–8).

The Crown was much less afraid of licentious than of seditious and heretical publications. The decrees it took to keep the profession under control were all meant to protect the political and religious order. The Council's decree of 1666 forbade the admission of any new printers to the Paris guild and led to the closing-down of twelve printing-works shortly after. The number of printing-works in Paris was fixed at thirty-six by another Councils decree of 1683. The latter decree was obviously ignored since there were still fifty-one printing-works in Paris in 1701. From 1715 to 1788, more than one-third of the applications for privileges were rejected, which did not prevent Diderot from publishing his works clandestinely and anonymously in Paris, with an imprint of The Hague or London (Lough 1978: 175–6).

This repressive policy naturally encouraged the development of big publishing centres elsewhere in Europe. Many seventeenth-century authors, such as Jean Balzac, Théophile de Viau, and Descartes, had already published their works in Amsterdam, which, by the end of the seventeenth century, was the second most important centre after Paris for the publication of French books (Febvre and Martin 1971: 281). Many of the major literary works published in the eighteenth century first appeared outside France: Montesquieu's *Lettres persanes* in Amsterdam under a bogus Cologne imprint, his *Esprit des lois* in Geneva, Prévost's *Manon Lescaut* in Amsterdam, Rousseau's *Discours sur l'inégalité*, *La Nouvelle Héloïse*, and *Le Contrat social* in Amsterdam (Lough 1978: 176).

The smuggling of such books into the country only incensed the government and led it to pass ever stricter regulations such as, for instance, the *règlements* of 1723 which confirmed the terms of the earlier ones about the privileges, adding only that the latter could now also be granted by the Warden of the Seal, as well as by the Chancellor. The number of censors reached 178 on the eve of the Revolution, though in practice control over the book trade was largely delegated to the *directeur de la librairie*. L'abbé Bignon was the first to hold this office in 1699 (Lough 1978: 174).

The Bastille often hosted the authors, the booksellers, or simply the carriers of banned books during the century. Voltaire was twice imprisoned in it, the first time for the Rohan business, the second time for a satirical poem against the Regent; and he would probably have paid a third visit to the prison, after the publication of *Les Lettres philosophiques*, had he not taken refuge in Lorraine. Diderot's *Encyclopédie* also did time in the Bastille after the church's campaign against it (Lough 1978: 179–86). Rousseau's *Emile* suffered an even worse fate: it was condemned by Parliament to be burnt by the hangman, and its author had to flee to Switzerland. Two young women found themselves in the Bastille in 1771 for trying to smuggle banned books into Paris under their skirts; the same year, the Widow Stockdorff of Strasburg was imprisoned for smuggling banned works into Paris. The second time she was arrested, she was sentenced to stand in the pillory and to be banished from Paris and Strasburg for nine years. After the fall of the Bastille in 1789, freedom of expression was officially recognized in article 11 of the *Déclaration des droits de l'homme*. This freedom was effective until 1792, but it gradually disappeared again after the Convention and Napoleon's arrival (Lough 1978: 190–1).

French authors had other grievances against the Crown: there was no law to clearly protect their rights and define literary property until 1793. The article on 'Droit de copie' published in *L'Encyclopédie* explains that once an author has transferred his work to a bookseller, 'the latter becomes as incontestably the owner and with the same prerogatives as those enjoyed by the author himself' (*Encyclopédie* 1778: my translation). The author is here considered as an ordinary worker or owner who, once he has sold the product of his work or his property, retains no right whatsoever in it. Diderot was not against such a practice; in a memorandum written in 1761, he defended perpetual copyright and the booksellers who, having inherited the privilege to publish La Fontaine's *Fables* and *Les Contes*, were deprived of the said privilege in favour of La Fontaine's grand-daughters by a Council's decree inspired by Malesherbes (Febvre and Martin 1971: 240–1).

However, more and more people in government, like Malesherbes himself or Sartines, realized that writers deserved a better treatment. In 1777, five decrees, complemented by a decree of July 1778, attempted to settle the matter by granting perpetual privilege to the author and a ten-year privilege to the bookseller who bought the right from the author; this legislation also guaranteed the author against piracy. But it was the decree of July 1793 which finally defined literary property and guaranteed not only the author's rights but those of his heirs for a period of ten years after his death; this period was extended to twenty years by Napoleon in 1810 (Febvre and Martin 1971: 241; Lough 1978: 198).

This brief, and necessarily fragmentary, presentation of the difficult relationship between the law and the book trade in eighteenth-century England and France necessitates a few comments. First, the English book trade, which was marked from the start by a degree of complicity between the profession and the law, was not greatly hampered in its development, whereas the French trade, which was subjected to very strict regulations and censorship, was not run in a businesslike manner until the nineteenth century. Second, the author's rights were recognized much earlier in England (after 1709) than in France (after 1777 and 1793) where even such a liberal writer as Diderot insisted on considering the author as a common craftsman. These differences had a considerable impact on the development of the novel in the two countries; it partly explains why the novel bloomed half a century earlier in England than in France.

## THE AUTHOR

In 1730, towards the end of his long career, Alexander Pope drew the following picture of the author's plight: 'I believe, if anyone, early in his life, should contemplate the dangerous fate of authors, he would scarce be of their number on any consideration. The life of a wit is a warfare on earth' (Collins 1973: 25). French authors certainly had many reasons to complain at that time, too, considering that their legal and economic status was even less secure; paradoxically, though, they probably had more power and influence socially than the authors on the other side of the Channel. Here, for instance, is what the French novelist and moralist Charles Duclos wrote about the *gens d'esprit* (the wits) most of them *gens de lettres*, in his *Considérations sur les mœurs de ce siècle* published in 1751: 'However, of all the empires, that of the wits though not visible, is the most far-reaching. The men of power can give orders, the wits govern because eventually they shape public opinion which, sooner or later, will conquer or defeat any kind of fanaticism' (Lough 1978: 244; my translation). Pope clearly assessed his plight in economic terms and Duclos in ideological and political ones, a clear sign that two different logics prevailed in their respective countries.

By the beginning of the eighteenth century, the old system of patronage had not totally been supplanted by the market, even in England. Charles Montagu, who had patronized Dryden, was still patronizing Addison, Congreve, and Newton (Collins 1973: 116–18). In Queen Anne's days, wealthy men would readily give from five to ten guineas for the dedication of a play (Plant 1965: 76). With the advent of George I, patronage decreased considerably, though it continued to be extended to poets like Pope, Young, Gay, and Thompson. The writers who benefited from patronage had to perform some incredible volte-faces, siding one day with the Tories, the next with the Whigs, as their interests dictated (Collins 1973: 162). Even some novelists were patronized, though less frequently than the poets; Fielding was helped financially by Allen, the Duke of Bedford, the Duke of Richmond, the Duke of Argyll, the Duke of Roxburgh, and Lord Lyttelton, to whom *Tom Jones* was dedicated (Collins 1973: 185).

Booksellers, being writers themselves in some cases, often had more consideration for authors than did the patrons. Not infrequently, an author lived close to, or even with, his publisher, correcting the proofs on the spot (Plant 1965: 68–70). Tonson offered to give his writer friends a weekly feast provided, explains Wittenberg, 'that they gave him the refusal of all their productions' (Wittenberg 1978: 22). This was the origin of the Kit-Kat Club which became an important meeting place for the wits and writers. Some writers paid tribute to their booksellers. When Boswell said to Johnson, who had received £1,575 for his dictionary: 'I am sorry, Sir, you did not get more for your Dictionary', Johnson answered: 'I am sorry too. But it was very well. The booksellers are generous, liberal-minded men' (Mumby 1967: 237).

Not all writers harboured such good feelings towards booksellers, however. Walpole was very bitter towards the profession: 'Literature must struggle with many difficulties. They who print for profit, print only for profit; we who print to entertain or instruct others, are the bubbles of our designs. Defrauded, abused, pirated' (Collins 1973: 23). In his *Enquiry into the Present State of Polite Learning in Europe*, written in 1758 but published in 1774, Goldsmith denounced the fact that the author was at the mercy of the bookseller: 'The author, when unpatronized by the Great, has naturally recourse to the bookseller. There cannot be, perhaps, imagined a combination more prejudicial to taste than this. It is the interest of the one to allow as little for writing, and of the other to write as much as possible' (Goldsmith 1966: 1, 316).

The dignitaries who still patronized literature were also very critical of the booksellers who deprived them of their influence and authority on the book trade. A group of them managed to fan the anger of some patronized writers and to set up with them, in 1736, the 'Society for the Encouragement of Learning' which was presided over by the Duke of Richmond; it counted Paul Whitehead and James Thompson in its managing committee. The Society's official goal was 'to assist authors in the publication, and to secure them the entire profits of their own works' (Mumby 1967: 233-4). The idea was to finance the printing of books, the Society getting its money back out of the profits without depriving the authors of their copyrights. This method was revived by the American 'Fiction Collective' in 1974. Ten years after the Society's demise in 1748, J. Ralph wrote the following post-mortem: 'Their plan was too narrow, – They also forgot, that the Booksellers were Master of all Avenues to every Market, and, by the Practice of one Night's Postage, could make any Work resemble *Jonah's Gourd* after the Worm had *smote* it' (Collins 1973: 210).

The reason why the booksellers eventually won the battle of

the book, of course, is that they were running a more and more profitable business and distributing more and more money to the authors. Until the seventeenth century, English authors were usually getting very little money from their booksellers. Milton received a paltry £5 from his printer Samuel Symons for *Paradise Lost*, and a further £5 when the first edition was exhausted; his widow eventually resigned the full copyright for a third and final payment of £8 (Mumby 1967: 167–8).

The situation gradually changed during the first half of the eighteenth century. Swift received £200 for *Gulliver's Travels* in 1726, Fielding £183 10s for his *Joseph Andrews* in 1742, then £700 in two payments for *Tom Jones*, and £1,000 for *Amelia*. Even so, novels and poems brought in much less money than history books, for example. Goldsmith received 800 guineas for his *History of Animated Nature*, £250 for his *Grecian History*, 250 guineas for his *History of Rome*, but only £21 for his poem *The Traveller*. As for Smollett, he got £2,000 for his *History of England* as against £210 for *Humphrey Clinker*. Neither he nor Sterne would have been able to support themselves for any length of time on the money they made from their novels. Sterne had to finance the printing of the first two volumes of his *Tristram Shandy* with a loan of £100; the novel being immediately successful, Dodsley offered £650 for the second edition and two more volumes (Collins 1973: 30–41).

The writer's situation did not improve so quickly or so substantially in France where patronage of one kind or another continued to prevail and where the market did not really manage to impose its law before the Revolution. In the seventeenth century, booksellers had sometimes started to pay good money for novels. The publisher of the third part of *L'Astrée* gave 1,000 French pounds plus sixty copies of the book to Honoré d'Urfé's servant to whom the author had surrendered his copyright. D'Urfé, who accepted the patronage of Marie de Médicis, declined to be paid by his publisher (Febvre and Martin 1971: 236). La Calprenède had no such qualms: he sold the second and third parts of his *Cléopàtre* in 1646 for 3,000 pounds; Scarron sold the second part of his *Roman comique* for 1,000 French pounds in 1657 and claimed to have sold his *Virgile travesti* for 11,000 pounds in 1648, a claim echoed by Febvre and Martin but which Lough refuses to take seriously (Febvre and Martin 1971: 236; Lough 1978: 86).

The tradition according to which Louis XIV was a generous patron seems largely unfounded. The maximum gift doled out to writers was 100,000 French pounds, in 1669, a sum which represented only half the cost of a single journey of the court to Versailles. Corneille never received more than 2,000 pounds, and, after 1673, he received nothing for nine years. Racine never got more than 2,000 pounds either, but he was appointed Treasurer of France in 1674, a sinecure with an income of 2,400 pounds. As for Molière, he received only 1,000 pounds (Collins 1973: 98–117).

Patronage remained a very important source of income for most writers in the eighteenth century. The *fermier-général* Helvétius helped Marivaux; Choiseul gave La Harpe 3,000 French pounds for his drama *Mélanie*. Mme Geoffrin, a wealthy lady, was extremely generous with writers; she offered annuities to d'Alembert, Thomas, and Morellet. The Duke of Orleans appointed the playwright Collé as *lecteur* in 1760, a sinecure which brought a salary of 1,800 pounds. Voltaire also obtained pensions from the Regent and Louis XV at the beginning of his career, and he was appointed Historiographer Royal and Gentleman of the Bedchamber. Sometimes, French writers were also supported by foreign sovereigns: Catherine the Great patronized Diderot for over 60,000 pounds, though the latter already had a secure income from his father's estate inherited in 1759; and when Voltaire had fallen into disgrace, he went to London and received 24,000 French pounds plus 6,000 pounds from George I. In 1785, just before the Revolution, Calonne substantially increased the pensions given to the men of letters (Collins 1973: 226–34).

Rousseau, who could hardly count on his egerias to make ends meet, was rarely patronized for his literary works. On the other hand, he received 3,600 pounds from Louis XV and Mme de Pompadour for his opera *Le Devin du village*. While his contemporary Buffon was making 15,000 pounds with each volume of his *Histoire naturelle*, he received only 2,160 pounds from his Amsterdam publisher for his *Nouvelle Héloïse* which was the bestseller of the century; *L'Emile* brought him 6,000 pounds. He got a great deal less for *Discours sur l'inégalité* (twenty-five *louis*), and his *Lettre à d'Alembert* (thirty *louis*). He sought to obtain an annuity for his complete works, but he failed to get it; his heirs later got 24,000 pounds for them (Febvre and Martin 1971: 239; Collins 1973: 210).

Except for Diderot, the more innovative authors of the eighteenth century made comparatively little money with their pen. The market had not expanded as quickly as in England so that their bargaining power with the booksellers was a great deal less. As Malesherbes, who had done a great deal to improve the economic and social status of the men of letters before the Revolution, remarked in his *Mémoires*, the writers had not attained a secure status, economically at least:

> In France the men of letters are a very dependent class of citizens, because it is not a profession which is useful in itself. Most of those who have undertaken it have been induced to do so by a thirst for conquest, they have sacrificed all hope of making a fortune to please themselves and seek glory. However, as one cannot live on glory alone, it is thanks to the court or to the sinecures granted by the court that they can hope to survive in their old age, now that comfort has become a necessity.
> 
> (Lough 1978: 238; my translation)

Paradoxically, the impecunious French writers may have enjoyed a greater freedom of expression than their much better-off English counterparts. It was easier for them to steer away from those who had helped them in the past, since they had to find new patrons or protectors all the time. This may partly explain why the French thinkers (but not the novelists) were more often creative during that period; since they were dependent neither upon one single patron nor on the market to support themselves, they could write essays and philosophical works without any concern about pleasing a given patron or making money. Their economic independence (and sheer poverty, at times) may partly account for what Sartre calls their 'generosity' in 'Qu'est-ce que la littérature?':

> Thus the confusion of his public and the crisis of the European conscience invested the writer with a new function. He now considered literature as the permanent pursuit of generosity. He still had to surrender to the narrow and rigid control of his peers but he could perceive, below him, an

inarticulate and passionate expectation, a more feminine and diffuse desire which freed him from censorship; he had disembodied the spiritual and separated his cause from that of the agonizing ideology; his books had become free appeals to the readers' freedom.
(Sartre 1948: 154; my translation)

Sartre does not mention the economic aspect of the problem, but how can it be ignored? The writer's 'generosity' is not only a manifestation of his desire to offer something new and priceless to his reader, but an effect of his economic independence. The public is not putting pressure on him, yet, to produce the kind of work it desires; so he can 'generously' offer the fruit of his cogitations and labour without any concern about his pay.

This generosity was the French writer's way of being self- rather than market-oriented. He had come to realize that his hope of attaining his artistic and ideological independence did not lie with his patrons or booksellers who, anyway, were often on the side of the Establishment, but with the more discriminating readers, people a little like himself, who alone could vindicate him in the near or remote future.

## THE PUBLIC

The writer's plight would not have improved so quickly in England if his audience had not expanded as it did during the century. Whereas in 1730 writers 'outnumbered the public', as Collins claims, by 1780 'the public could absorb more than writers could give' (Collins 1973: 216). What Eisenstein called the 'overpopulation of Parnassus' (Eisenstein 1979: 158) was no longer a problem, the book trade having finally succeeded in building up a sufficient demand for the products it was offering.

Education developed regularly during the century, after the Society for Promoting Christian Knowledge, founded in 1699, started its charity schools. It was truly the beginning of popular elementary education in England. By 1727, there were 1,389 charity schools in England and Wales, with an attendance of 27,854 children (Plant 1965: 53–4). Later, the Sunday Schools took over, teaching the three Rs to thousands upon thousands of children. Most of the common people, as Cohen explains, 'were supposed to be satisfied with enough practical knowledge to get them through their reading, accounting, and letter-writing with some grace' (Cohen 1977: 68); this knowledge was clearly inadequate to allow them to read novels like *Tom Jones*. The fact that print orders for full-size books rarely exceeded 2,000 copies is an indication of the limited public for either fiction or any other kind of literature, in the eighteenth century.

Among the potential readers of novels, Ian Watt claims that women represented a high percentage, though he does not provide any figure. He explains that the women in England enjoyed greater freedom than in France, especially when it came to choosing a husband, though their legal rights remained very limited, even after the Marriage Act of 1753 (Watt 1967: 138–49). But there was one place in the house, he insists, where they were free to do what they wanted, namely their closet:

> Another characteristic feature of the Georgian house is the closet, or small private apartment usually adjoining the bedroom. Typically, it stores not china and preserves but books, a writing desk and a standish; it is an early version of the room of one's own which Virginia Woolf saw as the prime requisite of a woman's emancipation; and it was much more characteristically the locus of woman's liberty and even licence than its French equivalent, the boudoir, for it was used, not to conceal gallants but to lock them out while Pamela writes her 'saucy journal' and Clarissa keeps Anna Howe abreast of the news.
>
> (188)

Many heroines in eighteenth-century novels are shown reading in their closets; Fielding caricatured this situation by describing Shamela as she is reading a dirty book, *Venus in the Closet*, in that private room.

It was probably the circulating libraries which allowed women to lay their hands on novels. The first one was opened in London at the time when *Pamela* was published, a fact which Collins takes as a striking coincidence (Collins 1973: 245). In his indictment of the novel, Henry Pye, later Poet Laureate, seems to state as evidence the fact that women are known to go to the circulating library: 'the general effect of novel-reading on the gentler sex is too obvious to be doubted; it excites and inflames the passion which is the principal subject of the tale, and the susceptibility of the female votary to the circulating library, is proverbial' (Day 1987: 126). It was probably easier for a woman to borrow a novel for a short period of time than to buy one, for in the latter case she had to keep it somewhere in her room, with the risk that it might fall into her husband's hands.

The novel was often considered as a cheap and light merchandise, both economically and culturally. Vamp, an eighteenth-century publisher, once wrote: 'Novels are a pretty light summer reading, and do very well at Tunbridge, Bristol, and other watering-places; no bad commodity either for the West India trade' (Collins 1973: 244). Certainly, the word 'commodity' would not have been used in reference to a literary work a century before, a clear indication that the novel was not yet considered to be a genuine work of art.

Another innovation which made novels more accessible was their publication in parts or instalments. In a letter to Clairaut, Richardson explains his reasons for preferring to publish *Sir Charles Grandison* in this way:

> I think to publish it at three several times; because there are some few Surprises in different Parts of it, which, were the Catastrophe known, would be lessen'd, and take off the Ardor of such Readers as should happen to approve of the Piece.
>
> (Day 1987: 135)

This practice, which would spread in the next century, allowed a certain amount of communication between author and readers, with the result, sometimes, that the denouement was influenced by the public or a particular reader, as in the case of *Clarissa* (Eaves and Kimpel 1971: 205-34).

Data on the reading public and reading practices in eighteenth-century France are also very scanty; they do not allow us, as yet, to have a comprehensive picture of the novel-reading public at that time. We know, thanks to Furet's research, that literacy developed steadily in France from the Renaissance until the beginning of the third Republic. Between 1686-90 and 1786-90, the percentage of men who could sign their names rose from 29 per cent to 47 per cent, and that of women from 14 per cent to 27 per cent (Furet and Sachs 1974: 714–37). There were significant differences between rural and urban populations; just before the Revolution, 74 per cent of the silk workers in Lyons were able to sign their marriage contracts, 77 per cent of the carpenters, 75 per cent of the bakers, and 60 per cent of the shoe-repairers (Chartier 1987: 170). But, of those who could sign their names, how many could read? And of those who could read, how many had the time or taste to read novels? There is, unfortunately, no way to answer these questions with the data available at the present.

There are signs that more people, even among the working classes, were beginning to acquire books. Chartier provides some interesting figures which show the level of book-ownership around 1700 and after. Judging from the inventories made after people's deaths, in Paris, in the middle of the eighteenth century, only 15 per cent of the merchants owned books, and 12 per cent of the craftsmen, as against 62 per cent of the lawyers, 62 per cent of the members of the clergy, and 58 per cent of the members of Parliament. In the cities of western France, 27.5 per cent of all inventories mentioned the presence of books in 1697–8, and 36.7% in 1757–8, a percentage which slightly decreased in the second half of the century (Chartier 1987: 168–9). These statistics tell us nothing about the proportion of novels in the inventories; we only know that, as a rule, there were many religious books.

Chartier also pays attention to the new furniture used for reading: *bergère, chaise longue ou duchesse, liseuse, bonheur-du-jour*, etc., and he studies the eighteenth-century paintings which represent a person (usually a woman) reading. He takes these elements as unmistakable signs that reading was becoming a very private business requiring comfort and isolation (ibid.: 200–1). People did not have to buy the books they read, of course; they could go to the circulating libraries which were beginning to open everywhere in France, too, and borrow books by the day or even the hour. In some cases, the book had to be divided into two or three sections when there was an excessive demand for it, as in the case of *La Nouvelle Héloïse*, for instance (ibid.: 195).

The scarcity of information about popular culture has always plagued the historians. It is not yet possible to draw a reliable picture of the novel-reading public, either in France or in England, at that time. Were there more men than women reading books (and novels in particular), as Watt seems to assume? More craftsmen than farmers, as Chartier's picture of the reading public suggests? One cannot tell. All the data currently available seem to point to at least one fact, namely that novels were being read silently and in private, whereas chapbooks and the books published by the *bibliothèque bleue* were often read aloud, as in the *veillées* (social evenings by the fire) in France. There continued to be people, such as James Fenimore Cooper, who read books aloud to their family; Dickens travelled around the country, almost around the world, to give public readings of his works. But these forms of reading did not constitute primarily oral practices as they had done until the fifteenth century when copies were very scarce and books had to be read in public, either by the author himself or by an appointed reader who voiced the text to make it available to many people at the same time. All the available facts suggest that the novel inaugurated a more private kind of reading, each reader having his or her own copy (either bought or borrowed) and reading it silently in private, just as it had been written by the author who, even before the development of printing, had always needed a great deal of privacy.

As a result, author and reader began to find themselves in symmetrical positions, as it were, silently communicating with each other through the printed text, often over many centuries. But, whereas in oral readings or storytelling there was always a great deal of feedback on the part of the audience, a fact which allowed the public reader or storyteller to check whether the communication process was working as planned, with silent and private reading no such monitoring is possible. The reader is as isolated from his social group and from his environment as the author himself, and this leaves him more freedom 'to lend an ear' to unconventional ideas or to indulge in unspeakable fantasies triggered by the text.

The 'pleasure of the text' extolled by Roland Barthes largely derives from this magic distance between author and reader imposed by the medium, the printed book, a distance which guarantees their respective privacy:

Is the fact that I am writing with pleasure a sufficient guarantee for me – as a writer – that my reader will also read with pleasure? Not in the least. I must seek out the reader (I must 'cruise'), *without ever knowing where he is*. A locus of bliss is hereby created. It is not the other as a 'person' that I want, it is the locus: the prospect of a dialectics of desire, of the *unpredictability* of bliss: the odds must not be decided from the start, there must be a stake.

(Barthes 1973a: 11; my translation)

The locus of bliss is none other than the printed text, the printed book, which brings author and reader together and yet keeps them apart.

## CONCLUSION

As Walter Ong pointed out in his important book on orality and literacy, the word 'text', whose root means 'to weave' (Barthes says that *Text* means *Tissu* [fabric]'; 1973a: 100), is 'more compatible etymologically with oral utterance than is "literature", which refers to letters etymologically (*literae*) of the alphabet' (Ong 1982: 13).

The French structuralists have often failed to make such distinctions, taking it for granted that a text is necessarily a literary, or even a printed text. Hence their insistence, when studying novels, on exalting the narrator and ignoring the author who, they claim, never enters the picture when one reads or analyses a text. The semiotician, whose chief preoccupation is to dissect the signifying object at hand without any other consideration than the grid he has developed and hopes to perfect, even refuses to consider the problem of the medium (the printed book). Derrida provided a philosophical theory to vindicate the semiotician's enterprise: he denounced the phonocentric fallacy revived, he said, by de Saussure, but which belongs implicitly to 'the totality of the great era covered by the history of metaphysics' (Derrida 1967: 24; my translation). He did not realize that he was describing the transition between secondary orality, which nurtured itself upon hallowed texts, and the present typographic age in which texts (above all literary texts) are read silently. It is true, as Derrida claims, that the silent reading of books taxed the readers eyes more than his ears, but it is not true that the printed text is purely visual, like a painting. It must be voiced, somehow, otherwise it will not make sense.

The printing press dramatically changed the nature of the communication process between author and reader, as Marshall McLuhan showed in *The Gutenberg Galaxy*. The author is now aware that he cannot totally regulate the flow of information generated by his writing once his book starts to circulate, so he must overcode his text to be sure that its language will 'come clear all by itself, with no existential context', as Ong says about chirographic communication in general (Ong 1982: 104). This compulsion to overcode has induced some contemporary novelists to saturate every single page of their novels with erudite information, lexical and grammatical ambiguities, etc. (*Finnegans Wake*, Nabokov's *Ada*, or Pynchon's *Gravity's Rainbow*). The luxuriance of Joyce's or Nabokov's vocabulary is partly a side-effect of Gutenberg's invention. As Ong explains, 'The lexical richness of grapholects begins with writing, but its fullness is due to print. For the resources of a modern grapholect are available largely through dictionaries' (1982: 107). Such resources are available not only to the writers, of course, but also to their readers, who can always look up words if they do not understand them.

The typographic author is also challenged, even more than the chirographic one, to work with and against other texts or intertexts, because print encourages the writing and wide distribution of texts. He must avoid plagiarism and imitation at all cost, and, when he handles those other texts, he must develop a strategy to appropriate them, to use them as referents, just as Balzac used Saumur or Angoulême in his novels.

This wealth of texts and linguistic resources made available to the writer by the printing press helps the writer beat his unconscious, his self, as Ong explains:

The writer finds his written words accessible for reconsideration, revision, and other manipulation until they are finally released to do their work. Under the author's eye the text lays out the beginning, the middle and the end, so that the writer is encouraged to think of his work as a self-contained, discrete unit, defined by closure.

(1982: 148)

This feature will be examined in depth in the following chapters; it accounts for many of the characteristics of the modern novel.

Print also gives a certain fixed finality to the text. In manuscript cultures, texts were considerably revised and sometimes distorted in the process of copying. The industry has developed such elaborate techniques that it can reproduce the text with nearly perfect accuracy; it is the industry, therefore, which is responsible for the clean and eminently readable aspect of the page and of the book. This is a guarantee for the reader that the printed text represents the words of the author in their 'definitive or "final" form' (Ong 1982: 133). Eisenstein insists a great deal on this:

> Certainly press variants did multiply and countless errata were issued. The fact remains that Erasmus or Bellarmin could issue errata; Jerome or Alcuin could not. The very act of publishing errata demonstrated a new capacity to locate textual errors with precision and to transmit this information simultaneously to scattered readers.
> (Eisenstein 1979: 80)

Although even the most demanding writers and proofreaders, and the most sophisticated computers will sometimes overlook gross misprints, the modern reader considers that he is entitled to have a pure and faultless text. All the variorum editions now available show indirectly that this requirement can be met. Hence the concept of 'Real Text' promoted by Pynchon. The 'Real Text' is not, of course, the body of representations and meanings pictured by the reader; it is the object, the manufactured product for which the author provided a blueprint.

Print does not only reify the word (Ong 1982: 119), it also reifies the book, turns it into an object which can be manipulated. The reader can now go through what Goody calls 'backward scanning' whenever he wants to erase apparent inconsistencies (Ong 1982: 104). This backward scanning was not easy with manuscripts which required a very patient reading because of their countless abbreviations, their reduced or non-existent spaces between words and paragraphs. Now, the reader can photograph the page (which in itself partly vindicates Derrida), and go back many pages. He can also make notes in the margin (a point never mentioned by Ong), since, in most cases, the book is now his property and can be appropriated as he likes. This patient scanning of the text is often necessary with the more innovative texts which strive very hard to confuse the reader.

Because the book is such a perfectly tooled object, the reader has the illusion that he owns it, as he does his car or his television set. So does, to some extent, the industry which has worked so hard to purify the primitive chirographic object handed over by the author. The book at hand can therefore be said to have a double origin: a linguistic one in the author, and a technological one in the industry. In 1762, Warburton used this argument to plead against literary property:

> The Property of an Inventor in his Machine, is in every respect similar to the exclusive Right claimed by the Author in his Copy. It is admitted, that at Common Law, the Inventor hath no Property in the Form of his Machine; can the Author claim any in his Copy?
>
> (Warburton 1762: 22)

This means that the inventor has a right in his idea, though he does not know how to guarantee it, but no right in the actual machines manufactured according to his blueprint.

Where books are concerned, all the agents of the trade, starting now from the agents themselves, the publishing houses with their editors, readers, and marketeers, the printing works, the distributors, and the book dealers, similarly own a share of the books they publish or sell. Yet, the author, who wrote the blueprint, must still be held as the prime source and chief owner of the book. The reader, once he has bought the book, does not owe anything to the industry, but still owes everything to the author with whom he is trying to communicate.

In the oral age, the communication between storyteller and public was fairly straightforward, the channel (the voice) bringing together in one place and at one time the interlocutors. With the development of print, the process has become more complex, especially after the industry started to be the accomplice of the law. The new communication process involved in writing and reading a book such as a novel could be represented in the following way:

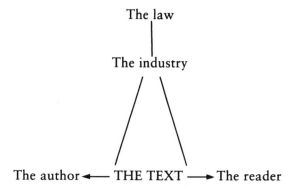

Writing and reading a printed book implies that author and reader enter upon a double communication process: an indirect one through the industry which manufactured and distributed the book, and a more direct one through the text which takes its roots both in the language itself and in the author who put the words together. Writing, especially in the post-Gutenberg era, 'is, indeed, at all levels, the word of the other' as Barthes explained (1964: 13; my translation). The other, or rather the Lacanian Other is present at the level of the language which constitutes the text, at the level of the law which controls its acceptability, and at the level of the industry which defines its marketability.

# Chapter 2

# The bookhood of the novel

'Novels are books and books are objects, and therefore they exist like other objects – they are a space in space', William Gass remarked once in a lecture (Gass 1983: 83). This seems a commonsensical view; yet so far few critics have taken into account the objecthood, the bookhood of the novel. The Russian formalists and the French structuralists fetishized the text, either as a linguistic construct begging to be deconstructed, or as a discourse teasing the discourse-analyst to reveal its structure. In either case, the bookhood of the novel is ignored since the only medium is held to be *l'écriture* (writing) and not print.

As we will see in the present chapter, the modern novel paraded its printhood and its bookhood from the start; by countless signs, it acknowledged the medium through which it would circulate until it reached its target, the reader.

## THE OBJECT

Medieval romances have come down to us as printed books, just like *Tom Jones* or *La Nouvelle Héloïse*, yet they were never meant to circulate in this form. The modern novel, on the other hand, is a product of the printing age manufactured in such a way as to make it more eminently transportable and readable by isolated readers.

### Presentation

As Febvre and Martin have shown, print gradually helped change the format of books. In the Middle Ages, the copyist's script was often of a comparatively large size; the manuscripts, which were usually kept in libraries and on lecterns, tended to be of a much larger format than printed books, which are meant to enter private homes (Febvre and Martin 1971: 130–3).

Most of the major eighteenth-century novels, on the other hand, were first printed in duodecimo volumes (usually around 16.5 by 9.7 cm in the copies I have consulted at the Huntington Library): *Pamela* in two such volumes, plus two more of the same format for part II, *Clarissa* in eight, *Joseph Andrews* in two, *Tom Jones* in six, *The Adventures of Roderick Random* in two. Only *Tristram Shandy* is of a slightly smaller format (probably the equivalent of a half-sheet in-octavo, since the signatures at the bottom of the pages run only from one to four, instead of one to six in the other cases). *La Nouvelle Héloïse* was published in the same format, along with most of the major French novels at that time in their first editions. It was comparatively easy to carry such books around and to hide them, if necessary.

Many of the earlier novels were bound in calf. According to Edward Newton, the 'small calf bound book continued to be the fashion until after the turn of the century: then with the increasing number of readers it was discovered that leather was expensive and paper BOARDS came into use' (Newton 1971: 16–17). Often, however, the bookseller would offer unbound copies to the public at a lower price, as Millar did for *Tom Jones*. This allowed book-owners to personalize their copies to the extent of putting their names or initials where one would expect to find the author's name and the title of the book.

The make-up of the page in eighteenth-century novels was still largely producer-oriented, whereas that of contemporary novels is clearly reader-oriented. All the copies of the first editions mentioned above which I have consulted at the Huntington Library present the same features in the page make-up: the pagination (which is in roman numerals for the many preambles and in arabic numerals for the text proper) is always given at the top, either in the centre when the title of the novel is not reprinted, or at the extreme right on the left-hand page and the extreme left on the right-hand page when the title is repeated (often split into two parts, one on each page).

At the bottom of the left-hand page, there is usually nothing, but at the bottom of the right-hand one there are always two kinds of information. First, there is the signature mark, that is, a letter which refers to the book section plus a figure which refers to the folio (the normal sequence for a duodecimo volume is A1, A2, A3, A4, A5, A6 plus six right-hand pages without the signature mark, then B1, B2, etc.; J, V, and W are omitted because it was the Latin alphabet that was normally used). The purpose of the signature mark is to enable the book sections to be gathered together in the right order (Glaister 1960: 376). In the right-hand corner, underneath the last word of the last line, is the catchword, that is, the first word of the next page. Its purpose was also 'to guide the binder in assembling' (Glaister 1960: 62). The practice began around 1500; it was to continue until the beginning of the nineteenth century (one finds it again in the 1801 edition of *Pamela*). Though this type of information was officially meant for the binder, there is little doubt that it was also exploited by the reader: it helped him not to interrupt his reading when he finished a page and turned to a new one, especially when he had to make a public reading of the text (Jennett 1973: *passim*).

The typographic presentation also demonstrates that writers and printers were still acutely aware of the oral dimension of the printed word. Italics were abundantly used, both to distinguish proper names from common nouns and to simulate handwriting. For instance, Clarissa's signature is always printed this way in Richardson's novel; her afterthoughts are sometimes printed crosswise in the margin, a clear indication that the author either did the composition of the text himself or closely supervised it (Richardson 1748: V, 239). Most common nouns are capitalized, as are sometimes the adjectives preceding prestigious titles, as, for instance, in *Jonathan Wild* 'Fatal Sisters' or 'Grand Monarch' (Fielding 1754: 186–7).

Richardson, who was his own printer, changed his policy in this respect between *Pamela* and *Clarissa*. In the first edition of *Pamela* he followed the normal practice of capitalizing all the nouns: 'Well, but God's Will must be done! – and so comes the Comfort, that I shall not be oblig'd to return back to be a Clog upon my dear Parents' (Richardson 1741a: I, 2). He maintained this practice in the preface of *Clarissa* but curiously abandoned it in the rest of the novel: 'Mr. Diggs, whom I sent for at the first hearing of the rencounter, to inquire, for *your* sake, how your brother was, told me, That there was no danger from the wound' (Richardson 1748: I, 2). Yet, he kept the habit, common in those days, of capitalizing the first word of a reported speech, as 'That' here. A few printers, like that of Donaldson's *Sir Barthlomew Sapskull* (1768), followed Richardson's new practice of not capitalizing the common nouns (Donaldson 1975).

There was a debate, in the eighteenth century, on this question of capitalization, as Cohen reports:

> All the language practitioners of the early part of the century agree that capitals should be used to indicate emphasis, but this recommendation brings them into conflict with 'Fashion' as Greenwood writes, especially the habits of printers.
>
> (Cohen 1977: 52)

The reference is to James Greenwood, who published *An Essay Towards a Practical English Grammar Describing the Genius and Nature of the English Tongue* in 1711. Others, Cohen reports, thought that there was 'visual beauty in the page that consistently marks the different parts of speech' (52–3). This is a point on which printers and authors (and even booksellers, we presume) obviously did not agree.

The same situation prevailed as far as punctuation was concerned. Dashes and suspension points were used abundantly, a practice which Sterne parodied extensively in his *Tristram Shandy*. Sentences, which usually ran on for many lines, tended to be divided into smaller units by commas, colons, or semicolons. Here is, for example, a passage from *Clarissa*:

> If any necessary matter be omitted in this my Will; or if any thing appear doubtful or contradictory, as possibly may be the case; since, besides my inexperience in these matters, I am now at this time very weak and ill; having put off the finishing hand a little too long, in hopes of obtaining the last forgiveness of my honoured friends; in which case I should have acknowledged the favour with a suitable warmth of duty, and filled up some blanks which I left to the very last, in a more agreeable manner to myself, than now I have been enabled to do –
>
> (Richardson 1748: VII, 309)

The sentence continues for many more lines. Richardson's punctuation not only underlines the articulations of the sentence but also provides the reader with breathing spaces every other line. One notices, by the way, that 'Will' is still capitalized in this passage, referring as it obviously does to the title of the document she is writing.

Most of our contemporary editions have 'standardized' punctuation (as well as capitalization or spelling); they have removed all the traces of orality that still remained in the early stages of the typographic era. Since writing is 'the Picture or Image of Speech', as Greenwood claimed, it should include marks 'adapted unto all the Material Circumstances of it' (Cohen 1977: 52). In his *English Grammar* published in 1712, Michael Maittaire explained that punctuation marks were important 'not only for the ease of breath, but also for the better understanding of the sense' (Cohen 1977: 51); in other words, the author must make sure, through his punctuation especially, that the text will be understood as he meant it. Greenwood went so far as to propose a sign to underline the irony of a text, '<' (Cohen 1977: 52). More recently, Alcanter de Brahm suggested in his *L'Ostensoir des ironies* (1899) that a reversed question mark be used for the purpose (Dupriez 1984: 265). Neither of these signs ever had much success. But, in *Tristram Shandy*, Sterne used the index finger 'to point out some important moral injunctions', as Watt explains (1965: xlv).

The presentation of our contemporary novels is more clearly reader-oriented. The words have now become mute graphs which the reader must voice by drawing the right inferences from the text itself. As we shall see in our last chapter, the so-called 'death of the author' is partly due to the development of typography which, after two centuries, has finally imposed its logic on the genre.

**Title-page**

The next important element to take into account is the title-page, which appeared towards the end of the fifteenth century. Since many books were sent out unbound, the first page often got soiled during transportation. It consequently became a habit to insert a blank page before the beginning of the text, a practice which unfortunately made it difficult to identify the book at its different stages of production. Hence the necessity of printing the title or some identifying information on the blank page, which also came to include the printer's colophon (Jennett 1973: 384).

In eighteenth-century novels, the title-page usually contained a great deal more text, though not necessarily more information, than in our contemporary novels. We now expect to find four kinds of data on a title-page: the title, the author's name, the publisher's name, and the date of publication (which now often appears on the back of the title-page). In Richardson's and Fielding's time, one usually found only three of these, the title, the date of publication, and the publisher's name and address. In exceptional cases, for example *Memoirs of a Woman of Pleasure*, the real publisher or bookseller refrained from giving his true name for fear of legal pursuit, but otherwise he always did so in order to protect his rights in the book.

Most of the titles of eighteenth-century novels are very long; they sometimes constitute texts in themselves. Usually, they give the name of the hero or heroine, but they preface it with a note underlining the historicity of the book:

*The Fortunes and Misfortunes of the Famous Moll Flanders, & c.*
*The Life and Adventures of Robinson Crusoe, & c.*
*An Apology for the Life of Mrs. Shamela Andrews*
*The History and the Adventures of Joseph Andrews and of his Friend Mr. Abraham Adams*
*The History of Tom Jones, A Foundling*
*The Adventures of Roderick Random*
*The Life and Opinions of Tristram Shandy, Gentleman*
*The Life and Adventures of Sir Bartholomew Sapskull.*

Such titles are reminiscent of the titles of the romances of chivalry parodied by Cervantes in *The Ingenious, Gentleman Don Quixote*.

In some cases, the hero or heroine's name is not even mentioned:

*Memoirs of a Woman of Pleasure* (which is now known as *Fanny Hill*)
*Memoirs of a Coxcomb* (also by John Cleland, 1751).

Such titles suggest that the book is going to deal with a type, as did the title of the picaresque English novel, *The English Rogue* (1665).

Richardson is the first one among the leading novelists of the century to have put the name of his heroine first:

*Pamela; or, Virtue Rewarded*
*Clarissa; or, the History of a Young Lady.*

Others followed his example, like John Shebbeare with his *Lydia; or, Filial Piety* (1755). Being the only professional printer Richardson was apparently more communication-conscious, realizing that a name would have a stronger impact on the reader than a programmatic formula. The other novelists were more anxious to give a brief (and sometimes ironic, as in the case of Sterne) hint about the content of the story itself or about the tradition which it perpetuated. Their titles have usually been pruned down since: we always refer to *Joseph Andrews*, *Tom Jones*, or *Fanny Hill*.

One can object, of course, that the titles as given above were grossly truncated, and that, for instance, the title of *Moll Flanders* actually is:

THE
FORTUNES
AND
MISFORTUNES
OF THE FAMOUS
Moll Flanders, &c.

Who was born in NEWGATE, and during a Life of continued Variety for Threescore Years, besides her Childhood, was Twelve Years a *Whore*, five times a *Wife*, (whereof once to her own Brother) Twelve year a *Thief*, Eight Year a Transported *Felon* in *Virginia*, at last grew *Rich*, liv'd *Honest*, and died a *Penitent*.

(Defoe 1970: 1)

Should the brief narrative be considered as part of the title? It is debatable. Such a narrative reads like an advertisement for the book, as did the subtitle of *The English Rogue*: 'Described in the Life of Meriton Latroom, a Witty Extravagant. Being a Compleat History of the Most Eminent Cheats of Both Sexes'

(Head 1961: n.p.). The additional information is clearly meant to hook the customer.

In those days, of course, there was no dust-jacket (it was invented in the nineteenth century) and therefore no blurb on the cover to advertise the book. All the advertising had to be done on the title-page. The subtitle of *Clarissa* reads quite clearly as an advertisement:

CLARISSA
OR, THE
HISTORY
OF A
YOUNG LADY
Comprehending
*The most* Important Concerns *of* Private Life
And particularly shewing,
The DISTRESSES that may attend the Misconduct
Both of PARENTS and CHILDREN,
In Relation to MARRIAGE

(Richardson 1748: I, n.p.)

There are many levels to be distinguished in this title: the title proper, plus the subtitle ('History of a Young Lady'), then an explanatory note ('The Most Important Concerns of Private Life'), and finally the moral lesson. Since Richardson was his own publisher (partly at least) and his own printer, we must consider that he inserted all these elements himself.

There is little doubt that some of these advertisement-like subtitles were composed (like the blurbs now) by the booksellers and publishers themselves rather than by the authors; hence the many changes in the following editions. The advertisement was meant to tickle the imagination of the reader; sometimes, also, it was used to protect the book against censorship, as in the case of *Moll Flanders*. There often was a reference to a celebrated work, as on the title-page of *Joseph Andrews*: 'Written in Imitation of The *Manner* of CERVANTES Author of *Don Quixote*' (Fielding 1742: I, n.p.) .

The title-page of *Tom Jones* contained no such advertisements but a Latin epigraph: '*Mores hominum multorum vidit*' (Fielding 1749: I, n.p.). This practice will be followed by Sterne on the title-pages of volumes 1, 3, 5, 7, and 9 of his *Tristram Shandy* (Sterne 1965). The epigraphs are from Epictetus, John of Salisbury, Erasmus, Pliny, and Burton; they were clearly provided by the author himself, who had hit upon this device to do his own advertising. Sterne and Fielding were obviously aware that the novel was not a very highly respected genre and needed all the help it could get from illustrious texts (preferably written in Greek or Latin) to be received favourably by the intelligentsia. Though these two arch-ironists wrote these epigraphs mostly to hint at the comic tone of their books, they probably used them, too, to claim a place for themselves in Parnassus. It would not have been very convenient, in the circumstances, for the bookseller or publisher to insert his own advertisement. So the device had the additional effect of keeping the industry out of the title-page while preserving the rights of the author.

This is the more paradoxical, in the case of *Tristram Shandy*, as the author's name does not appear on any of the title-pages. It was not only because he was a minister of the church and might have hesitated to sign such a risky novel that Sterne published his novel anonymously, but above all because *Tristram Shandy*, like *Moll Flanders*, was written in the first person by the eponymous character.

The epistolary novels were also published anonymously. On the title-page of *Pamela*, one merely finds the words: 'in a SERIES of FAMILIAR LETTERS FROM A Beautiful Young DAMSEL, To her PARENTS. Now first Published' (Richardson 1741a: I, n.p.); there is no reference, on this title-page, to any editor or compiler. On that of *Clarissa*, on the other hand, there is a note saying: '*Published by the* EDITOR *of* PAMELA', a confusing phrase, since the word 'published' can apply to the author as well (Richardson 1748). Richardson had obviously nothing to fear from censorship; his name appears on the title-page as that of the publisher: 'Printed for S. Richardson'. In fact, he published the novel with four other booksellers; Charles Rivington and John Osborn gave him twenty guineas for two-thirds of the copyright. When he published the second part the following year, he entered it at the Stationers' Company under his own name; then he obtained a Royal Licence for 'the sole printing, publishing, and sale of the four volumes' (Eaves and Kimpel 1971: 145). Rousseau's name does appear on the title-page of *La Nouvelle Héloïse* but not as that of the author: 'LETTRES DE DEUX AMANS Habitans d'une petite ville au pied des Alpes recueillies et publiées par J. J. Rouseau' (Rousseau 1964: 3). Rousseau claims only to be the compiler and editor of the book.

In the eighteenth century, one was evidently too close to the oral era when the storyteller was often both the author and the narrator of the story. It would have been self-defeating, it seems, for a novelist to sign his work when that work was supposed to be written by a narrator or a set of characters. Neither authors nor readers were yet ready to suspend their disbelief to the extent of accepting that the same narrative discourse could have a double origin. Later on, this practice became common, and Proust could insist that Marcel was a fictional character and not himself in *Remembrance of Things Past*. In the eighteenth century, the printed text had not yet acquired the ability it has now to generate a strong fiction effect as a result of all the manipulations it goes through; that is why, in those days, an author could not sign a text written supposedly by the eponymous character.

Neither Adrien Baillet, who published a book entitled *Auteurs déguisez sous des noms étrangers* in 1690, nor Halkett and Laing who published their *Dictionary of the Anonymous and Pseudonymous Literature of Great Britain* between 1882 and 1884, used this argument to account for anonymity or pseudonymity. Baillet cited among the chief motives: 'the *love* of Antiquity', '*prudence*', 'the *fear* of disgrace and penalties', 'the *shame* at producing or publishing something which would be unworthy of one's rank or profession', 'the *intention* to sound the minds on a subject which might seem new', ' the *fantasy* of hiding one's low birth or rank', and finally 'the *desire*' to hide a name which would not ring well (Laugaa 1986: 196; my translation). For Halkett and Laing, on the other hand, the chief motives are 'diffidence', 'fear of consequences', and 'shame' (Laugaa 1986: 229). Laugaa draws attention to the fact that, between 1650 and 1700, anonymity and pseudonymity developed at the same rate in literature as the fashion for masks in society (143–4), a point which we will keep in mind throughout our discussion of textual communication.

There is an article on this subject in Diderot's *Encyclopédie* which explains that anonymity can be praiseworthy, depending on the author's intentions: 'any writer who, out of shyness, modesty, or scorn for glory, refuses to attract notice at the beginning of his work deserves to be commended' (*Encyclopédie* 1778: 'Anonyme'; my translation). Yet the author of the article complains that the readers are often too favourably biased towards anonymous works, and that some writers have artificially tried to promote the sale of their books by publishing them anonymously. The article seems to suggest that secrecy does not necessarily make for quality.

One must also point out that booksellers were often all too pleased to publish books anonymously; while seemingly protecting the authors against censorship and the snooping public, they could claim the books as their property. The publication history of the *Lettres portugaises* is interesting in this respect. In 1668, a privilege was granted for the printing of 'a book intitled *Les Valantins, lettres portugaises, Epigrammes et Madrigaux* de Guilleraques [*sic*]'. The book was published anonymously by Barbin in 1669, but it bore a different title, *Lettres portugaises traduites en français* (Bray 1983: 59). Guilleragues, who was a member of the Parliament of Bordeaux and who became secretary to Louis XIV the same year, obviously had to protect himself. But, in the process, the publisher practically purloined the book: he wrote the address to the reader and claimed that the book had not been written in French. The hoax was so successful that there have been critics even in this century who claimed that the book was not written by Guilleragues.

Richardson, who was the author, the bookseller, and the printer of his books, had nothing to fear on that score, and considered anonymity to be a kind of game. In a letter he wrote to his brother-in-law a year after the publication of *Pamela*, he said that he 'did not intend [his authorship] should be known to more than 6 Friends, and those in Confidence' (Eaves and Kimpel 1971: 119). But when phoney sequels to the novel began to appear, he was more or less compelled to write two more volumes and to insist, on their title-pages, that they were being published 'By the Editor of the TWO FIRST' (Richardson 1742: III, n.p.). Also, he added an advertisement at the end of the fourth volume deploring the fact that imitations had been made, guaranteeing that this sequel is the only authentic one, and proclaiming that if it ever gets published, it should be 'solely, at the Assignment of Samuel Richardson, of *Salisbury-Court*, Fleetstreet, the Editor of these Four Volumes of *PAMELA*; or VIRTUE REWARDED' (IV, 472). Richardson was not claiming to be the author but only the editor of the book, a point which had not been made clear before; also, he wanted his readers to know that he was a member of the industry, as the Fleet Street address indicates.

Despite the harm being done to him by his imitators, Richardson immensely enjoyed the hoax. His long correspondence with Lady Bradshaigh about *Clarissa* shows that he liked to tease and be teased, keeping his enthusiastic (and sometimes prying) reader at a distance while, at the same time, wishing to draw nearer to her. He eventually arranged to meet her after she wrote that she had met him in the Park and had 'had an opportunity of surveying [him] unobserved' (Eaves and Kimpel 1971: 228). She had cleverly managed to reverse the roles and to rip off his mask; the author was suddenly at his reader's mercy! This must have been an unbearable situation. Richardson immediately arranged to meet the lady.

This celebrated correspondence is instructive as regards not only Richardson but all the novelists who declined to sign their works for other reasons than the fear of censorship. Not only did anonymity boost the authenticity of the manuscripts found and their realistic effect, but it guaranteed the inaccessibility and semi-godlike status of the author. The strategy is cleverly analysed by Sterne in *Tristram Shandy*. Tristram shuts out the bad readers in chapter IV of volume I, declaring that "tis wrote only for the curious and inquisitive' (Sterne 1965: 6). Then he compares writing to conversation, adding that the same discreetness is required in both cases:

> As no one, who knows what he is about in good company, would venture to talk all; – so no author, who understands the just boundaries of decorum and good breeding, would presume to think all: The truest respect which you can pay to the reader's understanding, is to halve this matter amicably, and leave him something to imagine, in his turn, as well as yourself.
>
> (83)

This very famous passage is ironic, of course; Tristram, or rather Sterne, knows that he is not giving a fair chance to his reader, that he does not 'halve this matter amicably' with him but snubs him (or her; more anon), making sure that his own privacy will never be invaded. Tristram is the full-proof mask of Sterne.

This did not prevent the latter from signing the first pages (not the title-pages) of volumes 5, 7, and 9 in some (the Huntington Library copy, for instance), and perhaps all copies, when they first came out. A. Edward Newton, who was a great bibliophile, provided the following explanation:

> Occasionally unscrupulous booksellers suggest that these were Sterne's own copies, whereas this was merely Sterne's way of indicating to his customers that they were buying the authorized edition of his book, which was so enormously successful that a pirated edition, printed in Dublin, almost immediately, made its appearance on the London market.
> (Newton 1971: 15)

The autograph had the same purpose, therefore, as Richardson's advertisement at the end of the fourth volume of *Pamela*: to guarantee his customers that they were buying the real text. Obviously, also, it was a way for the author to claim his rights in a book published anonymously.

Authors such as Richardson and Sterne clearly had ambiguous feelings on this matter: they thought they could not sign a work written in the first person by the eponymous character, and yet they did their best to claim their rights in the books. In a 1957 interview, Georges Bataille explained to Pierre Dumayet that the writer always feels guilty about writing, because 'Writing is, in spite of everything, the opposite of working', it is a kind of *'enfantillage'*: 'I believe that there is something essentially childish about literature' (Bataille 1988: 128; my translation). Richardson, who was a well-known printer, obviously felt this way about writing, and so did Sterne, the church minister. They both sensed that their writings exhibited another, perhaps less commendable, facet of their character which they were not totally ready to acknowledge at first.

We find an interesting fable on this theme in William Donaldson's *Sir Bartholomew Sapskull*, a novel published anonymously in 1768. The frontispiece shows the reverse of a man's head captioned 'The Reverse of Somebody', and it is followed by a comparatively long text which begins: 'The *reverse* of *Somebody* can be the likeness of *Nobody* ... so far the *frontispiece* is truly *original* ... and the *artist* cannot be charg'd with copying the *manner* of those important authors who make themselves the pre-*face* to their work' (Donaldson 1975: ii). Donaldson does not only criticize the authors who expose themselves too much but he also teases his readers while soliciting their admiration. This note is followed by a mock dedication 'To Somebody' which ends in the following way:

> SOMEBODY will be offended at this dedication, because I dissent from the establish'd doctrine of dedicators, and substitute myself the object of my idolatry! for in the vanity of my heart I have been led imperceptibly from my first view of inscribing this volume to some distant person, and brought the compliment home to myself, because in the writing of it I have all along consider'd myself SOMEBODY.
> (Donaldson 1975: viii)

Any author of an anonymously published novel is indeed 'SOMEBODY' craving respect and admiration. The author has always been vain and proud; Jean Guenot, a French novelist, once wrote that Danton's address to his executioner ('Samson, you must show my head to the people, it is worth exhibiting!') is one of the most telling statements about authorhood (Guenot 1982: 17; my translation). The author is childish, Guenot adds; he wants to sell his face, and now he is often encouraged in this enterprise by his publisher who readily puts his portrait (usually a photograph, but sometimes a caricature) on the back of the dust-jacket. Even such a haughty novelist as Nabokov agreed to exhibit his face in this manner, especially after the success of *Lolita*.

Of the major English novels we have mentioned so far, *Tom Jones* was the first to bear the author's name on the title-page: 'by Henry Fielding, Esq'. Fielding, who had published *Joseph Andrews* anonymously, finally consented to parade in the garb of the author. Yet he pursued the *'enfantillage'* in the opening chapters of each of the books which together constitute an anatomy of authorhood. He had apparently decided that overexposure of authorhood achieved the same effect as anonymity proper. And it is true, as we shall see in our fifth chapter, that, through this device, the author often becomes as much a fictional persona as Tristram Shandy himself.

**Advertisements and dedications**

The title-page was usually followed by various preambles such as those we found at the beginning of *Don Quixote*. The preambles were of two kinds: advertisements and dedications. The former were usually inserted by the bookseller who had financed the publication of the book, and the latter by the author himself who wanted to pay tribute to the person who had helped him financially.

Richardson had no patron; he financed the publication of his *Pamela* with Charles Rivington and John Osborn. When the novel came out in November 1740, it was prefaced by an anonymous letter to the editor praising the book. This letter, originally addressed to the author, had appeared earlier in the *Weekly Miscellany* (Eaves and Kimpel 1971: 91). The change from 'author' to 'editor' was naturally due to the fact that Richardson wanted his book to be authorless; yet this change was an implicit confession that some editing, or even rewriting, had been done by someone (or SOMEBODY!). After this letter, there was a eulogy written by Jean-Baptiste de Freval, for whom Richardson had already printed a book. Being his own publisher, Richardson hit upon this device to advertise his book without blowing his own trumpet. At the beginning of the second edition, not only do we find Freval's letter and the eulogy, but also an introduction including three more letters plus verses 'sent to the Bookseller, for the Unknown Author of the beautiful Piece call'd *PAMELA*' (Richardson 1741b: vii – xxxviii).

Sometimes, the bookseller would use this space to advertise the other books he had published. Here are, for example, the preambles at the beginning of the second edition of *Jonathan Wild*: the advertisement from the publisher to the reader mentioning that this is a revised edition and praising the author; the table of contents (a very common practice in the eighteenth century; Richardson's 'Contents' at the beginning of *Pamela* is a circumstantial summary of the novel); finally, a list of the books printed for A. Millar, opposite Catherine Street, in the Strand (among them *Joseph Andrews, Tom Jones, The Adventures of David Simple, Shakespeare Illustrated*) (Fielding 1754: n.p.).

The bookseller obviously felt he had a right to smuggle such advertisements into the book he was bringing out. The preamble was like a continuation of the title-page, a space which partly belonged to the bookseller, to the industry, rather than to the author himself. Nowadays, such advertisements usually appear at the end of the book rather than at the beginning. The space reserved by the publisher (advertisements, blurb, even the portrait of the author which amounts to an objectification of the author by the publisher himself) seems to have moved from the beginning to the end of the book as the author's rights have become better acknowledged. This 'migration' was preceded by another one: the publisher's colophon, which at first was printed at the end of the book, moved to the title-page, an indication that publishers and authors were now more or less on the same footing (Jennett 1973: 386).

From *Moll Flanders* until *Tom Jones*, none of the major novels I have examined has a dedication at the beginning. It is true, of course, that few books were then financed by wealthy patrons in England (or even by such charitable institutions as the Society for the Encouragement of Learning, of which, by the way, Richardson himself was a member). The industry had taken things in hand, and it was making sufficient profits not to expect any kind of official thanks from the authors. There were many authors who still depended on wealthy patrons to keep body and soul together while they were writing their books, however, but they could not easily acknowledge such kindnesses in dedications without giving away their own names. So, the necessity for the author to remain anonymous was also partly responsible for the disappearance of dedications in the first half of the century.

The first major novel beginning with a dedication is also the first one not to have been published anonymously, namely, *Tom Jones*. Fielding dedicated his novel 'To the Honorable George Lyttleton, Esq., One of the Lords Commissioners of the Treasury' (Fielding 1980: 35). Lyttleton did not finance the publication of the novel, of course, and neither did the Duke of Bedford, also mentioned in the dedication (nor Ralph Allen of Bath who is indirectly acknowledged, too). Andrew Millar covered all the costs, and he even gave £700 to Fielding into the bargain. But, while the latter was composing the novel, Lyttleton, who had encouraged him in this enterprise, granted him 'pecuniary "assistance"' (Dudden 1966: 584).

Lyttleton did not wish to be thanked by Fielding, as the dedication makes clear, but Fielding was adamant: 'I must still insist on my right to desire your protection of this work' (Fielding 1980: 35). In the following paragraphs, Fielding tries to find the reasons behind Lyttleton's refusal to 'the allowance of the honour which I have sollicited', and he comes up with the most favourable one: 'I suspect that your dislike of public praise is your true objection to granting my request' (36). Following the example of most dedicators in past centuries, he plays the part of the fawning courtier, exhibiting his unworthiness in front of the grandee who has granted him his patronage. But he immediately brushes aside his patron's 'modest aversion to panegyric': '[I] will consider not what my patron really deserves to have written, but what he will be best pleased to read' (36). Fielding obviously means: 'deserves to have written for him, or in his glory', but he intimates more flatly that his patron, who had urged him to write this book, may have lamented the fact that he had not written it himself.

The dedication, which has been forced upon the patron, turns after this into a presentation of the book and of the author's objectives. Fielding does not address George Lyttleton any more, but rather his reader: 'From the name of my patron, indeed, I hope my reader will be convinced, at his very entrance on this work, that he will find in the whole course of it nothing prejudicial to the cause of religion and virtue' (37). He invokes the name of his patron to commend the morality of the book and to protect himself against censorship. He does not only thank his benefactor; he uses his name and prestige to tell his readers that the novel has received the approval of a moral authority and cannot therefore be morally objectionable.

Fielding's dedication does not serve the same purpose, however, as did the dedications quoted in our first chapter; it is a preface of a kind, as he himself finally admits: 'I will detain you, sir, no longer. Indeed I have run into a preface while I professed to write a dedication' (38). The awkward tone of

The bookhood of the novel 69

this dedication, which strongly contrasts with the jocular tone of the novel itself, clearly suggests that Fielding was experiencing some difficulties in parading as an author. Though he was writing at a time when the novel was beginning to be better accepted as a genre, and though he was fairly confident in his achievement, he still felt that his status as a novelist was somewhat shaky. Hence his qualms, one suspects, when it came to signing his book.

After *Tom Jones*, more and more novels contained a dedication, whether they were published anonymously or not. *Lydia*, a novel written in the third person and published anonymously in 1755, was dedicated to William Berrow, Merchant in Bristol; the dedication is signed John Shebbeare, which seems to explode the author's incognito (Shebbeare 1974: n.p.). Charlotte Lennox dedicated her *Female Quixote* to the Earl of Middlesex in 1752; the novel was published anonymously, and the dedication is signed: 'The AUTHOR?' (Lennox 1974: vi). What is the question mark supposed to mean? It is hard to say, but it may have something to do with the fact that the author was a woman, and one who particularly lacked confidence, as is made clear in the dedication itself: 'The dread which a Writer feels of the public Censure; the still greater Dread of Neglect; and the eager Wish for Support and Protection, which is impressed by the Consciousness of Imbecillity; are unknown to those who have never adventured into the World' (Lennox 1974: iv).

No discussion of eighteenth-century dedications would be complete without a reference to *Tristram Shandy*. The first two volumes were published without a dedication. Sterne had looked for a patron to finance the venture, but he had not found one. Hence the sham dedication which appears in chapter VIII of the first volume:

My Lord,
I maintain this to be a dedication, notwithstanding its singularity in the three great essentials of matter, form, and place: I beg, therefore, you will accept it as such, and that you will permit me to lay it, with the most respectful humility, at your lordship's feet, – when you are upon them, – which you can be when you please; – and that is, my Lord,

whenever there is occasion for it, and I will add, to the best purposes too. I have the honour to be,
*My Lord,*
*Your Lordship's most obedient,*
*and most devoted,*
*and most humble servant,*
TRISTRAM SHANDY.
(Sterne 1965: 11–12)

Tristram Shandy offers this non-dedication to the highest bidder in the next chapter, and he promises, if somebody buys it, that 'in the next edition care shall be taken that this chapter be expunged' (13). In the second edition, Sterne wrote a dedication 'To the Right Honourable Mr. Pitt' and signed it: 'The Author'. Naturally, the said chapter was never 'expunged'. This was the first example, as far as we know, of a preamble finding its way into the body of a novel; it was going to be the fate of prefaces in the next century.

Incidentally, Sterne was perhaps parodying the old practice of selling fraudulent dedications; the forger, called a 'falconer', would travel around the country with his henchman, the 'mongrel', carrying samples of forthcoming books. As Brown explains, 'Arrived at the mansion of a local magnate, the mongrel, who carried a hand press, filled in the name of the particular noble, and the book was presented as dedicated to him alone' (Brown 1913: 6). Dr Johnson also loved to write dedications and often composed compliments to be later signed by others (Brown 1913: 7).

## PREFACES

In one of Barthelme's metafictional texts, a character sadly confesses: 'Endings are elusive, middles are nowhere to be found, but worst of all is to begin, to begin, to begin' (Barthelme 1976: 73). The opening of a text is indeed a critical moment both for the author and for the reader: two perfect strangers, one of them wearing a mask, are suddenly brought together without having been previously introduced by any mediating third person, except the industry, perhaps. Hence the need, acknowledged both by the author and the publisher, to advertise the text through the title-page, the dedication, the blurb, or even the portrait of the author on the cover

Until James, many novels began with a preface, be it an author's preface as in *Moll Flanders*, an editor's preface as in *Pamela*, or a double preface by the *éditeur* and then the *rédacteur*, as in *Les Liaisons dangereuses* by Choderlos de Laclos. Such prefaces, which in all three cases appeared in the first edition, show how difficult it was for the author to begin a novel and to start communicating with his unknown reader in the eighteenth century. They also raise the awkward problem of the limits and boundaries of the novelistic text.

The 'Author's Preface', at the beginning of *Moll Flanders*, is apparently meant to guarantee the truthfulness, the genuineness, of the story about to be told. However, this aim is immediately contradicted in the second paragraph: 'The author is here supposed to be writing her own history, and in the very beginning of her account she gives the reasons why she thinks fit to conceal her true name, after which there is no occasion to say any more about that' (Defoe 1966: 1). The author designated as such in this sentence is only the object of discourse of the other author mentioned in the title of the preface ('Author's Preface'), Daniel Defoe. Yet Defoe insists on representing himself only as the editor in the many allusions to the rewriting of the story, as for example in paragraph three:

> It is true that the original of this story is put into new words, and the style of the famous lady we here speak of is a little altered; particularly she is made to tell her own tale in modester words than she told it at first, the copy which came first to hand having been written in language more like one still in Newgate than one grown penitent and humble, as she afterwards pretends to be.
>
> (1)

The true author does his best to protect his incognito by using the impersonal 'we', passive forms such as 'is a little altered', 'is made to tell her own tale', or sheer ellipse ('came first to hand'; whose hand?). Defoe (whose name, let us not forget, appeared nowhere in the first edition) claims only to have rewritten Moll's crude tale.

Later, the preface turns into a vindication of the text as a good piece of writing or a novel, rather than as a genuine autobiography:

> It is suggested there cannot be the same life, the same brightness and beauty, in relating the penitent part as in the criminal part. If there is any truth in that suggestion, I must be allowed to say, 'tis because there is not the same taste and relish in the reading; and indeed it is too true that the difference lies not in the real worth of the subject so much as in the gust and palate of the reader.
>
> (2)

An autobiographer (especially one who is confessing her sins) is not really supposed to care about the 'brightness and beauty' of the text, but should primarily be concerned about the authenticity of the story told. It is the real author as editor who is here blaming the perverse reader for deriving more pleasure from the criminal part than from the penitent part of the book.

Defoe was clearly trying to ward off the attacks of the puritans and censors who were bound to object to his story of a London whore. He knew that he was violating a taboo, dealing with an unsayable and abject topic, so he took the precaution of prefacing the first-person narrative with these cautionary words to explain that he was not to blame for the sins committed by that unfortunate woman. He even took the precaution of passing judgement on her actions, underlining the fact that her sins always received their right retribution: 'there is not a wicked action in any part of it, but is first or last rendered unhappy and unfortunate' (3). Defoe behaves here like the champion of the moral laws which Moll so zestfully flouted; he explains to the righteous reader that he is on his, and not on Moll's side, and he suggests that whatever moral judgement this story may induce the reader to pass be aimed at Moll Flanders, not at the editor.

In the last two paragraphs, the editor informs his reader that the history is not quite carried 'to the end of the life of the famous Moll Flanders' and he laments the fact that 'nobody can write their own life to the full end of it, unless they can write it after they are dead' (5). Defoe was naturally aware that the narrative device he had adopted (first-person narrative by the protagonist, that is, homo- and intradiegetic narrator in

Genette's terminology) has its drawbacks: it does not allow one to give a dramatic or a climactic ending to the book. To conceal his embarrassment, Defoe mentions that Moll's husband 'gives a full account of them both, how long they lived together in that country, and how they came both to England again' (3). But he immediately goes on to explain that he could not use the husband's narrative, even though it covers an interesting part of Moll's life, because his narrative is not as elegant as that of Moll. Then, he flippantly concludes: 'so it is still to the more advantage that we break off here' (3), apparently hoping that his embarrassment will not be noticed by the hurried reader.

Our reading of this preface must conclude with a verdict of sloppy workmanship since Defoe confuses his two roles: that of author and that of editor. But could Defoe really do otherwise, considering both the times in which he was writing and the nature of his story? Censorship was a real threat, and if he wanted his novel to be read by a large public, he had to give evidence somewhere that he was on the side of the Establishment where morality was concerned. Being unable to do so under his own name, for the reasons explained earlier, but craving for recognition like all authors, he was caught in a difficult spot and adopted this ambiguous stance, parading here as the author, there as the editor, and doing his utmost to belittle the merits of Moll as a writer.

Even such a master of contemporary fiction as Joyce found it difficult to stick throughout to the role he had adopted. In *A Portrait of the Artist as a Young Man*, he made a slip similar to those committed by Defoe in his preface, switching roles as he was writing. This occurs at the beginning of chapter 4, during the evocation of Stephen's devotions:

> and at times his sense of such immediate repercussion was so lively that he seemed to feel his soul in devotion pressing like fingers the keyboard of a great cash register and to see the amount of his purchase start forth immediately in heaven, not as a number but as a frail column of incense or as a slender flower.
>
> (Joyce 1964: 137)

There are two phrases in this passage which are particularly disturbing: 'he seemed to feel his soul', and 'a great cash register'. In the first one, Joyce uses a semi-modal, 'seemed', which, like all modal auxiliaries (can, may, will, should) is by definition very ambiguous since it can reflect either the point of view of Stephen or that of the author. The second phrase, despite the transition implicit in the semi-modal, is rhetorically shocking: Stephen has been portrayed so far as a very passionate boy fully committed to everything he does. How could he, then, during this mystical stage inspired by a devouring sense of guilt, have thought up such a disparaging image as that of the 'great cash register' which casts doubts on the authenticity of his conversion? One cannot help but view this image as a comment made by the mature writer as he looks down upon his young protagonist's sudden and fugitive outburst of mysticism. Joyce confused his roles and violated the principle of absolute objectivity towards his protagonist which he had built into his novel, a clear sign that it was not easy, even two centuries after the publication of *Moll Flanders*, for a clever craftsman like him to know exactly where he stood as an author.

Since the invention of print, it has never been easy for the author to put a safe distance between himself and his reader without confusing his roles like this. In the eighteenth century, when the writer still lived in a mostly oral environment, this confusion was extremely difficult to avoid. The novelist felt the need to manage a kind of transition between the oral world of his daily life and the written world of the book. His failure to extricate himself from his narrative was fortunately not always as damaging to the book as we would expect; it often contributed to the fiction effect, as we shall see in the next chapter.

The 'Author's Preface', at the beginning of *Moll Flanders*, prefigured the editor's preface at the beginning of *Pamela*. Under the mask of the 'editor', Richardson begins by itemizing his aesthetic and didactic goals:

> If to *divert* and *entertain*, and at the same time to *instruct* and improve the minds of the YOUTH of *both sexes*. ... If these be laudable or worthy recommendations, the *Editor* of the following Letters, which have their foundation both in

*Truth* and *Nature*, ventures to assert, that all these ends are obtained here, together.

(Richardson 1980: 31)

He was apparently aware that a work which aims 'to *divert* and *entertain*', but also contains many passages which could be considered as morally objectionable, must display its didactic ambition from the start if it is to be read by a large public, and especially by impressionable girls. So, under the flimsy disguise of 'editor', the author (who was not known to be Richardson, let us not forget!) vouches for the purity of his intentions in publishing this book.

The editor presents himself above all as a reader of 'this little Work', explaining that his passions 'have been uncommonly moved in perusing it' (31). He does not even claim to have collected the letters or edited them, but simply to have stumbled upon a manuscript ready to print ('this little Work'). Richardson clearly confuses his many roles (author, editor, printer, and even publisher), though in the last line he insists that the role of the editor should not be confused with that of the author: 'an *Editor* can judge with an impartiality which is rarely to be found in an *Author*' (31). We may wonder who the author is in this sentence, for, if Pamela Andrews is supposed to have authored most of the letters and the journal, there are a few letters written by her parents also. It is not clear, therefore, whether Richardson has Pamela in mind when he mentions the author or another fictitious person who would have composed this series of letters.

The ambiguity still increases when we find the 'impartial' editor annotating the book, as for instance between letters XXXI and XXXII, to recount the circumstances of Pamela's abortive escape from Mr B.'s house. The editor never openly unmasks himself; he uses impersonal formulae: 'Here it is necessary the reader should know', or 'It is also to be observed' (123). In the summary (the 'Contents'), which was published only in the octavo edition, Richardson refers to this particular passage as follows: 'Here the Editor gives an account of Pamela's being carried to her master's seat in Lincolnshire, instead of to her father's' (35). The roles are not strictly defined: the editor's discourse is embedded in another writer's discourse. So, there are at least two replicas of Richardson in this book, not counting Pamela herself: the editor who wrote the preface and the other editor who wrote the table of contents and made of the first the object of his discourse. Strangely, the first editor never announces in his preface that he had to disregard some letters, to change the order in which they had been written, or to provide background information. Was it implicit in the title he had given himself ('editor')? We may wonder, for the only thing he seems to be doing in his preface is to promote a found manuscript to the rank of a printed book.

This confusion of roles is also obvious in Choderlos de Laclos's *Les Liaisons dangereuses* which begins with two prefaces: the 'Avertissement de l'editeur' ('Publisher's Note' in the translation) and then the 'Preface du Rédacteur' ('Editor's Preface' in the translation). The French word *éditeur* can mean either publisher or editor. It seems that this *éditeur*, like Richardson's first editor, is behaving like a printer or publisher: he plays no part in the writing of the book proper but merely hands over this risky text, warning the reader that it is probably a novel rather than a genuine collection of letters: 'we do not guarantee the collection and we have good reason to believe it is only a Novel' (Laclos 1924: 59). This implicitly confirms that, for most people at the time, the novel was a degraded form of history and certainly did not deserve to be called art. Later the *éditeur* explains that what induces him to think that this book is probably a novel is the fact that 'several of the characters he describes have such abominable morals that it is impossible to suppose they could have lived in our own century' (59). This commentary is obviously ironic; yet it confirms that immoral behaviour was not yet regarded as being verisimilar and could not be portrayed openly in print; the books that did portray it could only be pure fiction ('it is only a novel').

The 'Preface du Rédacteur' on the other hand, reads like an editor's preface. The *rédacteur* (the French word applies especially to newspaper editors) claims to have collected and sorted out the letters; he has even suppressed a few, as he 'honestly' confesses in a note: 'I have tried to preserve only those letters which seemed to me needed for the understanding of events or to reveal character' (61). The *rédacteur* is as aware as the *éditeur* of the depravity of the characters, and he expresses his fear that this collection of letters may appal many readers. Yet his moral qualms have little influence on his editorial decisions: he does not suppress letters because they are morally objectionable but because they might bore the reader, a clear indication that he behaves more as a novelist than as a genuine editor.

As these three celebrated examples indicate, the eighteenth-century novelists found it extremely difficult to launch their works. The *in media res* beginning favoured by Aristotle was uncalled for since those novels did not present themselves as works of fiction but as autobiographies (*Moll Flanders*) or collections of letters (*Pamela, Les Liaisons dangereuses*). The early novelists, from Cervantes to Defoe and Richardson, wanted to present their readers with irrefutable documents, usually written in the first person, for which they were not to be held responsible. They were simply turning manuscripts into printable (or even printed, in the case of Richardson) books, a clear indication that it was the printing press which gave birth to the novel. The growth of the industry had brought about a division of labour between the author, the editor, the publisher, and the printer; depending on the circumstances (on the kind of story to be told), the novelist could play any of the last three roles, letting his first-person narrator play the first. One could therefore claim that the modern novel was born with the reification of the text as printed book and with the author's refusal to acknowledge the authorship of the said book.

The elaborate strategies which have resulted from the author's refusal to parade as author compel the reader to play different roles, to put on different masks. The interpretative work done so far in this chapter exemplifies the kinds of adjustment a reader must make to occupy the right place in and towards the text. All these prefacers, the sham author in *Moll Flanders*, the editor in *Pamela*, the *éditeur* and the *rédacteur* in *Les Liaisons dangereuses*, proclaim themselves as existential subjects and real writers who do not belong to the stories proper. The reader, who by the simple gesture of opening the book evinces his willingness, his anxiety even, to interrelate with someone, spontaneously finds himself conversing with each of these interlocutors in turn and adapts his behaviour to each according to the generic names they go under. He agrees to be manipulated by these interlocutors as long as they stick to their self-proclaimed role, but he becomes restless when they start performing on two different stages at the same time.

In the 'Author's Preface' to *Moll Flanders*, for instance, how can one interrelate for very long with a writer who claims at one and the same time to be the author of this autobiography, then its editor, and finally a fiction-writer?

Such novelists put the reader in a paradoxical situation akin to the double bind a child can find himself in towards his parents. The Palo Alto communication theorists define the double bind as a pragmatic paradox in which an utterance and an utterance on the utterance (the meta-utterance) contradict each other. This paradoxical situation involves two or more persons engaged in an interaction of vital importance to all the interlocutors: someone makes an utterance in which he utters something and, at the same time, he utters something about his own utterance, the two utterances being contradictory. Some famous paradoxes given in *Pragmatics of Human Communication* are: 'Be spontaneous!' and 'You know that you are free to go, dear; don't worry if I start crying' (Watzlawick *et al.* 1967: 199–200). The mother who says 'Be spontaneous!' to her child makes him incapable of being spontaneous: either he starts acting more spontaneously, in which case he is simply following his mother's advice (or order), or he does not change his behaviour, in which case he must feel that he has failed to meet his mother's expectations. In either case, he remains under his mother's law and has no way of escaping. He is caught in a double bind because he is unable to get out of the frame set by the speaker, either by meta-communicating or by withdrawing from the interaction.

There are many famous examples of double binds in *Alice in Wonderland* and *Through the Looking Glass*. Tweedledum and Tweedledee are clever manipulators of paradoxes which put Alice in that situation; so is the Red Queen, as in the following conversation with Alice, for example:

'Do you know Languages? What's the French for fiddle-de-dee?'

'Fiddle-de-dee's not English,' Alice replied gravely.

'Who ever said it was?' said the Red Queen.

Alice thought she saw a way out of the difficulty, this time. 'If you'll tell me what language 'fiddle-de-dee' is, I'll tell you the French for it!' she exclaimed triumphantly.

But the Red Queen drew herself up rather stiffly, and said

'Queens never make bargains.'

'I wish Queens never asked questions,' Alice thought to herself.

(Carroll 1970: 323)

The syllogism implicit at the beginning of the conversation is this: if someone asks you to translate a word into a foreign language, he assumes that the word belongs to your native tongue. Alice reacts strongly by making a meta-utterance but gets further and further entangled in the Red Queen's queer logic. The latter, like many high-handed teachers, is not really asking a question but trying to intimidate a pupil who thought she could turn her teacher's logic to her own advantage. Alice does not realize that the Red Queen is indifferent to the content of the exchange but cares only about asserting her authority over her. As Humpty Dumpty unceremoniously puts it at the end of a similar conversation with Alice, 'The question is . . . which is to be master – that's all' (Carroll 1970: 269).

The prefaces which we have analysed here eventually manage to put us at a similar disadvantage as readers, no matter what their avowed didactic or aesthetic content was. The author insidiously enmeshes us in his paradoxes, that is to say in his fictions, by bringing us to interact with his fictionalized selves; he does his utmost to break down our defences in order to obtain our willing suspension of disbelief. These prefaces are not totally extra-textual and not yet fully intra-textual: they are what conditions the emergence of the fiction effect in the reader's mind.

Since Defoe, Richardson, and Laclos, and until James at least, many novelists have written prefaces of one kind or another. Melville prefaced his *Moby Dick* with two sets of texts: first his etymologies (four at least being partly erroneous, one being a joke) 'supplied by a late consumptive usher to a grammar school', and then his extracts, 'supplied by a sub-sub-librarian', and taken from various kinds of texts which deal with, or simply allude to, whales (Melville 1987: 75–91). Are these preambles part of the novel proper? Most of the extracts will be taken up again in the body of the novel which Melville clearly meant as a kind of encyclopaedia about whales. Yet they do not only announce the encyclopaedic project, they also suggest that the book follows a long tradition which has made of the whale an almost supernatural creature. They constitute (along with the etymologies) the textual raw material out of which the novel itself is going to evolve; Melville seems almost to be saying to his reader: 'Watch me, I am going to turn all these fragments into a complete story!'

The case of the 'Custom-House' piece, at the beginning of *The Scarlet Letter*, is more difficult to decide. Hawthorne does not simply claim to be the 'editor'; he explains the circumstances in which he supposedly found the manuscript from which he wrote the book, and he provides information on other subjects, such as the custom-house itself and its inmates.

The first paragraph begins like this: 'It is a little remarkable, that – though disinclined to talk over-much of myself and my affairs at the fireside, and to my personal friends – an autobiographical impulse should twice in my life have taken possession of me, in addressing the public' (Hawthorne 1962: 6). The first time was in *Mosses from an Old Manse*. Hawthorne seems to falter, realizing that there is something a little indecent in writing about oneself, but he trusts that 'an author may be autobiographical, without violating the reader's rights or his own' (7). Gide, Proust, and Joyce will make similar claims; their novels will give evidence that the peak of impersonal showing can be achieved by an author telling his own story. The 'reader's rights' are not defined but the author's duty is clearly hinted at in the first paragraph when Hawthorne speaks of 'the inmost Me behind its veil' (7): he must put on a mask in order to preserve his privacy and protect that of his reader. The printed book helps him achieve this goal but without guaranteeing that he will eventually succeed. When the author's voice is too clearly heard, the reader has the impression that his privacy has been invaded.

In the next pages, Hawthorne (who proclaims himself as author throughout) discusses the important business of the custom-house; many of his ancestors would have considered that, at long last, he was doing something really worthwhile: 'A writer of storybooks! What kind of a business in life, – what mode of glorifying God, or being serviceable to mankind in his day and generation, – may that be?' (12). Now he must be content with having his name printed on merchandise:

> No longer seeking nor caring that my name should be blazoned on title-pages, I smiled to think that it had now another kind of vogue. The Custom-House marker imprinted it, with a stencil and black paint, on pepper-bags, and baskets of anatto, and cigar-boxes, and bales of all kinds of dutiable merchandise.
>
> (24)

The name printed in black on those boxes is not the author's name, however; it it simply the name of the government representative who has examined the goods and levied the proper duties on them.

This detail, along with many others, begins to turn the custom-house into a book authored by Hawthorne himself. It is in the large room in 'the second story' that he finds the records of the custom-house and many other papers. The word 'story' is naturally ambiguous, Hawthorne having already introduced himself as 'a writer of storybooks'. Barth will exploit this word to its limits, in *The Tidewater Tales*, calling the boat in which the two protagonists journey and tell their endless stories 'The Story'. Among the papers found in that room, there are Jonathan Pue's papers which contain a strange piece of cloth, and, twisted in it, the 'small roll of dingy paper' which tells the story of Hester Prynne (27–8). Hester's story is therefore wrapped in a letter which is only one item among Pue's papers found in the large room in the second story – a clear case of syntactic and narrative embeddings.

Jonathan Pue's text, which Hawthorne claims to have in his possession (29), only served as a pre-text for the novel itself, the author having allowed himself 'as much license as if the facts had been entirely [his] own invention' where 'the dressing up of the tale, and imagining the motives' are concerned (29). Hawthorne claims to have totally rewritten the story, after leaving the custom-house.

Is this very famous piece really a preface? Hawthorne did not think so since he wrote a preface for the second edition of the novel in which he expressed his amusement that the introduction 'created an unprecedented excitement in the respectable community around him' (5). He agrees that this piece is not absolutely necessary:

The sketch might, perhaps, have been wholly omitted, without loss to the public, or detriment to the book; but, having undertaken to write it, he [the author] conceives that it could not have been done in a better or kindlier spirit, nor, so far as his abilities availed, with a livelier effect of truth.

(6)

Is it only another kind of *enfantillage*? Obviously not. Hawthorne is saying that he turned Pue's primitive narrative, itself made from 'oral testimony' (28), into a book, that he lent his pen to the *vox populi* of Puritan Salem. This introductory piece belongs intimately to the novel which is, after all, a kind of Salem saga: under the veil of autobiography, Hawthorne assumed the role of a bard, astride between two traditions, the oral and the typographic.

In *The Turn of the Screw*, James wrote an untitled introduction which has a great deal in common with the custom-house story; it could not easily be removed, without disfiguring the novel. It summarizes the circumstances in which the author (never named as such) discovered the manuscript which is going to constitute the main body of the novel. Here again, we are confronted with many embedded texts: first, the book written by the author from the manuscript; second, the fair copy of the manuscript made by the author; thirdly, the reading (publication?) of the manuscript by Douglas; lastly, the manuscript written by the governess.

Douglas had known the governess when he was twenty and she was thirty (she was his sister's governess); she was apparently in love with him. It was as a token of love, we presume, that she gave him the manuscript before she died at the age of fifty, and it was also as a token of love, we gather, that he kept it so long.

Without this introduction, we would know a great deal less about the governess and her tendency to fall in love with much younger boys or men. We would not know either that the oral delivery of the story, as well as the transfer of the manuscript from the governess all the way to the author, was prompted by love or friendship, feelings which, as we discover in the novel, may lessen one's ability to distinguish fact from fiction, the truth from a lie. Through this introduction, the author becomes involved in this story of mostly unrequited love, a fact which leads us to consider him not only as the author, but as another narrator, since he has a personal stake in the narrative. His extreme cautiousness in the manipulation of the manuscript and in the recording of the story (which is further underlined in the 1908 preface) generates the fiction effect, that is the gothic atmosphere, from the start. By the end of the nineteenth century, therefore, no introduction was necessary to show the reader into the main body of a novel. The respective places of author and of reader were very well established. This left the preface available for other purposes, as in the two cases we have just examined.

In the present century, the sham preface has become a metafictional device which often works very effectively, as for example in Nabokov's *Lolita*. In the built-in 'Foreword' of this novel, John Ray, the editor of the manuscript, explains the circumstances in which he received Humbert Humbert's text; he also explains that Lolita's surname was changed by the narrator himself:

> *Its author's bizarre cognomen is his own invention; and, of course, this mask – through which two hypnotic eyes seem to glow – had to remain unlifted in accordance with its wearer's wish. While 'Haze' only rhymes with the heroine's real surname, her first name is too closely interwound with the inmost fiber of the book to allow one to alter it.*
> (Nabokov 1970: 5–6)

Humbert, like Moll Flanders, is held responsible for these 'minor' changes. Of course, names do not play such a structuring or generative role in Defoe's novel as they do in Nabokov's. That Lolita's first name could not be changed enhances the genuineness of the story. Humbert seems to be saying that he could tamper with reality only up to a point, but that certain elements resisted his effort to put the story into his own writing. So, the foreword boosts the authenticity and the historicity of the story we are about to read, as did the 'Author's Preface' in *Moll Flanders*.

It also helps stigmatize the immorality of the story and to placate the censorious reader who would be tempted to blame the editor for it. John Ray, himself a psychiatrist, deprecates Humbert as '*a shining example of moral leprosy, a mixture of ferocity and jocularity that betrays supreme misery perhaps, but is not conducive to attractiveness'*, and he smugly concludes that Humbert *'is abnormal'* (7). This severe indictment of the pathetic but brilliant pervert should normally endear John Ray to the righteous reader; in fact, it merely fans his complicity with the protagonist as did the 'Author's Preface' at the beginning of *Moll Flanders*.

The illusion of historicity is further enhanced by the fact that the foreword summarily provides information about the *'destinies of the "real" people beyond the "true" story'* (6). We are told that Humbert died before the book was published, that Mona Dahl, one of Lo's friends, *'is a student in Paris'*. We are informed that one *'Mrs. "Richard F. Schiller" died in childbed, giving birth to a stillborn girl, on Christmas Day 1952'* (6). This obituary note does not, however, make sense at a first reading: how could the trusting reader who has just landed in this new 'universe of discourse' (one of Barthelme's pet phrases in *Snow White*) know that, under this name, there hides the heroine of the novel, Lolita? Instead of sticking to his self-proclaimed role, John Ray, the editor, is playing little games with the reader similar to those invented by his perverse patient in the main narrative.

John Ray's foreword does not therefore have the same functions as the 'Author's Preface' in *Moll Flanders*. John Ray does not call himself the author but the editor of the book: he merely claims to be handing over to us a somewhat delicate document, and unwittingly gets involved in the story because he refuses to stick to his self-appointed role as the editor of Humbert's text, and also because Humbert will get the better of him in the narrative. This foreword is obviously part of *Lolita*: since the cautionary words written by the sophomoric editor will be eclipsed by the poetic stunts of the narrator and protagonist, the reader spontaneously adopts an ironic stance towards preface and prefacer. The good reader, seduced by Humbert's skill, laughs at the didactic reading made by Ray and prefers the poetic one advocated by Humbert (7). Stanley Kubrick followed Nabokov's suggestions: he counted John Ray among the characters in the story. The foreword merely invites the reader to dissociate himself from the psychiatrist (who is necessarily a realist) and from the puritanical society whose order the psychiatrist helps maintain, and induces him to join forces with perverse Humbert. In the meantime, the reader has forgotten that he is being manipulated by an invisible author hiding behind the curtain, behind the black cover of the novel.

The postscript added by Nabokov in 1956, and which is now reprinted in most editions of *Lolita*, has a different status from the foreword, which it ridicules right from the start: 'After doing my impersonation of suave John Ray, the character in *Lolita* who pens the Foreword, any comments coming straight from me may strike one – may strike me, in fact – as an impersonation of Vladimir Nabokov talking about his own book' (Nabokov 1970: 313). Here, we find the same confusion of roles as in the novels we analysed earlier, but this time it is deliberate. After so many amusing impersonations, Nabokov wonders if he can still write under his own name and be taken seriously. He wants us to know that this postscript is not part of the novel and that it must be read as a direct address from him to us about the novel itself. This precaution suggests that it may be as difficult for a novelist to fade out of his text as it was to fade into it.

Nabokov wrote this piece to accompany the excerpts from Lolita which appeared in the *Anchor Review* in 1957; he meant it therefore as a vindication of the novel as well as an advertisement for it, in the hope that it would encourage an American publisher to publish it. This postscript does not belong to the book. It could easily have been dropped altogether. Yet, Nabokov insisted on keeping it, probably because he was still afraid of being considered a 'dirty old man' and wanted to make sure that no reader would confuse him with his protagonist. His tone is close to that of John Ray at times: 'my creature Humbert is a foreigner and an anarchist, and there are many things, besides nymphets, in which I disagree with him' (317). Yet there is a difference between the foreword and the postscript. The author emphatically ridicules Ray's didactic claims: '*Lolita* has no moral in tow' (316), and he refuses to praise Humbert's poetic talents about which Ray said: '*But how magically his singing violin can conjure up a tendresse, a compassion for Lolita that makes us entranced with the book while abhoring its author!*' (7). He cannot easily scorn Ray's aesthetic judgement since, in the circumstances, it matches his own. The respective roles of editor and author are not, therefore, as clearly defined as they seemed to be. The boundaries of the text remain largely undecided.

Richardson's postscript to *Clarissa*, which appeared at the end of the last volume, reads like Nabokov's postscript to *Lolita* in many ways. It also takes into account the readings which have been made of the book (or of its previous volumes) so far. It begins with a letter of F. J. de la Tour to John Bedford, explaining how Lovelace died after the duel; this letter has supposedly been translated from French, but a note suggests that it may have been written in English after all: 'Supposed to be written by Mr Bedford'. Then comes the postscript proper which begins: 'The author of the foregoing work has been favoured, in the course of its publication, with many anonymous letters, in which the writers have *differently* expressed their wishes as to what they apprehended of the catastrophe' (Richardson 1985: 1495). This statement contradicts what was said in the preface:

> But yet the editor to whom it was referred to publish the whole in such a way as he should think would be most acceptable to the public was so diffident in relation to the article of *length*, that he thought proper to submit the letters to the perusal of several judicious friends, whose opinion he desired of what might be best spared.
> (35)

Richardson, who posed as editor in the preface, poses as author in his postscript. He evidently found it difficult to distinguish between his various roles. Having reached the end of his long book, he felt the need to vindicate himself as far as the 'catastrophe' was concerned and to go on communicating with his public. He was obviously worried that his intentions might be misconstrued. There is not much difference between this postscript and that of *Lolita*: both evince their authors' lack of trust in the ability of the printed pages to convey their meanings and intentions. Such postscripts are the authors' last attempt to monitor our reading, as well as their last claim to authorship and authority over their books.

## TRISTRAM SHANDY: AN ANATOMY OF THE PRINTED BOOK

The novel is the first literary genre to display its bookhood and its printhood; plays and poems could be collected or published in books, yet until the end of the nineteenth century (say, until Flaubert's *La Tentation de Saint-Antoine* for drama, or Mallarmé's *Un coup de dé jamais n'abolira le hasard* for poetry), the fate of these two genres was only indirectly linked to the printing industry. Not so with the novel, which from the start acknowledged its bookhood, and exhibited it humorously as in *Tristram Shandy*, which we are now going to examine.

Sterne exhibits the bookhood and printhood of his novel on almost every page, playing on the confusion of roles which made most of his fellow novelists so uncomfortable. This novel would have been impossible to reproduce accurately before Gutenberg because of its many typographic games, such as the lines of dots, dashes, or asterisks, the italics, the fancy punctuation, etc. A writer of the chirographic age could not have taken such a risk since the copyists would inevitably have skipped or added a dash here, an asterisk there. It would not have made much difference in some cases, but in the following passage it would have made all the difference:

> – The chamber-maid had left no \*\*\*\*\*\*\* \*\*\* under the bed: — Cannot you contrive, master, quoth *Susannah*, lifting up the sash with one hand, as she spoke, and helping me up into the window seat with the other, — cannot you manage, my dear, for a single time to \*\*\*\* \*\*\* \*\* \*\*\* \*\*\*\*\*\*?
> (Sterne 1965: 284)

A copyist would not have bothered to check whether the number of asterisks really mattered. It does matter a great deal, in the circumstances, for a censored text hides behind the asterisks: 'chamber pot', and then 'piss out of the window'. When the reader finds out that such typographic signs can be used for this purpose (elsewhere, the words 'cod piece' are similarly censored; 244), he begins to wonder whether a ciphered text does not hide beneath the printed words throughout the novel.

Sterne exploited to the utmost the resources of the new technology to draw the attention of his reader to the materiality of the printed page. Chapters 18 and 19 of volume IX contain only two blank pages; these two chapters will be given later in chapter 25 of the same volume. Elsewhere, there are black pages, as in chapter 12 of volume I, which serve as an epitaph for 'poor YORICK', or again marbled pages as in chapter 36 of volume III. This latter stunt is particularly interesting since marbled pages are used to paste the printed sheets of the book to the boards of the cover. Sterne therefore turned the book inside out, putting the covers right in the middle. In another passage, he even skipped nine pages. In volume IV where pages are skipped, Sterne teases the bookbinder in the following way: 'No doubt, Sir—there is a whole chapter wanting here—and a chasm of ten pages made in the book by it—but the bookbinder is neither a fool, or a knave, or a puppy—nor is the book a jot more imperfect (at least upon the score)' (237). In the first edition, the page numbering skips in fact from 146 (a left-hand page) to 156 (the facing right-hand page, chapter 25), which means that all the left-hand pages remain odd-numbered until the end of the book (Sterne 1761: IV, 146–56). Sterne meant to skip ten pages and the printer skipped only nine; neither Sterne nor the proofreaders noticed. This mistake induced the printer to break his profession's rule concerning page numbering. Through this little anecdote, we see that a conflict was developing between the author and the industry. Sterne wanted the members of the industry to know that they were working for the author, and not the other way around. The printer was so intimidated, it seems, that he broke one more rule than was necessary.

These tricks (dashes, asterisks, dots, blank pages, black pages, marbled pages, missing pages) gradually coach the reader into realizing that he is holding a printed book in his hands, something which has been manufactured by the industry after the fastidious prescriptions of the author. By compelling the printer to pay a great deal of attention to every detail of his manuscript, Sterne also made sure that the product, the printed book, would look exactly as he (not the industry) meant it to look. Every single dash or asterisk is therefore a double signal addressed at one and the same time to the printer (who might be tempted to skip it since it is not properly verbal) and to the reader (who might similarly be tempted to pay attention only to the words proper). Every typographic sign is clamouring: 'This is a book, this is a printed book, and every little detail in it is important and has been carefully composed by the author'.

The industry was therefore beaten at its own game: it was because it had grown sufficiently dependable that the author could afford to play such typographic games and that the reader could be confident that in their printed form they accurately reflected the author's intention. One could say that the industry perfected the weapons which eventually lessened or, in some rare cases, annihilated its authority over the page. Naturally, it recouped its losses on the economic stage.

Here is a little anecdote to illustrate the point which has just been made. In the first edition of Nabokov's *Ada*, there is a pernicious misprint in a coded passage, '*xlic mujzikml*', which is supposed to mean: 'they embraced' (Nabokov 1969: 157). The code is very simple: 'One-letter words remained undisguised. In any longer word each letter was replaced by the one succeeding it in the alphabet at such an ordinal point – second, third, fourth, and so forth – which corresponded to the number of letters in that word' (160). In a word like 'lovely', or 'they', the sixth and fourth letters after the 'y' had to be capitalized to show that one was running into a new alphabet: '*xlic*' should therefore have been spelt '*xliC*'. Nabokov, or rather Van Veen, the narrator, concludes his explanation about the code with a flippant statement: 'Again, this is a nuisance to explain, and the explanation is fun to read only for the purpose (thwarted, I am afraid) of looking for errors in the examples' (161–2). Most readers obviously trusted Van's expertise and never bothered to check whether he had made any errors. The wary reader who has spotted it may wonder whether Van was taunting him by deliberately leaving this little mistake, or whether he, the narrator, or Nabokov, the author and proof-reader (and a very good one, as a rule), has not simply overlooked it. The latter interpretation turns out to be correct: in the following edition, the misprint was corrected.

This anecdote, like the one about the page numbering in *Tristram Shandy*, shows that the author must fight the battle of the book not only against his publisher, but also, and perhaps above all, against his reader who, having paid for the book, tends all too readily to impose his reading and his interpretation upon it and eventually to supplant the text with his own critical text.

Sterne also staged this second battle inside *Tristram Shandy*: he presented the anatomy of reading and showed how gamely the reader tries to get even with the author. Tristram, whose story is eclipsed by many other stories, except towards the end, teases the reader constantly through the two addressees built into the novel, Sir and Madam. The male addressee appears in the first chapter: 'Pray, what was your father saying?— Nothing' (Sterne 1965: 4). This dialogue goes on at the beginning of the next chapter: '——Then, positively, there is nothing in the question, that I can see, either good or bad.——Then let me tell you, Sir, it was a very unseasonable question at least' (4). Tristram has here staged the author's interlocutor who, in general, is only obliquely referred to in the body of a novel. 'Sir' is a persona, just like Tristram the author-in-the-book who is commonly called the narrator. Gerald Prince would call 'Sir' a 'narratee', 'that is to say the person whom the narrator addresses' (Prince 1973: 178). But this is no ordinary narratee, since a dialogue develops between him and Tristram, as if they were sharing the narrative task. Together, they are acting as if the book did not separate them in terms of space and time, as if the conversation (which writing is supposed to be, according to Tristram) could go on after the publication of the book.

This first addressee is soon joined by a second one, Madam, at the end of chapter 4: '——But pray, Sir, What was your father doing all *December,—January*, and February? ——Why, Madam—he was all that time afflicted with a Sciatica' (Sterne 1965: 7). Madam is a great deal more obtuse and straitlaced than Sir; whenever a sexual matter is raised, she is apostrophized by Tristram who seems to be doing his utmost to make her blush. She is a worse reader than the male addressee; she does not seem to be able to laugh at the dirty jokes Tristram cracks all the time nor to respond favourably to his innuendoes. She reacts very much like Uncle Toby (who is only half a man), while Sir often talks and behaves like Walter Shandy.

These built-in addressees raise a difficult problem. In *Tristram Shandy*, there is no preface or foreword, no postscript either. The text of the novel stands totally on its own, which was not the case with the other novels we have mentioned so far. At the same time, it stages a writer who is showing himself writing and two readers who are shown reading the text, or rather talking about it with the said writer as if they had been present at the time of the writing proper. Sterne was acutely aware of this complex communication problem. In a letter to Jane Fenton after he finished his first volume, he wrote:

> I have just finished one volume of *Shandy*, and I want to read it to some one who I know can taste and rellish humour – this by the way, is a little impudent in me – for I take the thing for granted, which their high Mightinesses the World have yet to determine – but I mean no such thing – I could wish only to have your opinion – shall I, in truth, give you mine? – I dare not – but I will; provided you keep it to yourself – know then, that I think there is more laughable humour, – with equal degree of Cervantik Satyr – if not more than in the last – but we are bad Judges of the merit of our Children.
>
> (Sterne 1980: 465)

We notice that Sterne had the same jerky, digressive prose in his letters as in his novel. Here, he deprecates 'their high Mightinesses' who will probably look down upon his book, but he wishes that someone, even a woman, could confirm his own favourable judgement of it. When he began his fifth volume, he wrote with much greater confidence to his friend John Hall-Stevenson: 'To-morrow morning, (if Heaven permit) I begin the fifth volume of Shandy – I care not a curse for the critics' (Sterne 1980: 466). His earlier volumes having been favourably received, he knew that he had made contact with people out there who understood what he was trying to do, who communicated with him in a satisfactory way.

## CONCLUSION

It apparently seemed something of a mystery in the eighteenth century that two strangers living in different 'universes of discourse' could communicate with each other through a printed book. Sterne devoted a whole novel to investigating this mystery, compounding the difficulty by representing inside his book the participants in this complex form of communication. He further confused the roles by attributing to one of his characters, Yorick, a sermon he had himself preached in York Minster, and by taking Tristram through the same journey he himself had made in France. He posed inside his novel the difficult problems that his predecessors had raised in the preambles, bringing his reader to raise insoluble problems such as: Who is the author, Sterne or Tristram? Is Tristram merely a mask for Sterne? Who are Sir and Madam? Merely bad readers who are teased to death by Tristram? Where do I stand as a reader? With whom am I communicating?

Gamely, the reader tries to extricate himself from the black box of the book in order to protect his sanity. He eliminates Madam, who is too obviously scorned by Tristram, then Sir, who lacks the culture and perceptiveness necessary to be a worthy interlocutor of Tristram, then Tristram himself, who is, after all, a character in the novel, though he is acting on the writing stage as much as on the 'storical' one. The reader is tempted to cry, like Yorick's starling: 'I can't get out', meaning of course, 'I can't get out of this book' (Sterne n.d.: 130)!

## Chapter 3
# The many births of the novel

So far, this study has dealt only with the novel as an *œuvre*, that which, to quote Barthes, 'we hold in our hand', leaving aside the *texte*, that which is held 'in the language' (Barthes 1973b: xv, 1016). The technological revolution described in the first chapter changed not only the appearance of the book and the relationship between author and reader; it also transformed the rhetoric of the text in a dramatic way.

### INTRODUCTION: THE NEW RHETORIC

Rhetoric was officially from the start a speech art, but, as Walter Ong points out, it 'was and had to be a product of writing' (Ong 1982: 9). It was only through writing that its theory could be formulated and developed. By the time of the Renaissance, this art had been subjected to a process called in Italian *letteraturizzarione*, which Kennedy defines as 'the tendency of rhetoric to shift its focus from persuasion to narration, from civic to personal contexts, and from discourse to literature, including poetry' (Kennedy 1980: 5). Rhetoric had gradually lost its political and forensic dimension; it was no longer a strategy to run the state and the nation in a more consensual way, but an instrument to give more pleasure to one's audience in literature, while projecting a better image of oneself.

In eighteenth-century England, rhetoric survived in four different forms, according to Wilbur S. Howell, who wrote a decisive book on the subject: that of the ancient Greek and Roman theorists, represented by the Ciceronians, which emphasized invention, arrangement, style, memory, and delivery; that of stylistic rhetoric, which served as an instrument for the analysis of literary works; that of the elocutionists, emphasizing oral delivery (liturgy, dialogues on stage, conversation); finally, that of the New Rhetoric, inherited from Bacon and Locke, and chiefly represented by Adam Smith and George Campbell. It became the general theory of literature, and provided standards of composition and criticism (Howell 1971: 696–7).

The New Rhetoric, says Cohen, was largely based on the Lockean principle that human communication involves ideas which are not in the 'real existence of things; but are the inventions and creatures of the understanding, made by it for its own use' (Cohen 1977: 39). Such ideas are merely the mind's perceptions of itself operating on ideas of sensation, and their signification 'is nothing but a relation that, by the mind of man, is added to them' (39). Like Antoine Arnauld, the chief author of the *Grammaire générale et raisonnée* (1660) and *Logique de Port-Royal* (1662), Locke made a distinction between the real and the nominal, realizing, two and a half centuries before Whorf, how language helps shape and give significance to reality.

The chief representative of the New Rhetoric was George Campbell, a Scottish pastor who published *The Philosophy of Rhetoric* in 1776; the book was very popular in the next century (forty printings between 1801 and 1887) but was then forgotten until its first twentieth-century reprint in 1963 (Howell 1971: 577–612). Campbell held rhetoric and eloquence to be synonymous; he defined the latter term in the following way: 'It is indeed the grand art of communication, not of ideas only, but of sentiments, passions, dispositions, and purposes' (Howell 1971: 580). And poetry was to him 'no other than a particular mode or form of certain branches of oratory' (590).

He was aware of Plato's harsh criticism of poetry and of rhetoric in general which could threaten the general good of the state and of its citizens: 'As the soul is of heavenly extraction, and the body of earthly, so the sense of the discourse ought to have its source in the invariable nature of truth and right' (595). But he interpreted the concept of truth in a very flexible sense, equating it to 'fiction' in a striking passage which could almost serve as the founding statement for our modern theory of verisimilitude:

We know that fiction may be as plausible as truth. A narration may be possessed of this quality in the highest degree, which we not only regard as improbable, but know to be false. Probability is a light darted on the object, from the proofs, which for this reason are pertinently enough styled *evidence*. Plausibility is a native lustre issuing directly from the object. The former is the aim of the historian, the latter of the poet.

(594)

This passage reads like a rewriting of the parable of the cave for the use of the novelist or of the romantic poet. The historian must found his reconstruction of the real on accepted evidence; the fiction-writer must create an object which radiates 'a native lustre', something close to what James was to call 'the air of reality' and Barthes the 'effet de réel'.

Campbell's theory, which would deserve a great deal more attention than we can give it here, shows how printing helped give birth to a new theory of knowledge as well as to a new poetics by creating a parallel world made of manufactured objects, the printed books which were gradually invading the 'real world' and undermining its traditional structures. Now, the author was not only an increaser but more and more a creator like God Himself; his creatures, Pamela Andrews or Tom Jones, looked often more real than Madame de Sévigné or Bonnie Prince Charlie, not because they performed more memorable deeds, but because they were made more compellingly real through a narrative discourse which at once simulated and improved upon a written discourse (letters, diary, history) in the world out there.

Marshall McLuhan suggested that print gave birth to the novel by allowing the development of the fixed point of view (McLuhan 1962: 126-7, 135-6). It might be more appropriate to say that it did so by encouraging the rise of the author. Before Gutenberg, narratives were above all the invention of a community, which used them to boost its consensus. The novel, on the other hand, was from the start the invention of an individual, who enjoyed a comparative immunity, partly guaranteed by the industry which mediated between him and the law. Under the mask of his inventions, the author could trot out his fantasies and his revolutionary ideas, provided he adhered to an acknowledged form of discourse, rather than to a fixed point of view.

In the present chapter, we shall analyse the three novelistic modes as they appeared in Europe between the sixteenth and the eighteenth century. Anna Laetitia Barbauld defined them in the following way, in 1804:

> There are three modes of carrying on a story: the narrative or epic as it may be called; in this the author relates himself the whole adventure; this is the manner of Cervantes in his *Don Quixote*, and of Fielding in his *Tom Jones* . . . Another mode is that of memoirs; where the subject of the adventures relates his own story. Smollett, in his *Roderick Random*, and Goldsmith in his *Vicar of Wakefield*, have adopted this mode . . . A third way remains, that of epistolary *correspondence*, carried on between the characters of the novel.
> (Allott 1980: 258–9)

The first mode is actually a genre (the epic), and the second and third ones are forms of discourse, memoirs and epistolary correspondence. This typology of the narrative modes closely matches the typology of the genres attributed, mistakenly says Genette (Genette 1986: *passim*), to Plato: the epic, the lyrical, and the dramatic. This confusion between modes, genres, and forms of discourse is still with us as the debate between Stanzel, Hamburger, and Genette testifies.

One hopes to shed some light on this awkward question in the present chapter. The novel was not born once, as we will show, but many times and at various stages. *Don Quixote* took up the epic mode where the old romance of chivalry had left it; Fielding did not create a new genre, in that respect, he only perfected the Cervantic mode in *Joseph Andrews* and *Tom Jones*. The picaresque novel, on the other hand, did not spring from a literary mode, the lyrical, but from a self-expressive mode of writing (autobiography and diary) which developed after the invention of print; from *The Life of Lazarillo de Tormes* to *Tristram Shandy*, the first-person narrative gradually adapted itself to print. The third mode, the epistolary, which was truly developed by an English printer, Richardson, did not spring from a literary mode, either, despite the fact that its dialogical form is reminiscent of drama, but from a new form of communication which developed on a grand scale during the Renaissance: letter-writing. It was print again which gradually turned this crude form of communication into an art, just as phonetic writing had earlier helped promote speech to the level of an art: rhetoric.

## MOCK EPICS

The third-person narrative is probably the oldest form of narrative. It is often equated with the epic, a narrative mode which unmistakably belongs to the oral age. The word 'epic', as Ong explains, 'has the same Proto-Indo-European root, *wekw-*, as the Latin word *vox* and its English equivalent "voice", and thus is grounded firmly in the vocal, the oral' (Ong 1982: 13–14). Exploiting the discoveries made by Milman Parry, Ong shows that the epic is the most primitive form of storytelling developed in the western world, a form which shares most of the characteristics of orality, including copiousness, conservatism, and homeostasis.

In the Middle Ages, the epic was revived in verse (*Beowulf*, the *chansons de geste*, Chrétien de Troyes's *Perceval*) and survived in this form until Milton's *Paradise Lost*. This is the Homeric form of narrative which Aristotle defined in the following manner in his *Poetics* (1459–60):

> Imitation through narrative in verse obviously must, like tragedy, have a dramatic plot structure; it must be concerned with one complete action, it must have a beginning, middles, and an end, in order that the whole narrative may attain the unity of a living organism and provide its own peculiar kind of pleasure. Its structure must be different from that of histories. History has to expound not one action but one period of time and all that happens within this period to one or more persons, however tenuous the connection between one event and the others.
> 
> (Aristotle 1958: 49)

The neighbouring genres of the epic, as this definition intimates, are tragedy, whose plot structure it must share, and history, whose looseness of action and diversity of characters it must avoid.

After the rediscovery of Aristotle's *Poetics* in the Middle Ages, much of the critical debate centred on the epic, from Roger Bacon to Cinthio, Rapin, Boileau, and Le Bossu. During the Restoration, in England, the debate was reopened by Davenant in his preface to *Gondibert* (1650), and by Hobbes in his *Answer to Davenant's Preface* (1650) and his preface to *A Translation of Homer* (1675); it continued with Dryden in his *Apology for Heroic Poetry* (1677), and later with Pope, Warton, Gibbon, Kames, and Johnson (in his *Life of Milton*, 1779, especially). The critics were chiefly concerned with the topics and heroes worthy of the genres, and with the treatment of plot, character, and poetic diction.

Concurrently, popular epics such as the romances of chivalry were beginning to develop in prose. Some (and perhaps most) of the cycles, for example the Arthurian cycle, had first been exploited in verse before such popular and post-Gutenberg books as Malory's *Morte D'Arthur* (finished in 1469–70 and published by Caxton in 1485) were composed. *Amadis de Gaul* was put into prose by Montalvo long after it had started to circulate orally. Don Quixote has a whole collection of these romances; among them, one finds *The Four Books of Amadis de Gaul*, *Palmerin de Oliva*, *Exploits of Esplandían*, *Platir the Knight*, *The Mirror of Chivalry*, and many others which were all published in the sixteenth century. There is also *La Galatea* by one Miguel de Cervantes (Cervantes 1949: 57)!

It was against this background of popular prose epics that Cervantes composed his *Don Quixote*, which is usually considered to be the first genuine novel. This book is truly a product of the printing age. We have already examined its preambles, which all proclaim its bookhood. The story is based on other printed books, which it parodies. If Don Quixote had been born a century earlier, he would not have had such an impressive collection of books; it was the printing industry which made available to him all those romances of chivalry. Cervantes's novel is therefore, among other things, a humorous reflection on the multiplicity of books which penetrated into all the spheres of life, and on their propensity to undermine reality by confronting it with a twin world which, to weaker minds, may have looked a great deal more appealing.

When the barber and the curate destroy Don Quixote's books, they merely mean to annihilate the bookish world in which he lives, hoping that he will settle down at last in their 'real' world. These two characters play an important role in the book: they help monitor reality for the bookish knight. So does Sancho Panza, but to a lesser extent because he has a personal stake in Don Quixote's wild quest (a governorship!). Still, he does try to open his master's eyes, as for example in the famous windmill scene:

> 'But look, your Grace, these are not giants but windmills, and what appear to be arms are their wings which, when whirled in the breeze, cause the millstone to go.'
> 'It is plain to be seen,' said Don Quixote, 'that you have had little experience in this matter of adventures.'
> (Cervantes 1949: 63)

Here, the oral (or 'real') world clashes with the bookish world which has kindled Don Quixote's imagination and perverted his perception of commonplace objects. As McKeon rightly puts it, this novel 'is a palimpsest of cultural layerings, a laminated cross-section of oral, scribal, and print cultures bonded together in a moment of contradictory coexistence' (McKeon 1987: 278). It is a book haunted by the ghosts of countless other books.

Though it preserves many features present in oral narratives, such as copiousness (digressiveness), closeness to the real world, and concreteness rather than abstractness (Ong 1982: 37–57), it is also and above all writerly and typographic in its structure, which is infinitely more complex than that of any book written before it. The opening paragraph presents two conflicting discourses:

> In a village of La Mancha the name of which I have no desire to recall, there lived not so long ago one of those gentlemen who always have a lance in the rack, an ancient buckler, a skinny nag, and a greyhound for the chase.
> (Cervantes 1949: 25)

One recognizes here the canonical opening of the oral tale: 'In a village of La Mancha . . . there lived', but it is immediately perverted by the subordinate clause ('the name of which I have no desire to recall'), just as the fairy-tale opening ('Once upon a time') will be perverted by a humorous aside ('and a good time it was') at the beginning of *A Portrait of the Artist as a Young Man*. Such canonical formulae are usually meant to give the illusion that the story, which has circulated orally for so long that it has virtually become public property, is telling itself without the intervention of any narrator; but the myth is here exploded.

Who is the storyteller who designates himself through the deictic 'I'? Cervantes? Of course not, though he does his utmost in the prologue to claim his rights in the book. Neither is it the market-goer who, in chapter IX, claims to have discovered the *History of Don Quixote de la Mancha, Written by Cid Hamete Benengeli, Arabic Historian*, in the marketplace of Toledo (72), but Cid Hamete himself, who deliberately chose to conceal the name of that village for the reasons stated on the last page of the second part:

> Such was the end of the Ingenious Gentleman of La Mancha, whose birthplace Cid Hamete was unwilling to designate exactly in order that all the towns and villages of La Mancha might contend among themselves for the right to adopt him and claim him as their own, just as the seven cities of Greece did in the case of Homer.
>
> (987)

Cid Hamete meant to write an epic in the Homeric tradition; he made sure that no one would have access to his 'sources' in order to give a double status to his story: historical (writerly) and mythical (oral) at one and the same time, in other words mock epic.

Between the opening and the closing of the novel, however, Cid Hamete's status changes considerably. In the first paragraph, he behaves as the oral storyteller who does not have to explain who he is since he is present at the time of the telling. At the end, he has become the object of another storyteller's discourse who uses him as the ultimate source of the story.

This strange reversal begins in chapter IX of part one: the nameless market-goer who buys the papers from a chapboy is above all a reader who has already read the first eight chapters of *The History of Don Quixote* but has been left stranded in the middle of a scuffle between the 'valorous Biscayan and the famous Don Quixote' (70). He badly wants to know what happened next:

> I was deeply grieved by such a circumstance, and the pleasure I had had in reading so slight a portion was turned into annoyance as I thought of how difficult it would be to come upon the greater part which it seemed to me must still be missing.
>
> (70)

This *scripta volent* topos will reappear in the epistolary novel. The modern novel founded much of its historicity upon it: the story told by the 'flying writings' may not be true, but the papers are real and must be taken seriously. They may contain some element of truth, some secret even, otherwise one could not account for the fact that some of them have survived and the rest have disappeared. This topos may well mark the origin of the unreliable narrator in nineteenth- and twentieth-century fiction. Someone, who had a personal stake in the papers, has tampered with them! The tampering now becomes the theme of the story, hence the metafictional effect.

In this case, the metafictional effect is emphasized by the fact that the market-goer reader is unable to read the papers because they are written in Arabic; he must use the services of an interpreter to decipher them. But the interpreter may himself be tampering with the text; here is how he introduces the continuation of the Biscayan's story: 'But, to come to the point, the second part, according to the translation, began as follows' (73). In the second part of the book, this interpreter or translator will openly interfere with the story, as for instance at the beginning of chapter V: 'As he comes to set down this fifth chapter of our history, the translator desires to make it plain that he looks upon it as apocryphal, since in it Sancho Panza speaks in a manner that does not appear to go with his limited intelligence' (538). This translator is also a critic; by denying the historicity of the characters, he simply boosts the writerly status of the story. This aside reads very much like that other aside by Cid Hamete himself in the margin of the papers: 'I cannot bring myself to believe that everything set down in the preceding chapter actually happened to the valiant Don Quixote' (665). Translator and 'author' obviously refuse to be duped; they let the reader know that whatever he does with the text is ultimately his responsibility.

The market-goer reader does take his responsibility for a

while and monitors our reading of the translation of Cid Hamete's text. He does not hand us the text proper but his reading of it, making Cid Hamete the object of his critical discourse: 'The learned Cid Hamete Benengeli tells us' (108), 'Cid Hamete Benengeli, the Arabic and Manchegan author ... informs us' (167). He faithfully reports, in reference to the events narrated in a chapter, that the author 'would prefer to pass over them in silence, as he fears that he will not be believed' (565). It is not the original translation we are reading, but rather the market-goer's reconstructed text, as the recurrence of the phrase: 'The history relates' intimates (728, 808, 978). He wants us to know that Cid Hamete is the author of the story, but at the same time he is tampering with the text by commenting upon it and by adopting a condescending attitude towards the author.

This embedding of narrative discourses (Cid Hamete ⟶ translator ⟶ market-goer reader) is not faultless. In the first paragraph of chapter XLIV of part two, the reader intimates that the translator has been tampering with the text:

> They say that in the original version of the history it is stated that the interpreter did not translate the present chapter as Cid Hamete had written it, owing to a kind of grudge that the Moor had against himself for having undertaken a story so dry and limited in scope as is this one of Don Quixote.
>
> (788)

The market-goer reader, who was monitoring our reading of the translation of Cid Hamete's text, has now been supplanted, it seems, by a reading community which had access to another text, the 'original version' in which the interpreter was himself part of the story as was Cid Hamete.

If the interpreter who tampered with Cid Hamete's text is the same person that worked for the market-goer reader, then the latter is also part of the story, and part of the papers since they belong to the same world, the same universe of discourse. His struggle to keep out of the story turns out to be a failure: he is a prisoner of the book, and Cid Hamete is his warden, his keeper.

The market-goer reader indirectly admits his defeat at the end when he quotes verbatim Cid Hamete's address to his pen which is a claim of authorship: 'For me alone Don Quixote was born and I for him; it was for him to act, for me to write, and we two are one in spite of that Tordesillesque pretender who had, and may have, the audacity to write with a coarse and ill-trimmed ostrich quill of the deeds of my valiant knight' (988). The reference is to Alonso Fernández de Avellaneda of Tordesillas whose name appeared on the title-page of the spurious second part of *Don Quixote*, published in 1614 (989). Cervantes had started his novel by saying that his *Don Quixote* was going to be a parody of the romances of chivalry, and now he concludes it by making a mocking reference to a book which plagiarized his own book. This novel apparently constitutes a major skirmish in the battle of the book which had been raging since the invention of print. Cervantes (like Richardson in the case of *Pamela*) was forced to write a second part to his *Don Quixote* in order to preserve his rights in his hero and his book (the two being virtually impossible to separate, in the circumstances).

To summarize, here are the chief protagonists in the battle of *Don Quixote*:

The nameless storyteller vs Don Quixote (the opening chapters)
Cid Hamete vs Don Quixote (chapter IX and after)
The translator vs Cid Hamete now (translator's remarks)
The market-goer vs the translator ('apocryphal')
The translator vs Cid Hamete in the 'original version'
Cid Hamete vs Avellaneda (address to his pen)

Most of the protagonists of the book trade and of the publishing industry play a part in this novel: the built-in author, the translator, the plagiarist, the chapman, and finally the built-in reader.

The present reader does not stand comfortably outside the black boxes: he is the one who tries desperately to nest the boxes but who eventually fails to do so, for the nesting is not perfect, the same protagonists appearing at different levels of the narrative, in different universes of discourse. The reader (this reader) is manipulated by the text and has to put on a new mask each time a new interlocutor comes on to the textual stage: he is first the tame listener to a jovial storyteller in the first chapters, then the accomplice of the market-goer after chapter IX, the critic of the unscrupulous translator in various passages, the solicitous confidant of Cid Hamete when the latter realizes that his story may be hard to believe, and finally a harsh critic of the plagiarist who has been trying to steal Cid Hamete's, or rather Cervantes's, work.

He is eventually faced with an at once poignant and exciting dilemma: who am I? To weasel out of this dilemma, he must first try to answer the insoluble question: what is the real text? He grows helpless, and cannot get out of the black box of the book to communicate on an equal footing with the author. The latter parades arrogantly in the prologue but hides throughout the novel, sometimes conspicuously, as at the end, when he puts on the cloak of his impersonator, Cid Hamete.

Fielding acknowledged his debt toward Cervantes on the title-page of *Joseph Andrews*: 'Written in Imitation of The Manner of Cervantes, Author of *Don Quixote*'. Though the English public was familiar with Cervantes's style, Fielding felt the need, in his preface, to define a reading contract for his book, which he did not call a novel but a romance:

> As it is possible the mere *English* reader may have a different Idea of Romance with the Author of these little Volumes, and may consequently expect a kind of Entertainment, not to be found, nor which was even intended, in the following Pages; it may not be improper to premise a few Words concerning this kind of Writing, which I do not remember to have seen hitherto attempted in our Language.
> (Fielding 1987: 3)

In the prologue to *Don Quixote*, Cervantes invented a persona (a solicitous friend) to preface his work and state humorously some of the writing principles he had adopted. Here, Fielding writes under his own generic name: he presents his book and tells his readers, who may not be familiar with the Cervantic conventions, how to read it. He invites his readers, whose bias in favour of such sentimental books as *Pamela* he is acutely aware of, to adopt a different stance towards this form of writing which does not exploit the then dominant *scripta volent* topos.

Fielding's efforts to promote the bookhood of his novel are obvious: he uses a highly intertextual book, *Don Quixote*, as his model; then, he defines his book as a mock epic, which he distinguishes from 'the Productions of Romance Writers on the one hand, and Burlesque Writers on the other' (8); and finally, he makes use of a well-known book, *Pamela* (and to a lesser extent *An Apology for the Life of Mr. Colley Cibber*), as a counter-model. Richardson's readers did not need to have read many other books to understand and take pleasure in *Pamela*. Not so with *Joseph Andrews* which, though supposedly 'copied from the Book of Nature' (8), is clearly addressed to an educated public; if its bookishness is not understood, it loses a great deal of its interest. It is therefore intensely metafictional, like *Don Quixote*.

Yet there is no such complex nesting of narrative discourses in it as in its model. The narrative voice heard in the first chapter is the same as that heard in the opening lines of the preface and again in the first chapter: 'In this Light I have always regarded those Biographers who have recorded the Actions of great and worthy Persons of both Sexes' (14). This 'I', which reappears in the opening chapters of each book, except the fourth, cannot be distinguished from the author's 'I' even when it appears in a narrative chapter: 'So I have seen, in the Hall of *Westminster*; where Serjeant *Bramble* hath been retained on the right Side, and Serjeant *Puzzle* on the left; the Balance of Opinion alternately incline to either Scale' (36). This authoritative person (or persona) who comments humorously on the common practices of Westminster Hall is the same one who addresses the reader in various passages, as for example at the end of chapter V: '*Joseph* retreated from the Room in a most disconsolate Condition, and writ that Letter which the Reader will find in the next Chapter' (24).

There is some confusion among the critics as to how this persona should be referred to. Stanzel believes that '[w]henever a piece of news is conveyed, whenever something is reported, there is a mediator – the voice of a narrator is audible' (Stanzel 1984: 4). It is true, as he explains, that '[m]ediacy is the generic characteristic which distinguishes narration from other forms of literary art' (4). But should the word 'narrator' be used so freely? And do such phrases as 'authorial third-person narrator' (90) really make sense? In the case of *Joseph Andrews*, we should then speak of an 'authorial first-person narrator', if we follow Stanzel's suggestion, since we find so many asides written in this way. The phrase sounds somewhat contradictory. Why not simply talk of the 'author' if the author is writing in his name (and under his own name, as in *Tom Jones*, where Fielding's name appears on the title-page)?

The elaborate strategies developed by novelists since Cervantes and Sterne (who, by the way, also claimed to write in the Cervantic vein) have bred a senseless fear among critics who are now so afraid of being duped by the inaccessible author that they never mention him by name, often preferring to use the term 'narrator' systematically instead. This fear is openly acknowledged by Wayne C. Booth in his discussion of irony. His *Rhetoric of Fiction* is an unsuccessful attempt to sort out the voices and appropriate the texts without any reference to the author. Writing about Fielding, he says:

> When Fielding comments, he gives us explicit evidence of a modifying process from work to work; no single version of Fielding emerges from reading the satirical *Jonathan Wild*, the two great 'comic epics in prose,' *Joseph Andrews* and *Tom Jones*, and that troublesome hybrid, *Amelia*.
> (Booth 1961: 71-2)

Because each book reflects a different facet of the novelist he prefers to say that the persona who parades on the writing stage as the 'author' is in fact the 'implied author', that is, neither the real author nor a bona fide narrator.

But does the 'implied author' of *Joseph Andrews* as we have already described him differ much from that of *Jonathan Wild* and *Tom Jones*? In the latter novel, there is no preface, but each opening chapter of the nine books reads as a preface of a kind. The first one begins like this: 'An author ought to consider himself, not as a gentleman who gives a private or eleemosynary treat, but rather as one who keeps a public ordinary, at which all persons are welcome for their money' (Fielding 1980: 51). In *Joseph Andrews*, the word 'author' appeared in the preface, not in the first chapter; but chapter I of book II, which was entitled 'Of Divisions in Authors' (Fielding 1987: 70), dealt with 'the Science of *Authoring*', that is to say with the way to make life easier for the reader, by providing titles at the beginning of each chapter, for instance. In the last paragraph of this particular chapter of *Joseph Andrews*, there is a comparison which is echoed in the opening metaphor of *Tom Jones*: 'I will dismiss this chapter with the following Observation: That it becomes an Author generally to divide a Book, as it doth a Butcher to joint his Meat, for such Assistance is of great help to both the Reader and the Carver' (72). Are not the fantasies and preoccupations of both 'implied authors' the same in the two books? Are we not entitled to say that Fielding was similarly aware in both cases of the rhetorical problems he had to solve in order to communicate efficiently with his public? There is no reason, it seems, to consider that the two implied authors are not one and the same person.

Booth's perspective is different from ours, of course. He considers that the problem must be viewed either from the author's or from the reader's viewpoint:

> Our reaction to his [the author's] various commitments, secret or overt, will help to determine our response to the work. The reader's role in this relationship I must save for chapter V. Our present problem is the intricate relationship of the so-called real author with his various official versions of himself.
>
> (Booth 1961: 71)

But is the 'implied author' implied by the author or by the reader? By the latter, of course, when he tries to appropriate the text and fantasizes an addressor with whom to communicate. This author, it is true, is not the 'real author'. The real author does not imply himself, he implicates himself no matter what; and it is because he cannot help implicating himself in his book that he must develop a strategy to keep his reader at a distance while giving him the illusion (through the banquet metaphor, for instance, in the first chapter of *Tom Jones*) of communicating directly, that is, without any mediation, with him.

So the two interlocutors are faced with the same dilemma in a symmetrical way: the author projects an image of himself in his novel and fantasizes a reader who will be tame enough and loving enough to enjoy the story, but who will also be a worthy interlocutor, capable of laughing or smiling at the right moment. He wants to be both the master of ceremonies and the chef, but also to sit at his guest's table incognito, while remaining in the one-up position. The reader, on the other hand, fantasizes an author who must be both demiurgic and tolerant, an author who remains inaccessible but gives evidence, at times, of appreciating his good taste.

The concept of 'implied author' is unsatisfactory because it seems to define once and for all the respective roles and places of the author and the reader. The restless critic seems to say: let us see where we stand exactly and then we shall be able to enjoy the book without any scruple or discomfort. This labelling amounts to considering a printed book as a genuine conversation between two persons (implied author and reader) who would know their places from the start.

The novelistic text is never so homogenous or stable, as we have seen in our study of *Don Quixote*. In *Tom Jones*, the many interventions of the self-proclaimed author (the so-called 'implied author') in the introductory chapters build up a metadiscourse. The opening chapter of book XVII of *Tom Jones* is very instructive, in that respect. Here is the first paragraph:

> When a comic writer hath made his principal characters as happy as he can; or when a tragic writer hath brought them to the highest pitch of human misery, they both conclude their business to be done, and their work is come to a period.
> (Fielding 1980: 777)

The person calling himself the writer is saying that playwrights are lucky people because they know that the plot must end according to certain conventions. Fielding, who had a great deal of experience as a playwright, naturally knew what he was talking about. Here, he laments the fact that the novelist must stay with his book throughout; he has no model to help him decide how to end his story. Hence his constant temptation to interfere with it and to curb the freedom of the characters he has invented:

> But to bring our favourites out of their present anguish and distress, and to land them at last on the shore of happiness, seems a much harder task; a task indeed so hard that we do not undertake to execute it. In regard to Sophia, it is more than probable, that we shall somewhere or other provide a good husband for her in the end ... and if our reader delights in seeing executions, I think he ought not to lose any time in taking a first row at Tyburn.
> (777)

What is the referent of 'our' and 'we' in this passage? The writer plus the reader, it seems, since they are both observers standing outside the story, and expecting Tom to meet a dire fate.

This interpretation is brought to naught, however, when we come upon the phrase 'our reader'. Here, the writer resumes his one-up position, bringing his reader down to the level of Sophia and Tom ('our'), forcing him, as it were, to come into the black box of the story as it is told in the other chapters. He does not want to be caught in the same box with his reader, as we see in the following passage:

> This I faithfully promise, that notwithstanding any affection, which we may be supposed to have for this rogue, whom we have unfortunately made our heroe, we will lend him none of that supernatural assistance with which we are entrusted, upon condition that we use it only on very important occasions.
>
> (777)

Here, the writer writes both in the first-person singular and in the first-person plural (the 'editorial we' whose use 'is prompted by a desire to avoid *I*', as the grammarian puts it (Quirk 1972: 208), as if he had a split personality. This 'we' is the more ambiguous as it sometimes includes the reader as an accomplice or a fellow spectator in the audience.

The 'writer' has apparently become like God Himself: he has created a number of characters, and now he claims to leave them free to save their necks or be hanged. If the novel had ended the way 'we' feared it might (Sophia marrying Blifil, and Tom going to the gallows), Fielding would not have needed to take such precautions. It was precisely because he intended to give it a happy ending that he was forced to reaffirm so emphatically his refusal to interfere with his creatures' fates. Hence the ambiguous 'we' behind which he concealed himself and through which he tried to intimidate his reader into total surrender. There was at least one reader, Mrs Barbauld, who bitterly took Fielding to task for forcing such a happy ending upon his novel: 'But what would have been the probability in real life?' (Day 1987: 199).

This strategy is not so different from that of Defoe at the beginning of *Moll Flanders* or that of Richardson throughout

*Pamela*. The author feels the need to create replicas of himself either at the beginning or in the course of his novel. The question he must solve is: how am I to get out of the book? The solution is always the same: by bringing the reader into it, either by apostrophizing him (Fielding 1980: 112, 254, 467, 546, 551, 769), by confronting him with different interlocutors, or by giving him the illusion that if he tries hard enough, he will eventually manage to corner the only worthwhile interlocutor, the AUTHOR. But, since the author's act of communication is necessarily over by the time the book gets published (and appropriated by the industry), the reader knows he will never make contact with him nor ever receive any confirmation that his interpretation is correct. The reader is caught in a double bind: he must try and make contact with an interlocutor if he wants to understand and enjoy the novel, but the very bookhood and printhood of the text tells him that his interlocutor is now dead and forever out of reach.

The invention of such personae as the 'implied author', the 'narrator', the 'model reader', and the 'narratee' has helped us to understand the process of textual communication a little better but it may also have deceived us. One must recognize that the novelistic text is intrinsically unstable, that its enunciative status keeps changing, and that the reader must pick up new interlocutors as he reads or performs the text. He does not choose these interlocutors arbitrarily of course; he uses the indices present in the text to decide how this and that passage must be interpreted. Reading a modern novel is like staging a complex play: the reader plays at one and the same time the role of the stage-manager and the roles of the actors. And he also apes the author who hides in the wings. In this respect, the third-person novel is often more complex than the first-person novel, as we shall see in our next chapter: it does not stage any identifiable and stable interlocutor but compels the reader to exert himself in order to project plausible ones.

## THE PICARESQUE NOVEL

The first-person narrative, whose first modern literary manifestation was the picaresque novel (*The Golden Ass* by Apuleius was already in the first person), probably started as a self-expressive form of writing. In sixteenth-century Europe, there appeared in all quarters a great need to write about and picture oneself. Delany has drawn attention to the fact that the 'first substantial English aubiography [Thomas Wythorne's *Autobiography*, written about 1576] and the first self-portrait by a native Englishman [Nicholas Hilliard's miniature self-portrait painted in 1577] were produced within a year of each other, so far as we can tell' (Delany 1969: 13). This desire to project an image of oneself may have been encouraged, says Delany (who borrows heavily here from Gusdorf), by the invention of glass mirrors which supplanted the old ones made of polished metal. Dürer's first recorded work is a drawing of himself with the inscription 'made out of a mirror'; and Rembrandt made over 100 self-portraits for which, obviously, he needed a good mirror (3).

Incidentally, the inventor of the printing press was also interested in developing new and better mirrors. One learns, through the proceedings of a legal dispute between Gutenberg and one of his Strasburg associates which took place in 1439, that he was not only trying to develop a new technique to print texts, but also helping to manufacture mirrors and to improve the technique for polishing gems (McMurtrie 1941: *passim*; Febvre and Martin 1971: 72–3). Gutenberg was obviously fascinated by surfaces, mineral or biological; he was struggling not only to picture the world (and himself) on mirrors but also trying to find new means to mechanically reproduce texts. This kinship between mirrors and print is spelled out beautifully by Borges in 'Tlön, Uqbar, Orbis Tertius'.

Neither Delany, who examined the British autobiographies of the seventeenth century, nor Fothergill, who made an extensive study of English diaries (Fothergill: 1974), nor again Lorna Martens, who wrote a comprehensive history of the diary novel (Martens: 1985), shows how the printing press could have had an influence on the rise of the autobiography or of the diary. As for Ong, he merely suggests that the 'kind of verbalized solipsistic reveries it [the diary] implies are a product of consciousness as shaped by print culture' (Ong 1982: 102). The suggestion is the more paradoxical as the diaries were not written for publication; neither were autobiographies, which were rediscovered, and sometimes printed, in the middle of the eighteenth century (Delany 1969:

108). Yet it is probably true that print, by encouraging the development of literacy, triggered in many educated people, such as Montaigne, a compulsive need to write and express themselves in prose. Before the invention of print, they would probably have expressed themselves through lyrical poetry, whose 'language, structure, and forms', Ong explains, 'could not readily be adapted to convey the story of a man's entire life' (1982: 102).

The picaresque novel appeared at almost the same time as the autobiography, and its period of development coincided with the period of development of both autobiography and diary. Bjornson suggests that the picaresque was an assertion of the self: 'In its broadest sense, the picaresque myth functions as one possible paradigm for the individual's unavoidable encounter with external reality and the act of cognition which precedes and shapes his attempts to cope with a dehumanizing society' (Bjornson 1977: 11). However, this assertion of the self is not so much reflected in the picaro's actions as in his first-person narrative through which he arrogantly exposes his view of the world and pits his values against those of the moral establishment. It is possible that the sixteenth-century picaresque was, partly at least, a reaction against the massive publication of religious books which took place after the invention of print.

The prologue to *The Life of Lazarillo de Tormes and his Fortunes and Adventures*, which opens with an arrogant 'I', announces that we are about to read a book, and probably a printed book:

> I think it well that things so remarkable, and mayhap never heard before of or seen, should come to the attention of many, and not be buried in the tomb of oblivion; since it is possible that some one who reads of them may find something to please him, and those who do not get so far as that it may divert; and in this connection Pliny says that there is no book, bad though it be, but has something good in it.
> 
> (*Life of Lazarillo* 1917: 1)

This 'writer' is clearly aware of writing to be published and to be read by a large audience. He obliquely acknowledges the new technology which, not being controlled by the church, as the old copying craft often was, can now afford to handle irreverent books. This evolution might account for the fact that *The Life of Lazarillo de Tormes* appeared around the same time (1554) as Rabelais's works (1533–64), which humorously denounce the intolerance and narrow-mindedness of the church.

In the last paragraph of the prologue, which reads like a dedication addressed to a person of high rank, the anonymous author emphasizes his didactic purpose in an ironic fashion:

> I entreat Your Worship to accept the poor hand-service of one who would make it richer, if his power and his desire conformed. And since Your Worship writes for me to write him and describe my case quite circumstantially; it seemed well not to take it up in the middle, but from the beginning, so that you may have a complete account of my person, and also that those who have inherited noble positions may reflect how little this is due to themselves, for fortune was partial to them, and how much more those have done to whom it was contrary, who rowing with vigour and skill have come home to a good port.
>
> (3)

Is this a genuine or a facetious dedication? We have no way of telling. The prefacer, who, in his reference to Pliny, announced his literary ambition while showing his awareness of an audience out there, now claims to be addressing only that noble person who asked him to write the book. This topos of the scurrilous story solicited by a noble person will reappear many times until the end of the eighteenth century (in *La Religieuse* and *Fanny Hill*, for example). At the same time, however, this prefacer is arrogantly saying to that person that he intends to demonstrate how morality is often conditioned by one's social origins and how the members of the higher classes are less deserving of praise for being virtuous than those of the lower classes.

The confusion of roles is again obvious: Lazarillo presents himself as a penman who has read Pliny and means to please a large audience. At the same time, he deprecates his talents in front of His Worship at whose invitation the book has been written, and he suggests that his poor penmanship may be due to his low social rank. We find here both the arrogance of the lordly author and the timidity of the grovelling menial. The communication process could be represented in the following way:

Lazarillo { as a follower of Pliny → the many readers
            as His Worship's servant → moral establishment

Lazarillo assumes two different roles and addresses his text to two different audiences. This is usually how the fiction effect begins to appear, as we have already suggested in our previous chapters.

One might hesitate to consider this book to be a novel proper because of the fact that the 'I' of the prologue is exactly the same as the 'I' we find at the beginning of the text itself, and the 'you', too:

> Then know Your Worship, before anything else that my name is Lazaro of Tormes, son of Thome Gonçales and Antona Perez, natives of Tejares, a hamlet near Salamanca. My birth took place in the river Tormes, for which reason I had the surname, and it was in this manner.
>
> (4)

If one considers the prologue to be part of the book, then the objection disappears: we are merely confronted with a homodiegetic narrator, that is, a narrator who is telling his own story. It is around this 'I' that the many incidents of the story will find their unity.

Incidentally, John Barth may have had Lazarillo in mind when he started his first novel, *The Floating Opera*. Here is how his narrator, Todd Andrews, a remote parent of Pamela and Joseph, and a fretful son who tries to understand, through his writing, why his father committed suicide, accounts for the title of his book:

> It always seemed a fine idea to me to build a showboat with just one big flat open deck on it, and to keep a play going continuously. The boat wouldn't be moored, but would drift up and down the river on the tide, and the audience would sit along both banks. They could catch whatever part of the plot happened to unfold as the boat floated past, and then they'd have to wait until the tide ran back again to catch

another snatch of it, if they still happened to be sitting there. To fill the gaps they'd have to use their imaginations, or ask more attentive neighbours, or hear the word passed along from up-river or down-river.

(Barth 1985: 13)

The word 'opera' must naturally be understood as the plural of 'opus'. Barth is here reversing the roles: it is the book which travels down the river while the readers are standing on the shore, trying to catch fragments of it as it sails past.

In *The Life of Lazarillo de Tormes*, the penman, born in his father's water-mill, seems to catch the stories as they drift past. Such is the narrative reversal which takes place between the picaresque novel of the sixteenth century and the post-modernist novel; the book supplants the 'I' of the penman until it eventually forces the reader to assume a much greater responsibility in reconstructing a unified reading out of drifting stories.

The chief English replica of *The Life of Lazarillo de Tormes* is Richard Head's *The English Rogue*, published in 1685. Head was the son of a chaplain to a nobleman in Ireland; he led a dissolute life as a literary hack, and he was probably drowned in 1686 while crossing to the Isle of Wight (Head 1961: i-ii). The text was heavily censored, apparently by the author himself; Shinagel, the editor of the 1961 edition, after mentioning that no copy of the unexpurgated version has survived, concludes, with unscholarly smugness, that it 'may be just as well' (i).

The book begins with the 'Epistle to the Reader', signed by Richard Head, and in which the author claims his authority and his rights in the book. Here are the opening lines:

Gentlemen,
It hath been too much the humour of late, for men rather to adventure on the Foreign crazy stilts of other mens inventions, than securely walk on the ground-work of their own home-spun fancies. What I here present ye with, is an original in your own *Mother*-tongue; and yet I may not improperly call it a translation, drawn from the Black Copy of mens wicked actions.

(x)

The reference to the Spanish picaresque novel, which had enjoyed a huge success in English translations, is obvious. English readers could afford to shrug off their moral principles when they read those foreign novels translated from a foreign language and narrating events which were supposed to have taken place (could only have taken place) in a foreign land.

The French public shared the same prejudices about picaresque novels, as the misadventures of *Gil Blas* testify. Lesage had published his *Nouvelles Aventures de Don Quichotte* in 1704 before he published *Gil Blas* in 1715, so the public was naturally inclined to consider the latter book as a new version or even a translation of a Spanish novel. The debate lasted more than a century. A Spanish priest, José Francisco de Isla y Royo, who obviously thought that the picaresque genre was the property of his country, translated the novel 'back' into Spanish under the following title: *Gil Blas de Santillana, robadas a España* [stolen from Spain] *y adapatadas en Francia por Lesage, restituidas a su patria y a su lengua por un español celoso que no sufre se burlan de su nación*. It was published in Madrid after his death in 1787 and 1788. Obviously, everybody thought that the picaresque novel was an exotic genre which belonged to Spain where Occident and Orient then met (*Dictionnaire des œuvres* 1984: 426–7).

Considering Lesage's difficulties with his public, Head was probably right to take the precautions he did in his 'Epistle to the Reader'. A book written in the first person and recounting the story of a rogue (*or pícaro*) could not be the work of an Englishman. People clearly thought at the time that no one would dare to parade his sins and vices in such a bald manner.

The bookhood and the printhood of the novel had again a great deal to do with the public's prejudices and the author's qualms. The development of print had not only given birth to censorship on a large scale, it had also added an intermediary between author and reader, namely the industry which claimed to control the production and circulation of books. Thanks to this intermediary, the author had a greater freedom to write his books and use obscene language if he so wished; but he had to pay a heavy price for this freedom and protection: he could not be sure that his rights would be acknowledged. Hence Head's claim at the end of his 'Epistle':

> It is a legitimate off-spring, I'll assure thee, begot by me singly and soly, and a person that dares in spight of canker'd Malice subscribe himself
>
> > A well-willer to his
> > Countries welfare,
> > Richard Head.
> > (Head 1961: xi)

This was the first time, perhaps, that an English writer was signing a first-person narrative telling the story of a rogue who was supposed to be none other than himself. Head, who was obviously worried that his readers might accuse him of plagiarism, chose to proclaim himself a sinner in order to be acknowledged as the author of the book.

He also claims, both in the 'Epistle' and in the text itself, that he wants his story to be a lesson to those who may be tempted to lead a life of roguery like himself. The first chapter, which begins with a flippant remark about his father's pedigree, ends with a note which echoes the 'Epistle':

> Now, to the intent I may deter others from perpetrating the like, and receive to myself absolution (according as it is promised) upon unfeigned repentance and ingenuous confession of my nefarious facts, I shall give the readers a summary relation of my life, from my nonage to the meridian of my days, hoping that my extravagancies and youthful exiliences have, in that state of life, their declination and period.
>
> > (7)

The word 'exiliences' appeared also in the 'Epistle'. If one compares this book to *Lolita*, for instance, one realizes that Richard Head is playing the part both of the editor, John Ray, who wrote the foreword, and of Humbert, the rogue who wrote down his story 'to save not [his] head, of course, but [his] soul' (Nabokov 1970: 310). He is urging his reader not to follow his example as a sinner while begging the moral establishment to forgive him, if only because he has had the courage to accuse himself in writing.

The autobiographical claim made in the 'Epistle' is soon undermined by a number of details in the narrative proper. The rogue's name is not Richard Head but Meriton Latroon. This ironic name is rarely used in the book but it nevertheless distances the protagonist from the narrator. Other more important elements tend to make us doubt that the prefacer is telling his own story. For instance the number and diversity of Meriton's adventures: he goes through two shipwrecks, is taken prisoner by the Turks, is sold as a slave (a clear echo of *Don Quixote*), escapes, travels to Ceylon, Siam, and other places; he marries many times, steals and fornicates in every chapter. No matter how eventful Head's life may have been, theere is no way he could have gone through so many adventures in those pre-jet days. It is all too obvious that he was exploiting a popular vein, that of the picaresque novel.

The language is often a mixture of preciosity and thieves' rhetoric. For instance, it contains four pages of canting vocabulary which are strongly reminiscent of Rabelais's list of such terms in his *Tiers Livre*, as well as of the catalogues of thieves' tropes published in chapbooks (30–4). Victor Hugo revived the tradition in *Notre Dame de Paris* by providing a great number of words picked up in the thieves' chief haunt in Paris, 'la cour des miracles'. Meriton Latroon is also taught how to tune his voice to 'raise compassion', what form of prayer he was to use 'upon such an occasion, what upon such, varying according to the humour of those persons that I begged of' (35). He also tells dirty anecdotes like the following with obvious gusto:

> That he, going about to correct me for this unlucky and mischievous fact, was by me shown a very shitten trick, which put him into a stinking condition, for having made myself laxative on purpose I squirted into his face upon the first lash given.
>
> (20)

Less than two pages further on, this scurrilous language is supplanted by mock preciosity:

> As then the early lark, the winged herald of the morning, had not with her pretty warbling notes summoned the bright watchmen of the night to prepare for a retreat, neither had Aurora opened the vermillion Oriental gate to make room for Sol's radiant beams, to dissipate that gloomy darkness that had muffled up our hemisphere in obscurity.
>
> (22)

We recognize here a number of poetic formulae used by Homer which, as Parry has shown, were meant to prop the memory of the storyteller. It is sheer parody in this case. Head wants his reader to know that he is no common rogue but is educated, too.

At the end of his long catalogue of evil deeds, Meriton Latroon concludes in the tone adopted by Head in the 'Epistle', apologizing for using 'expressions either scurrilous or obscene', and expressing his hope that 'he that hath sense will grow wiser by the folly that is presented him' (267). This didactic tirade strongly contrasts with the rest of the book in which the protagonist never shows compassion, or any kind of moral awareness. No reader can be fooled by this postscript. How could such a despicable character turn so easily into a moralist? The 'conversion' of Moll Flanders will be a little more plausible than that of Meriton Latroon.

This book could not, obviously, be a genuine autobiography. It was unthinkable that such a bad man could exist, let alone parade his vices in writing; so the book could only be a picaresque novel. Were Head's precautions purely a façade, then? Yes and no. If the censors had turned against him, he could have pointed out that the whole thing was a trick, that his character did not even bear his own name. On the other hand, he wanted his readers to know that he was no saint and that he had probably committed some of the evil deeds described in the book, though not all of them, obviously.

This strategy, which we find in most of the great novels written in the first person, such as *L'Immoraliste*, *Remembrance of Things Past*, and *Lolita*, has always been dictated to some extent by censorship. Most of these novels represent some kind of deviant sexual behaviour condemned by the law. The modern novel would be inconceivable without the existence of censorship, which, as we have seen, was itself a by-product of the printing press. Foucault indirectly confirms this in his discussion of the 'discursivization' of sex in the eighteenth century:

> Not only has the sphere of what one could say about sex been widened and not only have men been compelled to extend it even further; but above all one has plugged the discourse onto sex, according to a complex and multi-action mechanism which cannot run itself out in the mere subjection

to a banning law. Censorship against sex? On the contrary, one has set up a mechanism to generate about sex new discourses, ever more discourses, liable to function and to take effect in its very economy.

(Foucault 1976: 33; my translation)

Foucault does not mention the novel as one of those discourses, but what he writes can easily apply to it. The modern novel could be viewed as a specific strategy to make sex artistically sayable. It functions a little like the magic ring given by the Genii to Mangogul and Mirzoza, in Diderot's *Les bijoux indiscrets* (1748), which not only makes its wearer invisible but, when turned towards a woman, brings her jewel (her sex) to narrate its past experiences freely. A year before *Fanny Hill* and *Tom Jones*, Diderot wrote in this strange work what could be held to be the founding parable of the modern novel.

Print is responsible for the birth of the first-person novel, from *The Life of Lazarillo de Tormes* to *The English Rogue*, *Moll Flanders*, *Roderick Random* (strongly influenced by *Gil Blas*), and *Tristram Shandy*, not only indirectly, by encouraging the development of censorship, but also directly, by promoting a new kind of language. In the picaresque novel, there is a struggle between oral and typographic language. The picaresque novel retains many of the characteristics of orality listed by Walter Ong (1982: 37–46): it is 'additive rather than subordinative', 'aggregative rather than analytic', 'redundant or "copious"', 'close to the human lifeworld'. James objected to this kind of primitiveness; in his preface to *The Ambassadors*, he wrote that 'the first person, in the long piece, is a form foredoomed to looseness'; and he mentioned *Gil Blas* immediately after this (James 1934: 320). The historians of the picaresque novel have often put this looseness to the credit of the genre, explaining that it made for more realism: 'if literary pícaros are to be comprehensible', writes Bjornson, 'they and their situations must be somehow related to that which contemporary readers consider to be "real"' (Bjornson 1977: 13-14). The concept of realism Bjornson has in mind is intimately related to that of orality: the 'real' is that which has not yet been put into writing. This definition is more philosophically grounded than it may seem. French philosopher Clément Rosset defines the real as 'that of which there is no duplicate' (Rosset

1979: 25; my translation), that which has not yet been represented or put into words. The lower classes had not had access to writing before Gutenberg, whereas the upper classes usually had. The picaresque novel may have been the first attempt made by the lower (and so far illiterate) classes to put the world they lived in into printed narratives.

At the same time, this form of writing departed from the oral tradition in a number of ways. It was neither 'conservative or traditionalist', nor 'homeostatic', two important characteristics of orality for Walter Ong. Head and Defoe were acutely aware of undermining the moral and ideological foundations of the society they lived in, as their many precautions intimated. So is Diderot, who, in the first page of *La Religieuse*, describes the nun's determination to seek *M. le marquis* de Croismare's help. The latter opening is less 'oral' than the ones we have studied so far. The nun does not address the marquis; she writes: '*M. le marquis* de Croismare's answer, if he consents to send me one, will provide me with the first lines of this tale. Before writing to him, I wanted to know him' (Diderot 1962: 117; my translation). This reads almost like a passage from a diary: the nun is musing on the reasons why she must write the story of her life. Yet, the reference to that aristocrat whose 'sensitiveness . . . honour . . . honesty' (117) she has heard so much about has the same significance as Head's dedication to His Worship. Two worlds are here brought together: the old 'real', represented by the moral establishment, and the new 'real' which seeks access to writing and to print.

Also, the picaresque novel is not 'agonistically toned' in the sense defined by Ong, who gives the examples of African storytellers; neither is it 'empathetic and participatory'. Though the prefacer or narrator shows his anxiety to please his readers (as many of them as possible), he also puts them at a distance by promoting the bookhood and printhood of his text.

In a writerly picaresque novel such as *Tristram Shandy*, the author does gesture obliquely at his readers. The calligraphic games played by Tristram, his cheerful browbeating of the stupid Madam, his endless jokes, and sexual innuendoes create a very buoyant, even jubilant, atmosphere. Tristram considers the book to be a 'party' (Sterne 1965: 65) and the communication between author and reader the kind of exchange which develops between jester and jestee, mortgager and mortgagee:

> The *Mortgager* and *Mortgagée* differ the one from the other, not more in length of purse, than the *Jester* and *Jestée* do, in that of memory . . . the one raises a sum and the other a laugh at your expence, and think no more about it. Interest, however, still runs on in both cases.
>
> (21)

Here, Tristram describes a situation which is typically oral, as if author and reader were participating in a common ritual, and their laughter escalating through a kind of positive feedback
 This laughter may seem to have a great deal in common with carnival laughter as described by Bakhtin. In carnival laughter, it is not so much the content of the information that counts, Bakhtin explains, as the relationship and the quality of the symbolic exchange:

> It is, first of all, a festive laughter. Therefore it is not an individual reaction to some isolated 'comic' event. Carnival laughter is the laughter of all the people. Second, it is universal in scope; it is directed at all and everyone, including the carnival's participants. The entire world is seen in its droll aspect, in its gay relativity. Third, this laughter is ambivalent: it is gay, triumphant, and at the same time mocking, deriding. It asserts and denies, it buries and revives. Such is the laughter of carnival.
>
> (Bakhtin 1968: 11–12)

Carnival laughter is an elaborate kind of symbolic exchange in which the participants allow their identities to dissolve. There is no question of 'one-upmanship' (to borrow the vocabulary of Bateson), but a complete immersion in the seething whirl of the festival.
 Should Tristram's parable of the 'party' be taken literally? It is true that, in *Tristram Shandy*, the multiplicity of narratees and the confusion of roles gradually build up an intense jubilation in the reader which makes him obscurely feel at one with the author, even two centuries after the publication of the novel. The absence of closure paradoxically contributes to this effect: the reader is not left with a story which he could more or less adequately summarize, but with a body of words which

he can continue to play with. He feels that this text desires him, as Barthes expected the good texts to do (Barthes 1973a: 13). He must somehow show himself worthy of its infinite seductions, and reciprocate. A successful reading does not consist in decoding whatever the author has coded into his text; it consists in picking up the poetic gauntlet and appropriating the text.

The problem is that the reader knows from the start that he is bound to lose and will never be the ideal reader the author had in mind. The latter, despite his affirmations to the contrary, does not really want to communicate with the reader, but tries to erect an impressive body of words, that is, a printed book, which will guarantee his privacy. The parable of the party was just another of Tristram's jokes to snub us. A novel, especially when written in the first person, can generate a kind of euphoria, by simulating an oral form of communication akin to that of the carnival; but its obtrusive bookhood constantly reminds the reader that he is not at one with, nor in the presence of, the real author.

The picaresque novel managed a transition between the oral form of storytelling and the typographic one. The communication is still more oral than typographic in *The English Rogue* or *Moll Flanders*, but in *Tristram Shandy* it is mostly typographic, despite the many allusions to the oral world. But typographic communication is not one-directional. The author and the reader are still very much concerned with '*defining the nature of their relationship*' just like the speakers in ordinary conversations (Watzlawick 1967: 121). They are passionately signalling to each other over the abysmal array of printed words, evaluating the intensity of their relationship through their respective attempts to reach each other. The bookhood and printhood of the text guarantees that they will never put off their masks. There is no positive or negative feedback in or through a printed text comparable to the feedback in ordinary conversations or carnival laughter. The interlocutors cannot interrogate each other to regulate the flow and significance of their communication. The novel was based, from the start, on this necessary misunderstanding, the page being as it were like a twin-faced mirror on which author and reader project ideal images of themselves.

## THE EPISTOLARY NOVEL

Fielding obviously considered the epistolary novel to be a dramatic genre when he wrote, in his preface to Sarah Fielding's *Familiar Letters* in 1747:

> I know not of any essential difference between this, and any other way of writing novels, save only, that by making use of letters, the writer is freed from the regular beginnings and conclusions of stories, with some other formalities, in which the reader of taste finds no less ease and advantage, than the author himself.
>
> (Allott 1980: 249)

The chief advantage of the epistolary method, according to him, is that it allows the author to keep out of his text more easily and to avoid too direct a contact with his reader. It is not true, however, that the author of epistolary novels 'is freed from the regular beginnings and conclusions'; the editor's preface is as awkward a formality in many cases as whatever formality the author of a first- or third-person novel may choose to use.

At times, the epistolary novel is not as fundamentally different from the Spanish-imported picaresque novel as it may seem. Quevedo's *Cartas del caballero de la tenaza* (1627) was an epistolary novel but also a picaresque novel; and Manuel de León's *La Picaresca* (written between 1667 and 1680) was a collection of sixty-six letters exchanged between the Commissioner of the Inquisition in Toledo and a nun who was either his mistress or his daughter. On the other hand, an epistolary novel like *Pamela* turns into a diary when the heroine cannot communicate any more with her parents. And the two long letters which constitute *Fanny Hill* are very close in style and content to a memoir like *Moll Flanders*.

The letter is not, of course, a post-Gutenberg invention, as were the autobiography and the diary. It was an old form of communication which had also been exploited in literary works centuries before the rise of the modern novel. Versini, in his excellent study of the epistolary genre, mentions a number of Greek epistolary novels, such as Chariton's *Chaereas and Callirhoe* (written probably in the second century AD), Heliodorus's *Aethiopica* (written in the third century AD), or again

Xenophon Ephesius's *Ephesiaca* (written during the same period). Letters reappeared in the twelfth and thirteenth centuries with the troubadour *Salut d'amors*, the forerunner of the Italian *tenzone* and the Spanish *tenso*, which were both more chirographic than oral. Guillaume de Machaut's *Livre du voir-dit* (1363) is one of the first epistolary works written in prose as well as in verse: it is the amorous correspondence between an old poet and a seventeen-year-old girl, and consists of forty-six letters in prose, twenty-three from the poet and twenty-three from the girl, plus twenty-nine in verse from the poet, and twenty-six in verse from the girl. The transitions are provided by octosyllabic lines (Versini 1979: 10–12).

In the next two centuries, the epistolary romance, which began to flourish not only in France, but also in Italy and in Spain, started to develop concurrently with non-literary epistolary forms. The first collections of love letters, meant as epistolary models, were published in the sixteenth century; Michel d'Amboise's *Epîtres vénériennes* (1532) and Christophe de Barronso's *Jardin amoureux contenant toutes les règles d'amours* (written between 1530 and 1535) were among the most popular in France. Their purpose was not so much to teach a rhetoric of the letter as to promote a rhetoric of love. The 'secretaries', on the other hand, dealt with varied subjects; most of the French examples cited by Versini were meant for people living at or near the court: *Secrétaire des secrétaires* (1624), Jean Puget de la Serre's *Secrétaire de la cour* (1623) and his *Secrétaire à la mode* (1641), and, in the following century, Milleran's *Secrétaire des courtisans* (1714).

One of the earliest 'secretaries' published in England was William Fulwood's *The Enimie of Idleness: Teaching the manner and stile how to endite, compose and write all sorts of Epistles and Letters* (1568); many others appeared in the following centuries: *The Secretaries Study* (1652), *The Young Secretary Guide* (1687), *The Lover's Secretary* (1692), *The Experienc'd Secretary* (first published in 1699 and reissued many times), and *The Complete Letter Writer* (1755). One of the most famous examples, of course, is Richardson's *Letters Written to and for Particular Friends Directing the Requisite Style and Forms to be observed in Writing Familiar Letters* (1741) which prompted its author to write *Pamela* (Versini 1979: 29–31). The 'secretaries' or 'letter-writers' were essentially meant to teach the chirographic art to people who were learning to cast off the rags of orality. Yet the rhetoric they advocated was very close to that of oratory, as Versini explains: 'the letter, like a speech, must contain *salutatio, captatio benevolentiae, narratio, petitio, conclusio*' (48; my translation). The composition and many reissues of such books show how a new medium (here print), instead of destroying the old one (writing, and even oratory) as McLuhan claimed a little rashly, often helps promote it and make it even more sophisticated.

The transition from epistolary manuals to genuine letters like those of Guez de Balzac or Voiture, and finally to epistolary novels, took more than a century. The lost or stolen postal bag topos which developed from the beginning of the seventeenth century marked a very important stage in that evolution; some of the best examples are Nicholas Breton's *Poste with a Packet of Mad Letters* (1603), I.-W. Gent's *A Speedie Post with Certain New Letters* (1625), *A Flying Post with a Packet of Choice New Letters and Complements* (1678), Charles Gildon's *The Post-Boy Robb'd of his Mail, or The Packet broke open* (1692; Versini 1979: 34). What tickled the imagination of such writers was essentially the fact that letters could be 'purloined' or lost, that they could be read by other people than their rightful addressees.

The first epistolary novel to reach international fame, *Les Lettres portugaises* (1669), was based on this principle. The *éditeur* explains in his preface how he managed to get a good copy of the translation of these five letters addressed to an unknown gentleman now supposed to live in Portugal; he claims to be ignorant of the name of the addressee as well as that of the translator. All these stratagems made seventeenth-century readers wonder whether the letters were genuine. Some critics used the topographical errors in the fourth letter as evidence that the letters were a fake, but many believed that they were genuine. They were composed by Lavergne de Guilleragues, as now everybody recognizes (Bray 1983: 59–67).

This famous book, which was translated into English in 1678 and reissued many times (both in prose and in verse) in England before the publication of *Pamela*, served as a model for Aphra Behn's *Love Letters Between a Nobleman and His*

*Sister*, the first volume of which was published in 1684. This novel is an Arcadian French version of the love of Forde, Lord Grey of Werke, captain of Monmouth's horse, with his sister-in-law, Lady Henrietta Berkeley; such a relationship was considered as incestuous in the seventeenth century. Aphra Behn, like Richard Head in *The English Rogue*, acknowledges her foreign model: she passes off a real English scandal as a French one and transposes it into a well-known literary form to make the book more agreeable to her public. These narrative strategies, which were originally meant to fool the censors, largely boost the fiction effect by lending a double status to the text and by teasing the reader to find out what is genuine and what is fake.

The first volume begins with 'The Argument', written in the third person, which summarizes the events narrated in the letters; it ends with the following paragraph:

> After their flight these letters were found in their cabinets, at their house at St. *Denis*, where they both lived together, for the space of a year; and they are as exactly as possible placed in the order they were sent, and were those supposed to be written towards the latter part of their amours.
> 
> (Behn: 1987: 2)

There are at least three narrative dodges, the three passive phrases, in this passage: the first ('were found') allows the editor to omit the name of the person who found the letters; the second ('are . . . placed') serves as a screen for the editor himself; and the third ('are supposed') uses the authority of the *vox populi* to promote the historicity of the documents. This first volume contains only the letters of Sylvia and Philander; there is no date, no address at the beginning of the letters. And no reference is made to the communication problems that the exchange of letters usually implies.

The second volume (published in 1685) bears the same title as the first one, but it does not contain only letters; there are long narrative pieces, for instance the ten-page narrative at the beginning of the volume which opens like this:

> At the end of the first part of these letters, we left *Philander* impatiently waiting on the sea-shore for the approach of the lovely *Sylvia*; who accordingly came to him dressed like a

128 Textual communication

youth, to secure herself from a discovery. They stayed not long to caress each other, but he taking the welcome maid in his arms, with a transported joy bore her to a small vessel, that lay ready near the beach.

(113)

This third-person narrative is in the same Arcadian tone as *L'Astrée*, a fact which considerably undermines the realism of the letter scheme. This form of narrative gradually supplants the letters. The letter-writers' reactions will now be described, as in the following passage:

*Philander* having finished the reading of this, remained a while wholly without life or motion, when coming to himself, he sighed and cried, –'Why–farewell trifling life–if of the two extremes one must be chosen, rather than I'll abandon *Sylvia*, I'll stay and be delivered up a victim to incensed France'.

(121)

The commentator has now become an omniscient narrator of the Balzac kind, and can represent the protagonist's behaviour or 'quote' his thoughts. Two narrative discourses co-exist: that of the first-person letter-writers and that of the third-person omniscient narrator who begins to adopt an epic tone. The latter finally takes over in the third volume, published in 1687 under the title, 'The Amours of Philander and Sylvia'; this volume, which consists of a long narrative in the third person, contains only nine letters; there is not a single one in the last eighty pages (387-461).

This book, half novel, half romance, has probably not received enough attention. It constitutes a very important transition between romance and novel, between first- and third-person narrative, between genuine and fake epistolary literature, and more specifically between *Les Lettres portugaises* and *Pamela*. It is too Arcadian, too formulaic, to be realistic; at the same time, it is often very erotic, as when Philander tries to rouse Sylvia sexually by evoking 'her dress all negligent as when I saw her last, discovering a thousand ravishing graces, round, white, small breasts, delicate neck, and rising bosom' (3). The book reads a little like a hybrid of *L'Astrée* and Nabokov's *Ada*, which also describes an incestuous love and also contains a combination of first- and third-person narratives. It is suffused with the kind of passion which will devour Richardson's heroines.

*Pamela* is infinitely more elaborate than its French or English forerunners, not so much in its portrayal of sentiments and passions as in its communication pattern. We have already studied the editor's preface which, in many ways, was reminiscent of that of *Moll Flanders*. The editor does not retire into his ivory tower at the end of the preface, but continues to interfere with the narrative almost throughout the novel. The first time, he does so within the text itself: 'Here it is necessary the reader should know, that when Mr B. found Pamela's virtue was not to be subdued, and he had in vain tried to conquer his passion for her, he had ordered his Lincolnshire coachman to bring his travelling chariot from thence' (Richardson 1980: 123). Richardson had a difficult problem to solve here: he wanted to show that Mr B. had got in touch with Pamela's father without Pamela's knowledge, and this implied quoting a letter neither written by nor addressed to her. This section is very confused and reminds us of the tricks used by Aphra Behn in her second and third volumes.

The second time the editor's voice is heard, it is in a footnote to the diary: inside the letter Pamela has received from Mr Williams, there is a letter from her father which, obviously, she cannot quote since her diary is meant as a long letter to her father that she will mail when she regains her freedom. Quoting the letter would have amounted to sending it back to its author. Hence the editor's note: 'The following is a copy of her father's letter' (198).

In the body of the book itself, the narrative roles sometimes become terribly confused. There are far more people involved in this correspondence than in the examples we have analysed so far: there are Pamela's father, her mother, her parents (the same, and not the same), Mr Williams, Mr B., and some others; and inside the correspondence itself, there is the long diary. Many of the letter-writers often have two or more addressees in mind when they write. For instance, Pamela's father is not only addressing his daughter when he says, in his first letter: 'Everybody talks how you are come on, and what a genteel girl you are; and some say, you are very pretty; and, indeed, when I saw you last, which is about six months ago, I should have thought so myself, if you was not our child' (45).

A great deal of the information contained in this passage is clearly addressed to the reader rather than to Pamela herself: the reference to the *vox populi* to describe (or evoke) the pretty looks of the heroine is too conspicuous a trick; the modernist and postmodernist writers will use mirrors to write the portraits of their first-person narrators. The clumsiness of this notation is partly erased by the last notation, which suggests that the father may be in love with his daughter; Pamela's letters will perhaps serve to fan his repressed passion for her. The time reference ('about six months ago') is obviously meant for the reader, too, rather than for Pamela who knows very well when they saw each other for the last time.

The reader is therefore clearly the second addressee of that letter, just as Mrs Jewkes is the second addressee of the letter Pamela is going to write to her master: 'I went up to write my letter to my master; and, as I intended to shew it her [Mrs Jewkes], I wrote accordingly as to her part of it' (177). What looked at first like a clumsiness on the part of Richardson (the original addressor) is going to turn into one of the main narrative strategies of the novel: each individual text will likewise be given a double or triple narrative status, the reader being gradually teased to join this complex exchange as an objective and enlightened receiver.

In this novel, the manipulation of writing takes on a proportion unrivalled in eighteenth-century fiction. Pamela is an inveterate writer who is forbidden to write and communicate with the outside world, her parents especially. Confined as she is to the house or to her closet, she lives through her writing rather than through her actions and social intercourse. Doing nothing but write, she must interrupt herself at times because of outside interference: 'I must break off; here's somebody coming. / 'Tis only our Hannah with a message from Mrs Jervis. But here is somebody else. Well, it is only Rachel' (109). This reads like a sample of simultaneous writing. In another passage, she goes out into the garden between two paragraphs: 'But I will go into the garden, and resolve afterwards. / I have been in the garden, and to the back-door: and there I stood, my heart up at my mouth' (191). The garden gradually becomes the chief repository for her writing; at some point she says: 'I left them together, and retired to my closet, to write a letter for the tiles' (196). Pamela is not posting her letters, she commits them 'to the happy tiles, in the bosom of that earth, where I hope deliverance will take root' (162); later she will bury them 'under the rose-bush' (259). There is again an obvious parody of this in Nabokov's *Ada*.

She also gets to read letters not addressed to her. For instance, she manages to extort from farmer Monkton the letter Mr B. has sent him concerning her: 'I read its contents, and afterwards procured leave to take a copy of it; which follows' (138). The copy is supposed to be meant for her parents. She also accidentally reads a letter addressed to Mrs Jewkes, and Mrs Jewkes reads the one addressed to her (200ff.). Is this only an accident, or did Mr B. intend it that way? We are not sure. In another passage the postman (Colbrand in this case) hands her a letter which she was supposed to read only the next day (285). And she is so afraid that her own letters may not follow their proper course that she starts taking down copies of all of them (178).

The lost post-bag topos is here exploited with great effect: by drawing our attention to the misadventures that can befall her letters, Pamela forces us not only to read them from the points of view of all those unintended readers but to realize that she is writing only for herself. She once asks her father to keep her letters 'as it may be some little pleasure to me, perhaps, to read them to myself, when I am come to you, to remind me what I have gone through' (75). She is her own ultimate addressee: she sends her letters to her parents not only to communicate with them, but to safeguard her writing and eventually her story.

And when she is no longer able to send them, she begins to write her diary because she compulsively needs to analyse her feelings and adventures, and to turn them into a narrative. Mr B. understands her motives much better than she thinks; when he writes to her father that 'she has given herself up to the reading of novels and romances, and such idle stuff, and now takes it into her head, because her glass tells her she is pretty, that every body who looks upon her is in love with her' (24), he is not far off the mark. Pamela has been so much influenced by her readings that she now acts like a heroine in an epistolary novel. She acknowledges that much at the beginning of the second book: 'Well, my story, surely, would furnish out a surprising kind of novel, if it were to be well told' (181).

Once, she even addresses her parents in the same style Fielding and Sterne will use to tease their readers: 'O my dear parents! don't be frighted when you come to read this! But all will be over before you can see this' (208). This passage, as we shall learn later (263), marks the beginning of the stolen pages. Pamela has totally distanced herself from her present plight: she does her utmost to kindle her parents' imagination; then she tells them not to worry, that it will be all over by the time they read her report. She acts as if she were coaching novel-readers, tickling their imagination but also reminding them that it is pure fiction.

Mr B. finally becomes her chief reader; when he begs her to give him the beginning of her diary which she sent to her father, he says:

> As I have furnished you with a subject, I think I have a title to see how you manage it. Besides, there is such a pretty air of romance, as you tell your story, in *your* plots, and *my* plots, that I shall be better directed how to wind up the catastrophe of the pretty novel.
>
> (268)

He feels he has a right to see her letters and her diary since he plays such an important part in them and is in fact their chief inspirer. He, too, has become paper-hungry; she has teased him into seeing her as a body of writing, as an exciting fiction. He threatens to undress her to see if she does not keep her papers in her stays: ' "I never undressed a girl in my life; but I will now begin to strip my pretty Pamela, and hope I shall not go far before I find them." And he began to unpin my handkerchief' (271). This is one of the most erotic scenes in the novel. Mr B., who was originally (and still seems to be) the aggressor, has fallen into her trap: he does not so much want to see her naked body as to discover her naked self as it is exposed in her papers.

After he finally gets to read her diary, he asks her to continue writing: ' "I would have you," said he, "continue writing by all means; and I assure you, in the mind I am in, I will not ask you for any papers after these; except something very extraordinary happens" ' (275). Just as Desdemona loved Othello 'for the dangers [he] had passed', Mr B. loves her for the letters and the diary she has written. He is in love with a paper tease.

This book probably deserves to be called the first metafictional novel ever to have been written: the main narrator has fed her imagination upon books, and acts bookishly. She writes to be read not only by her official addressees but also by other readers, including Mr B. and herself later. The story becomes less and less that of her struggle against Mr B. and more and more that of her writing (both as a process and as a product to be manipulated) with which she tries to defeat time and space. Her writing is not only a report of all that happens to her, it is the very instrument with which she manages to defeat Mr B. and to turn him into a comparatively tame lover.

The reader is himself similarly tamed, being forced gradually to view her as the chief manipulator of the texts, when, in fact, the ultimate one is Richardson himself. Ian Watt acknowledges his unrest when he writes: 'The very lack of selectiveness, indeed, impels us to a more active involvement in the events and feelings described' (Watt 1967: 193). Such is generally the effect of genuine metafiction: it ensnares the reader into a tangle of texts from which he will never manage to extricate himself; it brings him to picture a godlike author pulling the strings from above, an ideal author who is always a step ahead and remains forever out of reach. The struggle is so exciting, though, that the reader feels he has acquired some rights in the text (just like Mr B. in Pamela's papers), almost as if he had partly authored it.

This illusion is, of course, bred by the medium itself, which keeps the author and the reader incommunicado. The reader's chief interlocutor is the editor of the preface who hands him the texts and tells him he is not part of them; but this editor does not stick to his role: he enters the black box of the novel, forcing the reader to do the same.

The communication situation can be represented like this:

```
Editor ↔ [(Pamela ↔ Parents) ↔ Mr B.] ↔ Reader
1              |_____|
2              |_____|
3       |_____|
```

## 134 Textual communication

In terms of communication, the first black box, the first system is the one which relates Pamela to her parents, and which refers to Mr B. as an object of discourse, not as an interlocutor. In the second black box, Pamela communicates with Mr B. who, through her writing, is now a subject, an interlocutor. The reader and the editor occupy symmetrical positions in the third box, or third system: they are communicating with each other through or over the texts within which the characters in the story are themselves communicating with each other. The diagram naturally leaves out the author, who has so cleverly managed to construct his little boxes that he has lured us into them, while himself staying outside them.

The diagram developed by Altman to explain the functioning of epistolary novels differs from mine in one important respect (Altman 1982: 200–1):

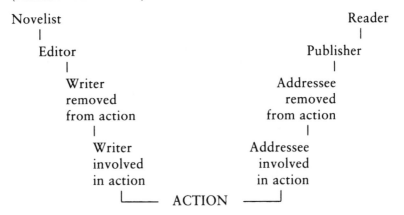

The editor and publisher occupy symmetrical positions in this diagram. As I have indicated from the start, the publisher is one of the addressors of the text; he is above this structure, but out of the text. Once he is removed from Altman's diagram, one realizes, indeed, that editor and reader occupy symmetrical positions.

This kind of communication would have been unthinkable without the intervention of the print industry. By appropriating the author's text in order to sell it to us, the industry, which can in no way be held to be its creator or possessor, induces us to retrieve it from its hands, to appropriate it poetically. This is what the above diagram reveals: that the author has withdrawn from the communication system, that he has faded out of it. The complex industrial and financial system which turns a single manuscript into thousands of books distributed around the world eventually gives an unprecedented freedom to the reader. It also grants an unprecedented stature to the author who, though he is the first and only sender, is out of his text which is left to fend for itself in the reader's hands.

The structure of *Clarissa* is more systematically epistolary than that of *Pamela*. There is no diary, here, and the number of correspondents is much greater. Only six out of the 537 letters are exchanged between Clarissa and Lovelace; there is not a single one by the latter in the first eighty pages of the novel. This leads Altman to suggest that the letters do not play an important role in the seduction game (1982: 22). She forgets that, here again, the tormentor will read many of the letters exchanged by Clarissa and her confidantes. Clarissa is aware that Lovelace is stealing her letters; one day, she writes to her favourite correspondent: 'I write this, my dear Miss Howe, only for a feint, and to see if it will go current. I shall write at large very soon, if not miserably prevented!!!' (Richardson 1985: 759). The letter will indeed be stolen by Lovelace and sent to John Bedford. Clarissa's stratagem has one important result: it informs Lovelace that she knows he is stealing her letters, and it turns him into another of her addressees.

Here, too, we find many textual embeddings. The editor interferes with the letter-scheme many times, as for instance in the following footnote: 'The whole of this black transaction is given by the injured lady to Miss Howe, in her subsequent letters, dated Thursday July 6. To which the reader is referred' (883). Elsewhere, his voice is heard within the text itself:

> Mr Lovelace gives her a very circumstantial relation of all that passed between the lady and Dorcas. But as he could only guess at her motives for refusing to go off, when Dorcas told her that she had engaged for her the protection of the dowager lady, it is thought proper to omit his relation, and to supply it by some *memoranda* of the lady's.
> 
> (926)

Laclos's *rédacteur* will often resort to such tricks in *Les Liaisons dangereuses*. The editor is censoring the text, as it were, deciding that one text is better than another, informing the reader that he is not being given all the elements to judge for himself since a selection has been made for his benefit. The editor does not obviously confine himself to his avowed role; he may even have a personal stake in the story.

Clarissa and Lovelace also act as editors, at times. Letter 22 contains two other letters, Letter 25, four, Letter 227, five, and Letter 405, nine. In the latter case, four of the nine copied letters are by Clarissa herself (1194–5). In Letter 229 addressed to John Bedford, Lovelace sends one of Anna Howe's letters to Miss Beaumont which he has received from Wilson; he does not bother to copy it, but he annotates it: 'Thou wilt see the margin of this cursed letter crowded with indices [here there is a pointed index]. I put them to mark the places devoted for vengeance, or requiring animadversion' (743). Lovelace does his utmost in his correspondence with his friend to show his ugly facet. In Letter 254 addressed to John Bedford, he quotes and annotates the marriage licence in the following way:

> *N. N. by divine permission, Lord Bishop of London, to our well beloved in Christ, Robert Lovelace* (Your servant, my good lord! What have I done to merit so much goodness, who never saw your lordship in my life?), *of the parish of St Martin's in the Fields* . . .
>
> (871)

Again, in Letter 261 to Bedford, he quotes papers he has received from Clarissa to show her mental daze: the first one is a letter to Anna which Clarissa tore into two pieces; the second is a letter to her father which is scratched through and which she had thrown under the table; the third and the following ones are notes more or less addressed to herself; the tenth is a poem containing echoes of and excerpts from Otway, Dryden, Garth, and Shakespeare. There are annotations in the margin at this point (893).

In this novel, the heroine neither manipulates nor tames her tormentor with her writing as Pamela did with Mr B. She does not even write in the same style as Lovelace, as William Farrell has remarked: 'Lovelace writes and even speaks in a style long associated with the courtly love letter while his victim resists his advances in the pathetic language of contemporary "she-tragedy" ' (Farrell: 1963: 365). Gopnik puts this difference of style in rhetorical perspective: 'Clarissa's typical verbal medium is non-rhetorical, often consciously anti-rhetorical; in its constant redefining and rephrasing her style is like Plato's dialectic, the language of sincerity and truth' (Gopnik 1970: 17). Clarissa is therefore rhetorically at a disadvantage: though she seeks our sympathy with her sincerity, we tend to side with her tormentor because he is a refined (and ruthless) rhetorician.

Here, the reader is not so evidently caught in the black box as in *Pamela*; he dispassionately debates with the editor the respective merits of the two antagonists. This novel prefigures the historical novel in which the reader will stand aside and never be intensely involved in the narrative structure. It is no coincidence, certainly, that so many historical events and personages, either contemporary (Louis XIV, Versailles, the tsar's cossacks) or classical (Pompey, Alexander, Tarquin), are mentioned. This novel is infinitely less metafictional than *Pamela*; it is more concerned with the strategies of love and deceit, with morality, than with the rhetoric of letters or texts in general.

When Richardson set out to write his *Meditations Collected from the Sacred Books; And Adapted to the Different Stages of a Deep Distress; gloriously surmounted by Patience, Piety, and Resignation. Being those mentioned in the History of Clarissa*, published in 1750, he simply extracted the moral marrow out of his novel. This book confirms that the novel was deeply grounded in the real and duplicated it somehow. Richardson was probably prompted to write this book by his readers' reactions to the denouement in which Clarissa's virtue did not receive its reward: he wanted to underline what, he thought, they had failed to see. This book of meditations is a second postscript in which the author tried to accompany his novel a little further into the dull-witted world.

A comparison between *Clarissa* and *Pamela* suggests that the concept of epistolarity may be misleading. A. L. Barbauld's famous statement about Richardson's epistolary form clearly applies more to the former than to the latter novel:

> The method . . . gives the feelings of the moment as the writers felt them at the moment. It allows a pleasing variety of stile, if the author has sufficient command of pen to assume it. It makes the whole work dramatic, since all the characters speak in their own persons. It accounts for the breaks in the story, by the omission or loss of letters. It is

incompatible with a rapid stile, but gives room for the graceful introduction of remark and sentiment, or any kind, almost, of digressive matter. But, on the other hand, it is highly fictitious; it is the most natural and the least probable way of telling a story.

(Allott 1980: 259)

Clarissa is indeed 'dramatic' in the sense defined by Mrs Barbauld: its style is varied, and each correspondent comes on stage in turn and retires afterwards, leaving the reader to judge of their actions and sentiments. This is the kind of epistolary novel Altman had in mind when she said of the epistolary confidant that he 'shares much more with his classical theater counterpart than he differs from him' (Altman 1982: 54). The epistolary novel would be, in this perspective, the narrative counterpart of drama, whereas the picaresque and the confessional novel would be a counterpart of lyrical poetry.

This structure does apparently allow the author to withdraw, as Richardson once said the author must withdraw: 'The pen is jealous of company. It expects, as I may say, to engross the writer's whole self: every body allows the writer to withdraw' (Watt 1967: 190). Yet the reader has the illusion of attending, from the auditorium, the same play as the author is himself attending from backstage. The asymmetry is still there, but it is less 'dramatic' than in the case of *Pamela*. The epistolary novel can be said to be genuinely dramatic when the reader is not lured into the black box of the story, as in *Clarissa*. Author and reader still occupy asymmetrical positions, but the author's withdrawal is not as obvious. In a metafictional novel like *Pamela*, on the other hand, this withdrawal is nearly total, at least in the first two volumes published in 1740.

## CONCLUSION: NOVEL VS ROMANCE

At the end of this chapter, we must address a question which has vexed the critics for over two centuries: what is, essentially, the difference between a novel and a romance? As Ioan Williams's anthology, *Novel and Romance, 1700–1800* (Williams 1970), his later book, *The Idea of the Novel in Europe, 1600–1700* (Williams 1979), and Geoffrey Day's more recent study, *From Fiction to the Novel* (Day 1987), show, the answers to this question have been varied and sometimes contradictory.

The distinction does not exist in French where the word 'roman' first appeared in the twelfth century with the meaning: 'A tale in French (in *roman*) verse adapted from the ancient legends of Latin literature and in which predominate prodigious and amorous adventures' (*Le Petit Robert* 1988: 1726; my translation). The concept is derived from the language itself: a *roman* or romance is a narrative composed in the vernacular. When, in the seventeenth century, such works as Scarron's *Roman comique* or Mme de Lafayette's *La Princesse de Clèves* were published, they were called by the same name, which suggests that in French literature the modern novel is merely felt to belong to the narrative tradition which started in the Middle Ages when the vernacular began to supplant Latin. The word 'romance', which appeared much latter, was used chiefly in its musical sense.

The Italian word *novella*, from which the English 'novel' and the French '*nouvelle*' are derived, designated a short narrative. In the early definitions of the word 'novel' the criterion of length was paramount; Johnson's *Dictionary* defines it as 'a small tale, generally of love' (Johnson 1755: 'Novel'). Lord Chesterfield also insisted on this criterion: 'A Novel is a kind of abbreviation of a Romance; for a Romance generally consists of twelve volumes, all filled with insipid love nonsense, and most incredible adventures' (Day 1987: 9). So the novel is first and foremost 'a little book' (this is the phrase used by most English novelists in the eighteenth century); we saw earlier that this usually meant a duodecimo edition in four to six volumes. The English novel therefore corresponded to a new publishing formula (like the chapbook): it was a small and comparatively cheap book meant for entertainment which could be read silently at home. Whereas the oral narrative tended to be copious, the typographic was supposed to be more compact.

The first English writer to have used the word 'novel' on a title-page was Congreve, in his *Incognita: or, Love and Duty Reconciled. A Novel* published in 1692. In his preface, he justified the use of the term in the following way:

> Romances are generally composed of the constant Loves and invincible Courages of Heros, Heroins, Kings and Queens, Mortals of the first Rank, and so forth; where lofty Language,

miraculous Contingencies and impossible Performances, elevate and surprize the Reader into a giddy Delight, which leaves him flat upon the Ground . . . Novels are of a more familiar nature; Come near us, and represent to us Intrigues in practice, delight us with Accidents and odd Events, but not such as are wholly unusual or unpresidented, such which not being so distant from our Belief bring also the pleasure nearer us. Romances give more of Wonder, Novels more delight.

(1)

It is not size but plausibility which justifies the use of the concept according to Congreve: the events narrated in romances cannot, on the whole, occur in our universe; those narrated in novels usually can.

This distinction will be echoed again and again throughout the eighteenth century. The romance never was supposed to tell the truth; that is why Johnson suggested in 1750 that it was amoral: 'In the romances formerly written every transaction and sentiment was so remote from all that passes among men, that the reader was in very little danger of making any applications to himself; the virtues and crimes were equally beyond his sphere of activity' (Williams 1970: 144). This criticism of the romance is reminiscent of Plato's indictment of the poets, which Ong now sees as a 'rejection of the pristine aggregative, paratactic, oral-style thinking perpetuated in Homer' (Ong 1982: 28).

The novel, on the other hand, is more truthful; it is not based on fabulous legends but on 'the Book of Nature', as Fielding explained in the preface to *Joseph Andrews* (Fielding 1987: 8) or as Richardson angrily reminded one of his correspondents: 'What a duce, do you think I am writing a Romance? Don't you see that I am copying Nature' (Allott 1980: 41).

But as the 'Book of Nature' has never been written, each writer may claim to be writing a new page of it, hence the fundamental individualism of the genre, as Ian Watt remarked:

> The novel is the form of literature which most fully reflects this individualist and innovating reorientation . . . The novel is thus the logical literary vehicle of a culture which, in the last few centuries, has set an unprecedented value on origi-

nality, on the novel; and it is therefore well named.

(Watt 1967: 13)

The novel constitutes an appropriation of the language for private purposes: it does not claim to project a consensual view of the world, based on metaphysical presuppositions or dogmas, but to propose an unprecedented one. It is not conservative, as the oral romance was; it is revolutionary, like the printed books which brought about the Reformation and the French Revolution.

Many conservative writers, like Owen Ruffhead in 1761, came to consider the novel as fundamentally immoral:

> The Genius of Romance seems to have been long since drooping among us; and has, of late, been generally displayed only for the basest purposes: either to raise the grin of Ideotism by its buffoonry, or stimulate the prurience of Sensuality by its obscenities. Novels, therefore, have circulated chiefly among the giddy and licentious of both sexes, who read, not for the sake of thinking, but for want of thought.
>
> (Day 1987: 8)

The satanic humour of Fielding, Smollett, and Sterne was obviously Ruffhead's chief target. Hugh Blair cannot help considering the English novels as 'inferior to the French' because they are less refined (Williams 1970: 250–1). Virginia Woolf will pass a similar judgement upon *Ulysses*: 'Genius it has, I think: but of the inferior water. The book is diffuse. It is brackish. It is pretentious. It is underbred, not only in the obvious sense, but in the literary sense' (Woolf 1978: 55–6). This is not only an aesthetic but a social judgement. Virginia Woolf and Hugh Blair consider that Fielding and Joyce, respectively, belong to the lower classes and lack refinement.

Another important criterion which helped distinguish the romance from the novel was that of unity of action. Here is what Arthur Murphy wrote in 1762 in his introduction to Fielding's *Works*: 'In the first place, the action has that unity, which is the boast of the great models of composition; it turns upon a single event, attended with many circumstances, and many subordinate incidents' (Day 1987: 19). Thomas Holcroft similarly insisted on the 'unity of design' in his Preface to

*Alwayn* in 1780 (Allott 1980: 46-7). Ong explains that it is print which created this unity: 'Print makes for more tightly closed verbal art forms, especially in narrative' (Ong 1982: 133), and later he tries to prove that the detective novel was a product of the printing age. He forgets to mention that the detective story did not begin as a novel but as a *nouvelle*, a short story, Poe's 'The Murders in the Rue Morgue'.

If one takes into consideration such novels as *Roderick Random* or *Tristram Shandy*, or the fragmented novels written by the postmodernists, it is clear that unity of action and of plot is not the genre's chief preoccupation. Lukacs excluded this criterion in his *Theory of the Novel*: 'The novel is the epic of an age in which the extensive totality of life is no longer directly given, in which the immanence of meaning in life has become a problem, yet which still thinks in terms of totality' (Lukacs 1971: 56). Unity of plot, which prevailed in drama, was a characteristic of the chirographic age, when societies were struggling to acquire their unity, not of the typographic age, which is above all the age of revolutions.

Marshall McLuhan and Ong's print-based criterion of the 'fixed point of view' is closely related to that of wholeness and unity of plot: 'With the fixed point of view, a fixed tone could now be preserved through the whole of a lengthy prose composition' (Ong 1982: 135). One could say exactly the contrary: print has allowed the novelist to multiply the points of view without making his book unreadable. Faulkner's *The Sound and the Fury* and Nabokov's *Pale Fire* would have been unthinkable in the chirographic and oral age. Here, Ong and McLuhan have probably confused many elements. Print did allow a more accurate simulation of genuine discourses, such as the diary, the letter, the dialogue, but this is a different matter.

Ong's general theory of the romance and the novel is more acceptable, however, than his discussion of the fixed point of view:

> Romances are the product of the chirographic culture, creations in a new written genre heavily reliant on oral modes of thought and expression, but not consciously imitating earlier oral forms as the 'art' epic did . . . . The novel is clearly a print genre, deeply interior, de-heroicized, and tending strongly to irony. Present-day de-plotted narrative forms are part

of the electronic age, deviously structured in abstruse codes (like computers).

(159)

Ong apparently realized that his theory of wholeness was somewhat contradicted by the contemporary novel, so he brought in, needlessly perhaps, another medium. The argument is sound, however: the chief criterion to distinguish between the romance and the novel is the medium through which they appeared and started to circulate.

Just as the French romance was originally characterized by the use of the vernacular as opposed to Latin, the English novel was characterized by the use of print as opposed to manuscript writing. The would-be coarseness of the English novel compared with the would-be refinement of the French one then becomes understandable: a new popular form of expression and communication was replacing the old aristocratic one. In many respects, one could say that the French started their novelistic revolution in the twelfth century when they began to use the vernacular in literary texts, and the English in the eighteenth century when they started to exploit the resources of the new technology invented by Gutenberg. There was no fundamental break in France between *Le Roman comique* and *La Princesse de Clèves*, on the one hand, and *Le Neveu de Rameau* and *La Nouvelle Héloïse* on the other. The transition from the medieval romance to the modern *roman* was gradual. In England, on the other hand, the transition was almost instantaneous when a printer, Richardson, suddenly began to write his letters.

Is the novel a genre, then? It is hard to say since it was born at least three times by simulating, in printed prose, three genres or modes of communication. No definition mentioning such elements as characterization, unity of plot, or point of view, will be able to take into account the French novels written in the late seventeenth century and the English novels written in the eighteenth century. The definition which can take into account all that happened during the period we have just studied could be the following: a novel is a small entertaining book, meant to be read silently and in private, which exhibits its bookhood, exploits the resources of the printing industry, contains important narrative elements, and simulates plausible discourses ('natural' or literary). This definition of the novel is medium-based, whereas definitions of literary genres are often based on subjects and diction. The fact that the novel has now become the chief literary genre, and a highly diversified one at that, may be an indication that it is not a genre in the traditional sense of the word, but the new name for printed literature.

# Chapter 4
# The modernist novel

The eighteenth-century novelist often had no proper status as an artist; within his novels, he tried one mask after another to find his place, not realizing that he was working with a new medium. In his dealings with his bookseller, the law, and the public, he was increasingly aware of acquiring a new role, a new function, but he often attributed those changes to political, economic, and social factors rather than to the growth of the printing industry.

At the beginning of the nineteenth century, the situation changed radically. The novel was now acknowledged, in most European countries, as a genuine form of art as well as a typical product of the industrial revolution. The historical novel *à la* Walter Scott and the realistic novel *à la* Balzac considerably helped boost the new bourgeois consensus, assuming in many cases the homeostatic and conservative functions that the old oral narratives had played before Gutenberg. They provided a transition between two periods. It was mostly in the 1850s that the novel, having strengthened its position on the market, became again a revolutionary genre. During the modernist era, which, for the novel, extends from 1850 to 1930 approximately, the status of the author changed considerably and, with it, the nature of his interaction with his reader.

## THE ENVIRONMENT

### The market

The Walter Scott phenomenon in the early decades of the

century had considerable effects on the book market. In England, the number of new novels printed every year rose constantly. Here are some figures collected by Malcolm Bradbury (Bradbury 1972: 206–13):

| Date | Books printed | New novels |
|---|---|---|
| 1850 | 2,600 | 381 |
| 1896 | – | 969 |
| 1899 | – | 1,825 |
| 1901 | 6,044 | – |
| 1913 | 12,379 | – |
| 1937 | – | 2,153 |

The ratio between the number of books printed every year and the number of new novels remains practically the same: one in eight. These figures do not take into account the number of copies printed, of course.

In France, too, Walter Scott was extremely popular. Between 1816 and 1851, his complete works were reissued twenty times and individual novels were printed or reprinted seventy-four times (Lyons 1987: 132–4). During the same period, Rousseau's *Nouvelle Héloïse* was reissued fifty-five times; the number of copies printed must have been around 75,000 to 120,000 (Lyons 1987: 96). This was a time when the book trade was developing rapidly, as the estimations made by Robert Estivals show (Lyons 1987: 12): 1,000 titles a year were published before the Revolution; 3,000 to 4,000 were published around 1815; 7,000 to 8,000 were published during the Restoration; 12,000 were published under Napoleon III; 13,000 to 14,000 were published at the end of the century.

In 1820, theology represented 10 per cent of the titles, law 5 per cent, education 5 per cent, arts and sciences 25 to 30 per cent, history 15 per cent, and *belles lettres* (which we would now call literature) 40 per cent. According to Louandre's estimation of 1840, 210 new novels were published that year, plus twenty reprints of eighteenth-century classics, plus about 100 translations, a total of roughly 330 novels for that year.

These figures seem to suggest that the novel represented 4 to 5 per cent of the total production of books in France at the time, that is infinitely less than in England (Lyons 1987: 14). Yet more and more novels already appeared at the top of the bestseller list around the middle of the nineteenth century: between 1846 and 1850, one finds, just after Saint-Ouen's *History of France*, La Fontaine's *Fables*, Florian's *Fables*, Fleury's *Catéchisme historique*, Béranger's *Chansons*, works of fiction like *The Thousand and One Nights*, Dumas's *Le Comte de Monte-Cristo*, *Les Trois Mousquetaires*, Fénelon's *Télémaque*, and Defoe's *Robinson Crusoe*. A generation before, that is, between 1811 and 1815, none of the eighteenth-century classics were in the top ten (Lyons 1987: 76–93).

This 'triumph of the book', as Lyons calls it, was brought about by a number of factors. First of all, more and more people could read. In England, male literacy rose from 63.3 per cent in 1841 to 92.2 per cent in 1900 (Bradbury 1972: 204). This does not mean that the same percentage could or wished to read such heavy books as novels; Walter Besant estimated that there were about 50,000 accessible readers in England around 1830 (Sutherland 1976: 12). In France, 50 per cent of new recruits in the army were illiterate in 1835, 30 per cent in 1863 and only 5 per cent in 1904 (Lyons 1987: 29). In the period between 1871 and 1875, 78 per cent of men and 66 per cent of women could sign their names in the marriage registers (Lough 1978: 276–7). The generalization of education, after the Education Act of 1870 in England and the *Lois Jules Ferry* of 1880–1 in France, did not immediately change the structure of the book market, but it substantially increased the potential audience of all books, and of novels in particular, by improving the reading competence of the majority of the people.

Printing technology, which had not changed much since Gutenberg, was now beginning to develop at a very fast rate. The first automatic press licensed by König and Bauer in 1810 was acquired the following year in London by Thomas Bentley; it was able to print 800 copies an hour. In 1812, the first cylinder press was invented; it was considerably improved in the following years and could print 4,000 to 5,000 copies an hour by 1827. The first rotary press was licensed by William

Bullock in 1863. At the same time, paper, which began to be made from wood pulp after 1844, was becoming a great deal cheaper (Dreyfus and Richaudeau 1985: 201–2).

All these technological improvements made it possible for the publishers to produce more and cheaper books. The price of novels, which, in England, had gone down regularly during the eighteenth century, steadied at about 3s a volume in 1790; it rose sharply during the Napoleonic wars to reach the one-guinea mark per volume in 1820. The first attempt to sell books to the millions at a very low price was made by Constable in the 1820s, but it ended in bankruptcy in 1826, though the firm had once held the copyrights in the *Encyclopaedia Britannica* and the *Edinburgh Review*. Many other attempts were made to sell volumes at 6s or 8s between 1833 and 1853, but they all failed. After many unsuccessful attempts, Bentley finally put out fifty-seven titles in 1865, thirty-one of them costing less than £1; fifteen were 31s 6d novels, and three 21s novels. By that time, reprints cost only 6s to 3s (Sutherland 1976: 11–19). The railway, or 'yellow-back' novel (popular reprints, mostly) which began to appear in the 1840s sold for less than 1s or 1s 6d; in 1896, Newnes started their popular Penny Library. By that time, Dickens's works were sometimes given away with tea (Bradbury 1972: 204–5).

While the chapbooks were slowly disappearing, a double fiction market was beginning to develop again. The first market was almost totally restricted to the three-decker novel, which continued to be published until the end of the century, for the circulating libraries, mainly. According to the *Publisher's Circular,* six times as many three-deckers were published in 1887 as in 1837 (184 against 31; Sutherland 1976: 24). The three-decker usually sold for 31s 6d, which was a comparatively high price. But, as the *Westminster* noted in 1852, it was a convenient formula for the publishers who found 'it easier and more profitable to sell 500 copies of a work at a guinea and a half per copy, than 5,000 at half a crown, or 50,000 at a shilling' (Sutherland 1976: 15). The Net Book Agreement of 1898, which established the 6s to 7s 6d novel for the next thirty years, stabilized the market until the rise of the paperback (Sutherland 1978: 173).

Here are, for instance, the publication ledger figures for

Trollope's *The Three Clerks,* published in 1857 (Sutherland 1976: 14):

|  | £ | s | d |  | £ | s | d |
|---|---|---|---|---|---|---|---|
| Printing 1,000 | 130 | 5 | 6 | 38 presented | | | |
| Paper | 91 | 0 | 6 | 500 Mudie | 288 | 0 | 0 |
| Binding 750 | 47 | 10 | 3 | 210 sold | 227 | 8 | 9 |
| A. Trollope | | | | 119 sold | 115 | 12 | 6 |
| (payment in full) | 250 | 0 | 0 | 23 sold | 24 | 19 | 0 |
| Advertising | 63 | 7 | 8 | | | | |

The publisher made a profit of approximately £100, that is to say much less than the author. But he usually made more money on reprints for which he did not have to pay additional money to the author.

Mudie, who was the owner of the largest circulating library, bought half the print run of Trollope's *The Three Clerks,* and at a little more than half a guinea a copy. He was, according to an article published in the *Saturday Review* in 1860, 'in a position to make himself dictator of literature', being the largest purchaser of novels in the world (Sutherland 1976: 26). He bought about one million volumes between 1853 and 1862, and half of them were novels. Of the 3,864 novels Bentley sold by subscription in 1864, 1,962 were bought by him (Sutherland 1976: 25–9). This circulating library disappeared in 1937 when public libraries started to take over.

The second market concerned a much larger public and was covered chiefly by two formulae: part issue, and serial publication in periodicals. Part issue publication of novels, which had started almost two centuries before, took a considerable share of the market around the middle of the nineteenth century. Chapman and Hall, the publishers of The *Pickwick Papers,* designed the book from the start to be published in 1s parts, which allowed as many as 60,000 subscribers to have the fiction '"warm from the brain" and usually before any critical judgement could be imposed on it' (Sutherland 1976: 21). A novel the size of a three-decker cost around £1 in easy payments with this formula; it was usually large-paged, well printed and amply illustrated. All of Dickens's novels except two were brought out this way, four of Thackeray's six novels, and many of Ainsworth's, Trollope's, and George Eliot's.

The other cheap formula was serial publication in newspapers and magazines. In the middle of the century, many English publishers, such as Bradbury and Evans, Smith, Macmillan, and Bentley, established magazines and weeklies with a very large circulation which, like *Blackwood's,* began to serialize novels (Sutherland 1976: 38). In France, newspapers and magazines such as *Le Siècle* and *La Presse* published Dumas, Balzac and Eugène Sue; *Le Journal des Débats* published Dumas's *Comte de Monte-Cristo* (1844–5), Hugo's *Mystères de Paris* (1842), and more popular novels like *François de Champi* (1847–8) (Lyons 1987: 146).

The author could draw colossal profits through these publishing formulae when his novels became popular. Dickens received £10,000 from Chapman and Hall for the part issue of *Our Mutual Friend,* and he died a wealthy man, leaving an estate of £93,000 (Sutherland 1976: 22). The successful novelists were therefore becoming more affluent. By 1913, Arnold Bennett was reporting an income of over £300 a week, though not all of it was from fiction-writing (Bradbury 1972: 155). On the other hand, three-quarters of the novels published in the second half of the century were being published partly and totally at their authors' costs. When Hardy published his first book, *Desperate Remedies,* in 1871, he had to pay £75 to have it printed. Gissing invested £125 of his own money in his first novel, *Workers in the Dawn* (1880), and he got two-thirds of the profits, that is, a paltry £2! Later, he managed to make £150 per novel but finally had to turn to literary agents, first to A. P. Watt and then to J. B. Pinker (two of the most prominent literary agents at the time), to market his manuscripts and run his publishing business (Bradbury 1972: 154–7).

French authors also had to publish at their own cost in many cases. *Remembrance of Things Past* is now so famous that one tends to forget that Proust financed the printing of the first volume published by Bernard Grasset. Though he had published articles in such a popular newspaper as *Le Figaro,* and had many influential friends, such as Calmette, Lucien Daudet, or Jacques Copeau of the *Nouvelle Revue Française (NRF),* he spent four difficult years (between 1909 and 1913) trying to find a publisher for his first volume. As the recent book *Marcel Proust à la recherche d'un éditeur* reveals, he did not really trust the publishers; after the *NRF* turned down the manuscript (Gide, who had been asked to read the manuscript for the *NRF*, rejected it without reading it), he decided to publish his novel at his own cost and to divide his profits with Grasset in order to keep control over the publication. This allowed him to rewrite many passages on the proofsheets (Lhomeau and Coelho 1988: 188). One wonders what would have happened to this masterpiece if Proust had not been a man of independent means.

To defend their rights, the less independent authors founded societies in France and in England which functioned a little like labour unions. The *Société des gens de lettres*, founded in 1838, counted Hugo, Dumas, and Soulié among its first members. In 1839, Balzac became its president. The same year, Sainte-Beuve criticized the enterprise in an essay entitled 'La littérature industrielle' (Lyons 1987: 60). The English Society of Authors was founded much later, in 1883, by Walter Besant to safeguard the rights and needs of the authors; it published a monthly review entitled *The Author*. George Gissing joined the Society but he found it 'a mere gathering of tradesmen' (Bradbury 1972: 135). Still, such societies fulfilled a very important need: the author's income was regularly declining as a result of the profession's becoming somewhat overcrowded; and the industry was in a much stronger position to dictate its conditions to the author who often had to beg to be published. At the beginning of the twentieth century, publishers, who often preferred to sell cheap, non-copyrighted books, accepted only a limited number of new titles.

Many of the most famous modernist authors had very small incomes. Henry James was making so little money from his writing at the end of his life that Edith Wharton arranged to have some of her royalties diverted into his account so that he would not know how small his audience was (Bradbury 1972: 156). Virginia Woolf and James Joyce did not earn much for part of their lives. The former's income from her fiction between 1920 and 1924 was £106 5s 10d the first year, £10 10s 8d the second, £33 13s 0d the third, £40 0s 5d the fourth, and £70 0s 0d the fifth (Sutherland 1978: 110); she was earning only £520 a year from her books when she was forty-seven (Bradbury 1972: 150). Joyce had to teach in Zürich for quite a while to keep body and soul together; he made nothing from *Chamber Music* published in 1907, and was assisted by patrons like Harriet Shaw Weaver during the war. It was only after Sylvia Beach published his *Ulysses* in Paris in 1922 that he began to receive a proper income (Ellmann 1959: 514–63 *passim*).

**The law**

The trade-off between the industry and the state which still prevailed to some extent until the end of the eighteenth century diseappeared gradually during the nineteenth century. The state increasingly tried to curb the power of the industry by protecting the rights of authors and imposing stricter censorship rules without having to grant any additional guarantees in return.

In England, three Copyright Acts (1814, 1833, and 1842) substantially improved the protection of the author; the third one guaranteed his rights in his lifetime and those of his heirs for seven years after his death. It still provided that the books should be registered at the Stationers' Hall, but it did not confirm the authority of the Company to police the market. The Copyright Act of 1911 further protected the rights of the author or rather of his heirs who retained the rights for fifty years after the author's death; it granted no compensation to the industry (McFarlane 1982: 2–3; Mumby 1982: 19). By that time, an international agreement, the Berne Convention, which had been signed by seventeen countries, including Britain and France, and had gone into effect in 1887, protected unpublished works of citizens of Conventions states, provided the said works had been published in a Convention state (Wittenberg 1978: 116).

The United States did not sign the Convention because it was contrary to the Constitution which, in its Article I, Section 8, provides that the 'Congress shall have power . . . To promote the Progress of Science and useful Arts, by securing for limited Times to Authors and Inventors the exclusive Right to their respective Writings and Discoveries'. Congress voted the first US Copyright Act in 1790, protecting the author's rights for fourteen years and a possible extension of another fourteen years. The Copyright Act of 1891 allowed the US to enter into treaties with other countries, but insisted that only the books 'printed from type set within the limits of the United States' would be protected. The Copyright Act of 1909, which remained the law regulating copyright until 1978, extended the 'term of copyright for an original period of twenty-eight years' which could be renewed for another twenty-eight years (Wittenberg 1978: 34–7).

The American and British states were not only trying to protect the authors against the publishers but increasingly brought their authority to bear on the market to ban obscene literature. Until the eighteenth century, English law was comparatively helpless to ban dirty books, despite pressure from political figures and members of the church. On 1 June 1778, William Wilberforce, backed by the Archbishop of Canterbury, brought the Crown to issue 'A Proclamation for the Encouragement of Piety and Virtue, and for preventing and punishing of Vice, Profaneness, and Immorality'. Wilberforce also petitioned to suppress 'all loose and licentious Prints, Books, and Publications dispersing Poison to the Minds of the Young and Unwary, and to punish the Publishers and Vendors thereof' (Thomas 1969: 113). Realizing that the government was incapable of imposing its authority in this matter, he founded the Proclamation Society to implement the rules stated in the Proclamation. At the start, the Society was constituted of seventeen bishops, six dukes, and eleven peers. It was only moderately successful. In 1801, another society, the Vice Society, was founded; it also petitioned to suppress the publication of 'Licentious and Obscene Books and Prints' (Thomas 1969: 189). It was apparently more successful: according to Lord Campbell who, in the mid-nineteenth century, was pleading for stricter regulations against dirty books, it brought 159 cases against pornographers in the first fifty years of its life and won 154 of them (Thomas 1969: 213).

In 1857, the legislator finally decided to take things in hand by passing the very strict Obscene Publications Act. This Act, which came to be called the Campbell Act, has been held responsible for the puritanical mood of much Victorian literature. In the first case tried under it in 1868, Alexander Cockburn gave a definition of obscenity which was also to be used in the US: 'The test of obscenity is whether the tendency of the matter charged is to deprave and corrupt those whose minds are open to such immoral influences and into whose hands a publication of this sort may fall' (Lewis 1976: 7–8). The Act did not prevent the publication and circulation of such pornographic works as Edward Sellon's *The New Epicurean* in 1865, *The Romance of Lust* in 1873, or 'Colonel Spanker's' *Experimental Lectures* in 1879, or again such reviews as the *Pearl* (1879–80), *Cremone* (1882), or the *Boudoir* (1883). On the other hand, it certainly did much to keep many great novels out of England for decades.

In America, Massachusetts, first as a colony, and then as a state, led the battle against erotica. In 1668, Marmaduke Johnson, a printer of Cambridge, was fined £5 for possessing Henry Neville's *The Isle of Pines* (Thomas 1969: 2–3). It was again a Massachusetts court which suppressed *Fanny Hill* in 1821. The first federal decision against erotica was the Customs Law of 1842 which was meant to prevent 'the importation of all indecent and obscene prints, paintings, lithographs, engravings and transparencies' (Thomas 1969: 7). In the following decades, Anthony Comstock, the head of the YMCA, conducted a campaign against erotica and led Congress to pass the so-called Comstock Law of 1873 excluding obscene matter from the mails. As a Post Office agent, he helped ban *The Lustful Turk*, *Curtain Drawn Up*, *Madame Célestine*, and *Fanny Hill*; the New York Supreme Court rejected his bid to ban *The Decameron*, the *Heptameron*, *The Arabian Nights*, *Gargantua*, *Pantagruel*, and *Tom Jones* but the Act that bears his name continued to be invoked until 1966 (Thomas 1969: 11–28).

Many of the great modernist novels, from *Madame Bovary* (1857) to *Ulysses* (1922), were subjected to censorship. When Du Camp bought *Madame Bovary* for 2,000 francs to publish it in his *Revue de Paris* in 1856, he asked Flaubert to remove the more scabrous passages, but Flaubert refused. Du Camp started to bring it out in October in a bowdlerized version. Flaubert protested in the 15 December issue, but to no avail. He then sold his rights in the novel for five years (against a payment of 800 francs to which a bonus of 500 francs was added) to Michel Lévy who wanted to publish it in book form, and was summoned, in January 1857, before the *6e chambre du Tribunal correctionnel* who intended to ban the book.

The Imperial Prosecutor, Maître Pinard, who was also an

enlightened reader, remarked in his indictment speech that Flaubert was a talented author who knew all too well how to paint up the more erotic scenes: 'Do you know, in the world, gentlemen, a more expressive language? Have you ever seen a more lascivious tableau?' (Flaubert 1961: 424; my translation). He almost got carried away at one point: 'What the author exhibits here is the very poetry of adultery' (425; my translation). He obviously enjoyed the novel a great deal; but, as he explained later in his indictment, one had to protect the weaker sex against such books: 'Who reads M. Flaubert's novel? The men who attend to political or social economy? No! The frivolous pages of *Madame Bovary* fall into the more frivolous hands of girls, and even of married women sometimes' (435; my translation). Such a novel could not hurt people like him, he claimed, but it might induce married women to follow Emma's example. It was a matter of public health and safety to ban the book. His conclusion is interesting for it could serve as one of the ruling principles of the modern novel: 'Art without rules is not art; it is like a woman who would discard all her clothes. Submitting art to the only rule of public decency is not to subjugate it but to honour it. One can only progress with a rule' (437; my translation). One is a little 'shocked' to find such a risky comparison in this indictment. Had not Maître Pinard fallen under the spell of that terrible novel? He was right, of course, when he said that art needs rules. The modern novel is indirectly the child of censorship. Flaubert himself had to develop sophisticated devices to say or suggest the unspeakable in a scene like that of the *fiacre* which the prosecutor was prompt to stigmatize.

Maître Sénard, the attorney for the defence, was (or probably had to be) a much less perceptive reader. He insists on the morality of the book, showing how Emma had to suffer for her sins, how the novel teaches girls and young women to be good and pure: 'you will have noticed in that love the platitudes of married life' (444; my translation). He forgets to mention that there never was any real love between her and Charles. He also extols the virtues of Charles against the depravity of his wife, claiming that Nemesis is always on the side of the law, which, of course, is not true. Despite this lame defence, Flaubert was acquitted and the novel was allowed to come out in book form, which it did in April of the same year with great success.

This trial is exemplary in many respects. It shows that the nineteenth-century bourgeois acutely sensed the subversiveness of the novel, the danger it constituted for one of the strongest institutions at the time, marriage. Besides, it confirms the impression we have had from the start that the narrative devices developed in the modern novel are often meant to fool the censor and to protect the author. In this particular trial, the attorney for the defence could pick and choose and come out with conclusions which were diametrically opposed to those of the Imperial Prosecutor. The verdict eventually shows how difficult it was for the law to prosecute the novelist for the sins committed by one of his protagonists.

In a number of cases, the publishers themselves became censors in order to protect their reputations or their financial interests. Nine months after the publication of Dreiser's *Sister Carrie* in 1900 in the US, Comstock's successor, John Sumner, complained that the book 'contained seventeen profane and seventy-five lewd words' and managed to draw the attention of two postal inspectors to the book. The publisher, John Lane, was so intimidated that he recalled all the copies remaining in the bookstores. It was only in 1923 that an unexpurgated version was brought out by Liveright (Lewis 1976: 67–9).

Sometimes, a publisher would bring out a novel only after censoring it. In his interesting little book on the genesis of *The Rainbow* (a novel which was suppressed by the police as soon as it came out in 1915) and of *Women in Love*, C. L. Ross shows how Lawrence was gradually brought to change his projects (Ross 1979). The typescript of *Women in Love* circulated for a long time before the book was published, and Lawrence revised the text many times as a result of his readers' reactions and in the face of all his difficulties to find a publisher. The American publisher, Seltzer, retained the typescript so that Lawrence would not have it at hand when reading the proofs (124–7). His English publisher, Martin Secker, suggested that Lawrence remove 'the references [in chapter 7] to the unconventional manner in which the occupants of [Halliday's] flat used to sit about in the morning', that is, naked. Lawrence complied with his request and described Birkin not 'in a state of nudity' but in 'white pyjamas' (126–7).

Ross also shows how Secker altered the text without Lawrence's knowledge in the passage where Birkin talks about the sexual dimension of *Blutbrüderschaft*. The following passage appears in the page proofs and the Seltzer edition, but not in the Secker edition:

> Gerald moved uneasily. 'You know I can't feel that,' said he. 'Surely there can never be anything as strong between man and man as sex love is between man and woman. Nature doesn't provide the basis.'
> 'Well, of course, I think she does. And I don't think we shall ever be happy till we establish ourselves on this basis. You've got to get rid of the *exclusiveness* of married love. And you've got to admit the unadmitted love of man for man. It makes for a greater freedom for everybody, a greater power of individuality both in man and woman.'
>
> (128–9)

The publisher, considering no doubt that such a passage would endanger the commercial success of the novel, censored it without informing the author.

The difficulties of publishing sexually explicit fiction were clearly increasing both in the US and in England. Joyce had to publish his *Ulysses* (1922) in France, and Lawrence his *Lady Chatterley's Lover* (1928) in Italy. If *Ulysses* had been a French novel, and *Lady Chatterley's Lover* an Italian one, it is doubtful, however, whether they would have come out so easily in these two countries. In the eighteenth century, French novelists had similarly evaded censorship by publishing their works in Amsterdam or Geneva.

This permissiveness towards foreign novels is well demonstrated in the fact that, in 1933, a US court allowed *Ulysses* into the United States. In the preceding years, many novels which we now consider classics were banned in the US, and especially in Boston: Cabell's *Jurgen*, Dreiser's *An American Tragedy*, Lewis's *Elmer Gantry*, Dos Passos's *Manhattan Transfer*, Faulkner's *Mosquitoes*, etc. Judge Woolsey, of the US District Court of New York, was as perceptive a reader as Maître Pinard. He praised Joyce's technique of representing the stream of consciousness as well as his sincerity. After defining the obscene as that which tends 'to stir the sex impulse or to lead to sexually impure and lustful thoughts', he remarked:

> Whether a particular book would tend to excite such impulses and thoughts must be tested by the court's opinion as to its effect on a person with average sex instincts – what the French would call *l'homme moyen sensuel*. It is only with the normal person that the law is concerned.
>
> (Lewis 1976: 127)

Though he considered the novel somewhat 'emetic' at times, he finally gave it a clean bill of health. Judge Manton refused to accept literary merit as a redeeming criterion and argued, in a dissenting opinion, that the weaker people must be protected by the law: 'If we disregard the protection of the morals of the susceptible, are we to consider merely the benefits and pleasures derived from letters by those who pose as the more highly developed and intelligent?' (Lewis 1976: 129).

This case shows not only that the courts tend to be more tolerant towards foreign books where obscenity is concerned, but also that they find it more difficult to rule against technically complex novels. Lawrence lost the battle of the book, in the case of *Women in Love*, because he had failed to saturate his text, so that his publishers managed to rewrite it wherever they wanted to tone down risky passages. Joyce won that battle because he made his text so complex, so poetic at times, that his publishers had only two options: either to turn down the novel or to publish it verbatim. *Ulysses* is so elaborately coded that it does not lend itself to either erotic recuperation or prudish deletions.

## TWIN-VOICED OPENINGS

The 'triumph of the book' and the growth of institutional censorship which it automatically encouraged brought about a dramatic change in the novelistic discourse. The bookhood of the novel being now acknowledged by everyone, novelists and readers alike began to grant a kind of organic existence to the object and to the characters themselves. At the same time, the fear that the censors might prosecute their books forced the novelists to distance story and characters so as to avoid being accused of the latter's sins. Flaubert, though he considered himself to be Madame Bovary, managed to distance himself so much from his novel that he eventually felt as if it were almost a foreign body; in a letter written to Louise Colet in 1853, he said: 'What is making me go so slowly is that nothing in this book is derived from myself; never has my personality been of less use to me' (Flaubert 1965: 314). Here, the archetypal modernist novelist does not only confess his fear, he also formulates what was to become the chief modernist dogma: text and characters must stand on their own, without any assistance from the author.

This necessity largely helps account for novelists' reluctance, during that period, to write first-person narratives. Such a form of narrative usually induces the reader to view the book as an autobiographical disclosure. This refusal to say 'I' and the rejection of everything that might be construed as a trace of the author's discourse is nowhere more visible, perhaps, than in the opening paragraph of *Bleak House*:

> London. Michaelmas term lately over, and the Lord Chancellor sitting in Lincoln's Inn Hall. Implacable November weather. As much mud in the streets, as if the waters had but newly retired from the face of the earth, and it would not be wonderful to meet a Megalosaurus, forty feet long or so, waddling like an elephantine lizard up Holborn Hill. Smoke lowering down from chimney-pots, making a soft black drizzle with flakes of soot in it as big as full-grown snowflakes – gone into mourning, one might imagine, for the death of the sun. Dogs, undistinguishable in mire. Horses, scarcely better; splashed to their very blinkers. Foot passengers, jostling one another's umbrellas, in a general infection of ill temper.
>
> (Dickens 1971: 49)

The first word, because it is not part of a complete sentence, can be understood in different ways: as a label on an object, as the title of a book, a guide book for instance, or again as the writerly transcription of the ostentatious gesture made from a vantage-point by a guide presenting the town to a foreign visitor. In all cases, the author is positing the existence of London as extra-textual, and he strongly appeals to the reader's imagination to picture it in this particular weather.

The first notation was spatial, the second is temporal. Dickens specifies that the story begins after the 'Michaelmas term', in November. These two notations, by providing a referential context, help reduce the unrest the reader usually experiences when he opens a new novel. Besides, the verbless sentences suggest that the story must take place in the historical present: the deleted verbs, in elliptical sentences, are usually supposed to be conjugated in the present tense, even in such extreme forms of narrative discourse as so-called interior monologue.

The deletion of the verbs does not eliminate the tenses only, it also eliminates the traces of the person who is speaking. One assumes that most of the deleted verbs would be conjugated in the third person: 'Here is London. The Michaelmas term is lately over, and the Lord Chancellor is sitting in Lincoln's Inn Hall.' The expansion of the syntax becomes more difficult, however, in the next sentence: 'Implacable November weather'; unless the word order is changed ('the November weather is implacable'), it is difficult to provide an acceptable deep structure. This is due to the fact that the adjective 'implacable' does not occupy a predicate position in the elliptical sentence, which implies that a predicative verb ('have' for instance) and a subject other than 'November weather' must be inserted to complete the sentence. What the elliptical forms obscure most, therefore, is the person of the verbs, and, consequently, the narrative voice. Dickens is doing his utmost here to make the referent speak for itself, as it were.

A detailed description *à la* Balzac would have done a great deal more than simply present a given world to the reader's imagination: it would have established the authority of a godlike, omniscient, narrator. Here, for example, is the opening of *Le Père Goriot*:

> Madame Vauquer, née de Conflans, is an old woman who, for forty years, has been running a bourgeois boarding-house in Paris, rue Neuve-Sainte-Geneviève, between the Latin Quarter and the Faubourg Saint-Marceau. The boarding-house, known as the Maison Vauquer, is open to both men and women, young and old people, and never has scandal-

mongering sullied the good name of the respectable establishment.

(Balzac 1967: 27; my translation)

This description of the boarding-house which continues for many more lines could not have been made by any of the characters in the novel; no character, no first-person narrator, is privileged to know as much about places and people as Balzac's so-called omniscient narrator. At the end of the first paragraph, the obtrusive narrator apostrophizes the reader in a most un-Sternian style:

So you will do, you who are holding this book in your white hand, you who are snuggling in a plush armchair saying to yourself: Perhaps this is going to amuse me. Once you have read about the secret misfortunes of old man Goriot, you will dine with good appetite, blaming the author for your callousness, taxing him with exaggeration, accusing him of having written poetry.

(28; my translation)

This passage, in which Balzac tries to boost the historicity of the events about to be narrated while undermining their bookhood (a word synonymous here with 'poetry'), is a clumsy rejection of authorhood ('blaming the author for your callousness'). It revives, all too seriously, the 'Book of Nature' myth which we found in Fielding's humorous prefaces.

Dickens's technique at the beginning of *Bleak House* is infinitely more subtle. His elliptical, impressionistic, style manages a convenient transition between the real world and the fictitious world without making too conspicuous the withdrawal of the master of ceremonies. Dickens's opening is voiceless, as are many of the postmodernist openings we will analyse later. Naturally, Dickens could not have continued very long in the same style; a true narrative cannot be launched until the language becomes more articulate, that is to say, predicative, and 'vocalizable'. Dickens gradually begins to embed full sentences in elliptical ones, as at the end of the first paragraph: 'and losing their foot-hold at street-corners, where tens of thousands of other foot passengers have been slipping and sliding since the day broke (if this day ever broke)'

(Dickens 1971: 49). The predicative process now seems to be primed, and it espouses the contour of reality.

The language also becomes more figurative, which in itself testifies to the involvement of a specific imagination: 'waddling like an elephantine lizard', 'as big as full-grown snowflakes', 'gone into mourning, one might imagine', 'composed interest', or 'as if they were up in a balloon'. There is also a growing number of modal auxiliaries: 'and it would not be wonderful', 'ought to be sitting here – as here he is', 'where he can see nothing but fog', 'members of the High Court of Chancery bar ought to be – as here they are' (49–50). The first parts of each sentence, containing mostly epistemic modals, seem to echo the *vox populi*, but the second parts, which are assertive ('as here he is'), apparently simulate the interior monologue of a witness who would sit next to Miss Flite, the 'little mad old woman' (51).

In the second opening of *Bleak House*, in chapter 3, Esther's first-person narrative supplants the third-person narrative:

> I have a great deal of difficulty in beginning to write my portion of these pages, for I know I am not clever. I always knew that. I can remember, when I was a very little girl indeed, I used to say to my doll, when we were alone together, 'Now Dolly, I am not clever, you know very well, and you must be patient with me, like a dear! '

(62)

This second opening prefigures, in reverse, the second opening of *Remembrance of Things Past*, in *Un Amour de Swann* where the third-person narrative supplants the first-person narrative of the first opening. The predicative process is emphatically proclaimed in the opening 'I'. The text is focused not so much on the content, the referent, as on the relationship that the narratrix wants to develop with her prospective reader. Her doll stands for the absent, and perhaps restive reader, to whom she addresses her narrative and whom she begs to see things from her point of view and pity her.

These two openings lend a dramatic dimension to the novel. The first one reads like the stage directions with which the playwright prescribes how the story, told mainly in Esther's narrative, should be staged in our minds and imaginations. Or it could be the 'dumb voice' of the silent witness, Miss Flite, who has followed all the developments of the Jarndyce and Jarndyce case from the beginning. This narrative persona is therefore clearly a non-person, a text-bound fiction which has nothing to do with the people we meet in actual life. Hence our difficulty in knowing exactly where we stand: being unable to decide who is addressing us, we are restless and try on mask after mask, without much success, until we come across Esther's first-person narrative. Then we begin to empathize with the girl; being her confidant and analyst, we know at last where we stand.

At the beginning of *Madame Bovary,* Flaubert adopted a narrative strategy which is exactly the opposite of that of Dickens. He began his novel with an almost arrogant *nous* ('we') which he then gradually allowed to fade out of the narrative in the next pages:

> We were in class when the headmaster came in, followed by a new boy, not wearing the school uniform, and a school servant carrying a large desk. Those who had been asleep woke up, and every one rose as if just surprised at his work.
> 
> The headmaster made a sign to us to sit down. Then, turning to the teacher, he said to him in a low voice:
> 
> 'Monsieur Roger, here is a pupil whom I recommend to your care; he'll be in the second. If his work and conduct are satisfactory, he will go into one of the upper classes, as becomes his age.'
> 
> (Flaubert 1965: 1)

The narrator's 'I' is here fused in the 'we' representing the pupils who saw Charles Bovary arrive at school that morning. The reader is almost invited to take a seat among the pupils, and to see for himself how ridiculous Charles looked.

In the following paragraphs, the 'we' is used again, but sparingly: 'We began reciting the lesson', 'When we came back to work, we were in the habit of throwing our caps on the ground' (2). Then it disappears completely: 'There was a burst of laughter from the boys' (not 'from us'), 'The same sputtering of syllables was heard' (not 'we heard the same'), '(they yelled, barked, stamped, repeated "Charbovari! Charbovari!")' (2– 3). Through the impersonal formula ('There was') and the passive form ('was heard'), the first-person narrative gradually becomes a third-person narrative ('they yelled', which, at the beginning, would have read 'we yelled'). This opening 'we' will continue to haunt us throughout the novel whenever Charles Bovary is being ridiculed. We are never allowed to forget that someone, who once knew Charles at school, explained right from the start how clumsy the poor boy was, how gullible, too.

Maître Sénard did not draw attention to this opening, of course; it would have invalidated that part of his defence in which he claimed that 'M. Flaubert constantly enhances the superiority of the husband over his wife, and what a superiority, if you please?' (Flaubert 1961: 467; my translation). It is partly because of this opening that one tends to side with Emma rather than with her husband in the novel. Flaubert did deserve to be censored, after all (according to the laws of his days, that is): in a way, he was condoning Emma's sins. The last lines of the book confirm this:

> Since Bovary's death three doctors have succeeded one another in Yonville without any success, so effectively did Homais hasten to eradicate them. He has more customers than there are sinners in hell; the authorities treat him kindly and he has the public on his side.
>
> He has just been given the cross of the Legion of Honor.
>
> (Flaubert 1965: 255)

The passionless and imaginationless bourgeois has won the battle. He reaps the profits of Charles's shortcomings, of Emma's sins, and of the whole tragedy; the Other, the state, thanks him for it, while Flaubert curses him without having to say so.

The person or persona behind the 'we' does not deserve to be called a narrator: he never takes any active part in the story. He does not mediate between us and the story but shows us into it, begging us to consider Charles and Emma objectively. He is clearly much closer to the author himself as well as to the reader than to any of the characters in the story, including the schoolboys mentioned in the opening scene. He is the counter-Other who pits his values, moral and aesthetic, against those of Homais and his likes. This opening, like that of *Bleak House*, is intensely dramatic: it reads like the proceedings of a trial, with Maître Pinard as prosecutor, and Maître Sénard as counsel for the defence.

The persona standing behind the 'I' at the beginning of James's *What Maisie Knew* shares many features with that behind the 'we'. This novel, which is also written in the third person, begins with the evocation of yet another trial. Here is the first occurrence of the 'I' in the introduction: 'so that the only solution finally meeting all the difficulties was, save that of sending Maisie to a Home, the partition of the tutelary office in the manner I have mentioned' (James 1954: 18). This 'I' points towards a person who is as well informed about the whole affair as was Miss Flite in *Bleak House*, a person who has taken it upon himself to narrate the whole story. It is genuinely an authorial 'I'. Later in the novel, this person discusses some of the writing problems he had to face:

> It was granted her at this time to arrive at divinations so ample that I shall have no room for the goal if I attempt to trace the stages; as to which, therefore, I must be content to say that the fullest expression we may give to Sir Claude's conduct is a poor and pale copy of the picture it presented to his young friend.
>
> (164)

The 'I' wants us to know not only that he is not interfering in any way with the story but that he is accurately rendering all these events, though, in fact, he never had access to them.

In this novel, James managed to simulate a discourse which is essentially unvocalizable, that of a little girl's becoming more and more aware of what is happening around her as well as within her. His 'I' lends a modicum of verisimilitude to the narrative while producing the fiction effect. The concept of 'implied author' would not be of much help here, either, for it would divert our attention from the fact that the text is a non-discourse, and cannot be attributed to one and the same subject throughout. As Maisie grows up, the narrative discourse espouses her thoughts, her interior discourse, more and more, though it is still monitored by or filtered through another consciousness.

In *L'Immoraliste,* Gide's attempt to withdraw from his story is almost pathetic. The novel opens with an epigraph taken from the Psalms. Then it continues with a preface, written for the second edition published in 1902 by *Le Mercure de France*, in which the author, not implied in the least, presents his book 'pour ce qu'il vaut' (for what it's worth). In this preface, Gide tries to defend his good name, insisting that he should not be confused with his protagonist, Michel:

> That if I had given this book as a bill of indictment against Michel, I would hardly have done better, for nobody was grateful to me for the indignation they felt with my hero; people seemed to experience this indignation in spite of me; from Michel it extended to me; people all but wanted to confuse me with him.
>
> (Gide 1958: 367; my translation)

Gide seems to talk like Maître Sénard: he prides himself on having underlined the depravity of Michel while exalting the virtues of the latter's wife, Marceline. He inveighs against his thankless readers (like Francis Jammes, for instance) who had failed to see that the indignation they felt towards Michel had actually been triggered by the text itself. They should have been grateful to him for stigmatizing Michel's perversion, instead of turning against him and claiming that he had written a complacent self-portrait.

But Gide contradicts himself immediately after this: 'But in this book I have neither tried to accuse nor to extol, and I have refrained from judging' (367; my translation). After blaming his bad readers for failing to notice that their revulsion against Michel comes in fact from the text itself, he declares that he did his utmost not to pass judgement on his protagonist. One is here reminded of Defoe's contradictory statements in the preface to *Moll Flanders*. Gide seems to make a distinction between his own values and the values implicitly conveyed by his novel, and he blames his public for not making the same distinction.

The novel begins with a letter which is supposed to accompany the transcript of Michel's confession. This letter is addressed to 'Monsieur D.R. President du Conseil' (the Prime Minister; 369). Its author, who claims to have heard Michel tell his story, is the brother of the same 'Monsieur D.R.' whom he begs to find a job for Michel. He hesitates to post the manuscript, being aware that its improper content is liable to horrify his correspondent: 'but now that the time has come to send it, I still hesitate, and the more I reread it the more horrible it looks to me' (369; my translation). This letter is another version of the author's preface. The Prime Minister's brother, who is acting the part of a messenger only, wants to get rid of an offensive text; he pities Michel and envies him at the same time. However, sending this story to his brother is probably not the best solution to the problem of finding a job for his friend.

These two prefaces, one genuine, the other fake, designate two sets of addressees. In the first one, Gide makes a distinction between the naïve readers (real readers, not narratees), who spontaneously decide that Michel is a replica of the author, and more sophisticated readers, who consider like him that 'to set down a problem correctly one must not consider it in advance as already solved' (367; my translation). The second preface, the letter, is supposed to have only one addressee, the Prime Minister, but actually it has two: first the understanding brother who knows Michel personally and who, presumably, is broad-minded enough to offer him a job in spite of everything, and secondly the same person, as a representative of law and order, of the Other. These two addressees turn out to be the same as those of Gide in his preface (the same, too, as those of John Ray in his foreword to *Lolita*): the hedonist on the one hand, and the puritan on the other, that is, Gide himself with all his contradictions.

*L'Immoraliste* constitutes a very important stage in the history of the novel: it was the first time that, in a realistic and uncensored novel, a first-person narrator was openly allowed to exhibit his perversion as if he were confiding his secret to us and begging us to understand him and therefore to disregard the values we may live by. Gide should have congratulated himself that his readers were passing such critical judgements on his protagonist; it was a clear sign that the bookhood of *L'Immoraliste* had successfully been erased, and that his readers had surrendered to the illusion that this was reality. But he did not, because his guilt was so acute that he felt almost transparent. He wrote to his friend Scheffer: 'That there is a bud of Michel in me, it goes without saying. But how many buds we carry within us, dear Scheffer, which will never bloom in our books' (1515; my translation).

Gide never considered *L'Immoraliste* to be a novel. In the introduction to the *Pléiade* edition, Nadeau described Gide's attitude towards the novel in the following way:

> The novel depends upon a convention which André Gide cannot accept because it rests upon a double deceit: The author feigns to be reproducing life, creating a life more authentic than life itself; the reader feigns to accept the transcription of life for life itself. Now, art, which is the antinomy of nature, is not life; it is a style given to life.
>
> (xxxi; my translation)

Gide could not accept the double bind inherent in the bookhood of the genre. He took up the debate where Plato had left it in the *Republic,* but this time it was not writing which he was denouncing but print, which undeniably creates a strong mirror effect, both for the writer and for the reader. His dilemma was essentially that of *Narcisse romancier,* to borrow the excellent title of Rousset's book on the novel: he was too much involved in everything he wrote to consider it as fiction. This excess of self-consciousness would lead some French writers in the following generation either to write essays, like Barthes, or to sacrifice the story, like Robbe-Grillet and the New Novelists.

Proust was also reluctant to use the word *roman* to designate the book he was writing. *Remembrance of Things Past* began as an essay against Sainte-Beuve in which he intended to refute that critic's method of explaining a writer's work in reference to his life. In a letter to Valette, he explained why the preface was to come at the end:

> Sainte-Beuve's name does not come up haphazardly. The book does end with a conversation about Sainte-Beuve and aesthetics and when one has finished reading the book, one will realize (I would like to work it out this way) that the whole novel is but a device to put into practice the artistic principles propounded in that last part, a kind of preface, if you life, but put off till the end.
>
> (Lhomeau and Coelho 1988: 33–4; my translation)

He will call the book an *essai-roman* for a while (Lhomeau and Coelho 1988: 42). The evolution which eventually led to the novel as we know it now shows that Proust was not too sure what reading-contract he wished to propose to his readers. He wanted to express his views on literary criticism, not didactically, however, but in action.

The opening of *Remembrance of Things Past* reflects this

ambiguity. The person, who will call himself 'Marcel' throughout the book, is playing on two or three stages at the same time:

> For many years, I went to bed early. Sometimes, immediately after putting out my candle, my eyes would close so quickly that I wouldn't have time to say to myself: 'I'm going to sleep'. And half an hour later, the idea that it was time to look for sleep would awaken me; I would want to lay down the volume that I thought I still had in my hands, and to blow out my light; while sleeping, I hadn't ceased to reflect upon what I had just been reading but these reflections had assumed a very particular twist; I seemed to have become the subject of my book.
> (Proust 1954: 33; my translation)

The first 'I' does not point so much towards the protagonist who used to go to bed early, as towards the enunciator, the narrator. The second one is more referential than deictic: it designates the child who, in his interior monologue, did not manage to distinguish between himself as enunciator and himself as existential subject.

This shuttling back and forth between narrating subject and existential or historical subject (it tends to be toned down in Scott-Moncrieff's translation; Proust 1934: 3) continues in the following line where the narrator explains that in his dream or reverie he, as a child, used to picture himself as the protagonist of the book he had been reading. This *mise en abyme* of the narrative process confuses the reader, who desperately looks for a narrator to converse with but only finds two unlikely replicas: the child saying to himself that he is falling asleep, and the dreamer, another character in a way, who thinks he is the character described by the book which the child has been reading. This is another version of Alice's dilemma when she learns that she may be part of another person's dream.

This opening is more straightforward, at first sight, than that of *Bleak House* or *Madame Bovary*. The problem, of course, is that it can read either as the opening of a novel or as the opening of an autobiography. Some critics have listed the many discrepancies between the novel and Proust's life to settle the question. Genette, who based his now famous study of the '*Discours du récit*' on this novel, acknowledges the similarities but chooses to ignore them in his analysis:

> This does not mean, of course, that the narrative content of *Remembrance* is for me without any connection with its author's life: but this connection is simply not of such a nature as the latter can be used for a precise analysis of the former (the reverse either).
>
> (Genette 1972: 73; my translation)

This is a very apposite remark, but it is not clear how Genette manages to differentiate Proust from his so-called '*narrateur supposé*' or 'supposed narrator' (73) who is considered throughout *Figures III* as the only subject worth writing about, if not communicating with.

Genette does not put the problem in communicational terms, but in semiotic ones. Here is the founding statement of his theory:

> Since any '*récit*' – be it as extended and as complex as *Remembrance of Things Past*, is a linguistic production relating one or several events, it may be legitimate to treat it as the development, as monstrous as you like, of a *verbal* form, taking this word in its grammatical sense: the expansion of the verb.
>
> (75; my translation)

Elsewhere (71), he provides definitions of the '*récit*' which are clearly reminiscent of the rhetorical categories (*inventio, positio, elocutio*) as if he wanted to reify it and avoid dealing with the main 'subject'.

His unease is obvious when, after quoting Vendryes's linguistic definition of the 'voice' as the 'Aspect of the verbal action in its relationship with the subject', he comments:

> Naturally, the subject involved here is that of the utterance, whereas for us the *voice* will designate the relationship with the subject (and more generally the instance) of enunciation: once again, these are only borrowings of terms which do not claim to be based on strict homologies.
>
> (76; my translation)

When he talks about 'the relationship with the subject (and more generally the instance) of enunciation', he does not seem to realize that 'relationship' (*rapport* in French) is a transitive word: in the underlying syntax, 'the relationship of X with Y', he offhandedly erases X. And when he realizes that the narrative voice is not a proper voice, he immediately reformulates the concept abstractly as 'instance . . . of enunciation', a concept which has worked havoc in French structuralism. An 'instance' is nothing but a text-bound abstraction lending itself to semiotic recuperation.

Genette's study of *Remembrance of Things Past* is based on a fallacy: that a single subject, the '*narrateur supposé*', is controlling the '*récit*'. His '*Discours du récit*' is a study of the discursive distortions (in terms of time, mode, and voice) imposed by this '*narrateur supposé*' on the story of his life. But, as Proust himself made clear, the chief story of his *essai-roman* is about how Marcel became an artist and decided to write the book we are reading (hence the preface at the end). There are two storylines, that of Marcel's life, and that of the writing of the book, and two subjects, the existential one and the artist, who are constantly playing hide-and-seek with each other. We can hardly guess, until *Le Temps retrouvé*, that the structure is so complex, but, as our brief study of the opening has already suggested, we immediately sense that this is no common autobiography and that we are interacting with endlessly embedded discourses and with different subjects.

Proust's first-person narrative eventually absents the original subject, that is, the author himself; it burdens the reader with the difficult task of having to decide whom he is really communicating with. The 'I' of the opening sentence is a mirror through which the reader tries to catch a glimpse of the elusive author but in which, eventually, he sees only a reflection of himself seeking to communicate with the author. It does not only point towards the enunciator, it also and above all points in our direction: it represents the ultimate Other that Lacan writes about, the language as law (the law of representation and communication) which brings people together, because they intensively need to communicate, but also keeps them apart because they need secrecy to impose a favourable image of themselves.

## THE PROTAGONIST'S 'I'

With Gide and Proust, we have gradually shifted from the authorial 'I', which at once binds together and keeps apart the interlocutors (author and reader) while allowing at least one of them to remain outside the black box, to the 'I' within the black box, that of the individual characters whom the semioticians and neo-rhetoricians would like to call narrators (genuine or supposed). In the present section, we are going to examine two kinds of discourse developed in the modernist novel which simulate or have the coherence of real discourses: the dialogue, and the so-called interior monologue.

### The dialogue

The modern novelist has always tried to 'quote' his protagonists verbatim if only to prove that he is honestly doing his job as a historian. He has always acted a little like Mrs Honour in *Tom Jones* who, when being blamed by Sophia for talking against Tom, quotes her fellow servants to defend herself:

> 'I am sorry, I have offended your ladyship', answered Mrs Honour, 'I am sure I hate Molly Seagrim as much as your ladyship can, and as for abusing Squire Jones, I can call all the servants in the house to witness, that whenever any talk hath been about bastards, I have always taken his part: "for which of you," says I to the footmen, "would not be a bastard, if he could, to be made a gentleman of? and," says I, "I am sure he is a very fine gentleman."'
> (Fielding 1980: 196–7)

Mrs Honour evades the question: she is not saying that she takes Tom's side, but simply shows that whenever someone abuses him she immediately asks that person whether he would not rather be in Tom's place than in his own. She breaks the line of communication between Sophia and herself and proposes a new one between Sophia and the impertinent servants who censure her Tom. The dynamics of dialogue in modern fiction is wonderfully demonstrated in this passage: the author, like Mrs Honour, withdraws from the stage by making his characters speak for themselves.

Many dialogues, in bad novels especially, are simply meant

to provide the reader with background information which would sound too flat in a third-person narrative. Such dialogues serve to promote, somewhat flatly, however, the showing effect of the text. Some of Flaubert's dialogues in *Madame Bovary* belong to this category. Here, for example, is the first conversation between Emma and Léon at the inn:

> 'Do you at least have some walks in the neighborhood?' continued Madame Bovary, speaking to the young man.
> 'Oh, very few,' he answered. 'There is a place they call La Pâture, on the top of the hill, on the edge of the forest. Sometimes, on Sundays, I go and stay there with a book, watching the sunset.' 'I think there is nothing so beautiful as sunsets,' she resumed; 'but especially by the seashore.'
> 'Oh, I love the sea!' said Monsieur Léon.
> (Flaubert 1965: 57–8)

Here Flaubert seems to be presenting the romantic map of the Yonville region. This is not a true conversation, of course, but the parody of a conversation: it does not 'show' the country around Yonville but suggests that Léon and Emma have been brought up on romantic clichés.

In *Bleak House*, one finds dialogues like the following, which sound like authentic dialogues:

> My guardian stood before me, contemplating the birds, and I had no need to look beyond him.
> 'And what do you call these little fellows, ma'am?' said he in his pleasant voice. 'Have they any names?'
> 'I can answer for Miss Flite that they have,' said I, 'for she promised to tell us what they were. Ada remembers?'
> Ada remembered very well.
> 'Did I?' said Miss Flite – 'Who's that at my door? What are you listening at my door for, Krook?'
> The old man of the house, pushing it open before him, appeared there with his fur cap in his hand, and his cat at his heels.
> 'I warn't listening, Miss Flite,' he said. 'I was going to give a rap with my knuckles, only you're so quick!'
> 'Make your cat go down. Drive her away!' the old lady angrily exclaimed.
> (Dickens 1971: 252)

Miss Flite is not allowed to answer Mr Jarndyce right away; Esther takes over after his question to remind Ada of a thing Miss Flite said earlier. Then Miss Flite brings into the conversation a new character whose arrival has not yet been mentioned in any narratorial aside. Since there is no description of the scene, the reader must try and picture it: Miss Flite turning her attention away from her guests and looking towards the door, and Krook standing there, probably eavesdropping. The showing effect is produced by many elements in this dialogue: Esther's intervention, her appeal to Ada, Miss Flite's hesitation, her turning to Krook, and Krook's arrival which occurs before it is described.

This scene produces a strong showing effect akin to what Barthes calls the 'effet de réel' that is, 'the pure encounter of an object and of its expression' (Barthes 1968: 89; my translation). This 'effet de réel' has very much to do with the author's apparent non-interference in the narrative process. The critics' objection to 'telling' has always been based on the principle that unmediated information exposes the author to a direct communication with the reader.

What eventually makes a dialogue truly present in the reader's mind is its complex texthood, its eminent 'commentability' or, in theatrical terms, its representability. To illustrate this point, we will analyse a dialogue from James's *The Bostonians*, which is possibly one of the most complex and genuine dialogues ever composed in English fiction, namely the conversation between Verena and Olive, just after the party at the Tarrants' house during which Olive was officially presented to Verena's parents. When Olive decides to leave, because she is annoyed by the young men's fawning attitude towards her protégée, she asks Verena to follow her outside. Here is the beginning of their conversation:

> 'I can see that you are angry at something,' Verena said to Olive, as the two stood there in the starlight. 'I hope it isn't me. What have I done?'
> 'I am not angry – I am anxious. I am so afraid I shall lose you. Verena don't fail me – don't fail me!' Olive spoke low, with a kind of passion.
> 'Fail you? How can I fail?'

'You can't, of course you can't. Your star is above you. But don't listen to *them*.'

(James 1981: 116)

Verena senses that her friend has been irritated by the whole performance; she knows why but still hopes she will not be reprimanded. Hence the ambiguous 'something' which after the predicative 'angry' can only stand for 'somebody'. We gather, through these approximations, that Verena is intently watching Olive's reactions to decide whether she guessed correctly. James does not describe the interlocutors' reactions; he leaves it to his reader to picture the scene. Apparently, Olive did not react in any conspicuous way since Verena eventually admits, somewhat sheepishly, that she feels guilty, before begging Olive to tell her what she has done. At the same time, of course, she is challenging mute Olive to say what is on her mind: she exposes herself in order to force her friend to do the same.

Olive, who always strives to keep her good image in front of her spiritual daughter, parries the attack as best she can. She is not ready to speak out yet, but tries to keep Verena on the defensive: 'I am not angry – I am anxious.' This is a marvellous example of what Freud calls *Verneinung*, or negation. Olive is not negating the proposition presented by Verena ('you are angry at me') but countering the allegation, unbearable to her, that she is capable of getting angry despite her spiritual elevation. She wields the negation to confuse her 'daughter' and to prevent her from going deeper into a matter which is too embarrassing. She conscientiously erases everything she dislikes in Verena's accusation, sensing that anger could be regarded not only as a flaw in her, but also as a sign of her excessive concern for, and therefore attachment to, Verena.

As the reader begins to understand, she is in love with Verena, though she is not aware of it yet; she refuses to acknowledge the fact because it is morally and psychologically unacceptable. The adjective 'anxious' doesn't have the same negative connotation as 'angry', and that is presumably why she inserts it in the conversation to give a better image of herself; 'anxious' tends to be intransitive, subject-oriented, whereas 'angry' tends to be transitive, object-oriented, hence the correction.

The tightrope stunt performed here by Olive between transitive and intransitive forms continues in the following passage. She uses a verb, 'fail', which can be both transitive and intransitive. She uses it transitively but ambiguously, saying both 'don't let me down' and 'don't disappoint me'. In the first interpretation she is beseeching Verena to continue to love her; in the second, she is admonishing her to remain faithful to the cause, feminism, intimating that she herself strongly believes in her.

By a process of conversational mimicry which is well-known to discourse analysts (a grammatical structure or a key word uttered by one of the speakers is echoed by the others), Verena appropriates the verb she has just heard but detransitivizes it: 'Fail you? How can I fail?' She erases the first interpretation of Olive's words and retains only the second one, intimating that she takes Olive's affection for granted though she strongly resents her lack of trust. Her self-confidence, which comes naturally from her being loved by many people, Olive included, is not as strong as it seemed: it is gradually undermined by Olive's doubts. So, in her echoing answer, Verena does not simply defy her spiritual mother, she asks her how she could go wrong, how she could 'fall' (a verb which, by the way, is always intransitive) rather than 'fail'.

It is not clear, in Olive's answer, exactly what are the words deleted after 'can': 'fail me' or simply 'fail'? Besides the modal auxiliary 'can' has at least two meanings in this case: either 'it is not possible that' or 'you mustn't', the latter interpretation being capable of being paraphrased as 'I won't allow it to happen'. To Verena's expression of panic, Olive responds by saying that nothing bad can happen to her as long as she, Olive, stands by her and tells her what to do. The star which is supposed to be above her is none other, therefore, than Olive herself, who is terribly self-centred and tries to bring her protégé back into her orbit.

This dialogue, which has been analysed more extensively elsewhere (Souchu 1984: 195–207), looks very much like an authentic conversation: it is not telling the reader anything about the place, the other characters, or the two interlocutors that he did not know before. It simply shows, in a dramatized way, how the two protagonists interact with each other, how cunningly aggressive they can be without losing their good image. The reader has the illusion of witnessing a scene of jealousy he was not supposed to witness. He is a voyeur and an analyst at one and the same time. He is not analysing the author's discourse this time, but that of the protagonists, who are exposing themselves shamelessly. The 'I' has at long last been objectified: it is not a screen behind which the author hides, it is a signifier, a text-bound object upon which the reader must practise his know-how in order to extract all its significance and stage the scene properly in his mind. The perfect simulation of a discourse like this has the effect of absenting the author; the reader seems to be stumbling upon an *objet trouvé* which he must analyse and account for.

## The interior monologue

The reader has a comparable feeling in the presence of so-called interior monologue which Dujardin, one of the first writers to use it extensively in *Les Lauriers sont coupés* (1887), defined in the following way:

> The interior monologue is, in the order of poetry, the unspoken discourse without an audience, by which a character expresses his most intimate thought, that closest to the unconscious, prior to all logical organization, that is to say, in its nascent state, by means of direct sentences reduced to a syntactic minimum.
>
> (Banfield 1982: 136)

This definition was echoed, with only slight alterations, by Melvin Friedman in his *Stream of Consciousness: A Study in Literary Method* (Friedman 1955: 7) and by Robert Humphrey in his *Stream of Consciousness in the Modern Novel* (Humphrey 1954: 24). Friedman insists on calling 'stream of consciousness' a genre, like the ode or the sonnet, and the 'interior monologue' a form of discourse practised in that genre (Friedman 1955: 3–4).

Here is a non-discursive sample lifted from the 'Hades' chapter of *Ulysses*:

> Tail gone now.
> One of those chaps would make short work of a fellow. Pick the bones clean no matter who it was. Ordinary meat

for them. A corpse is meat gone bad. Well and what's cheese? Corpse of milk. I read in that *Voyages in China* that the Chinese say a white man smells like a corpse. Cremation better. Priests dead against it. Deviling for the other firm. Wholesale burners and Dutch oven dealers. Time of the plague. Quicklime fever pits to eat them. Lethal chamber. Ashes to ashes.

(Joyce 1969: 116)

This reverie has been triggered in Bloom's mind by the appearance of a rat moving in and out of the graves, and perhaps also by the name on the grave, 'Robert Emery', which reminds him of Robert Emmet, an Irish patriot who tried to get Napoleon's help against the English. The name may also evoke in his mind (preconsciously at least) the word 'emetic' (meaning 'inducing to vomit'), for the whole passage is a sickening evocation of death as rot. This word was used, we remember, by Justice Woolsey in his 1933 verdict. The description ('Tail gone now') which follows may be ambiguous, too. The tail is that of the rat, of course, but it is also, perhaps, Robert Emery's sex which the rats have probably eaten up by now. Hence the following reverie in which Bloom pictures the rats' feast over the dead bodies.

Neither of these two interpretations is offered by Gifford and Seidman in their substantial commentary on the novel (Gifford and Seidman 1974: 97). They mention, on the other hand, that *Voyages in China* will appear later on Bloom's bookshelves and explain the church's attitude towards cremation, etc. The difference of analysis is interesting: it shows that such a poorly predicated passage lends itself to different kinds of interpretation. This is not a discourse, with an 'I' pulling the strings and talking through a mask, except in the sentence 'I read in that *Voyages in China*'. It is simply a concatenation of images and affects whose logic cannot be reconstructed in any definite way. There is no one to confirm our interpretation; Bloom himself would not be able to explain what led him from one image or idea to the other. And readers of these lines may think that my sexual interpretation of the word 'tail' reveals more about this reader's obsessions than about those of Bloom.

In James's dialogue, which we analysed earlier, we were dealing with a prose which had all the attributes of a genuine discourse; we could depend upon our preconceptions and our scientific knowledge concerning verbal communication and psychology (if not psychoanalysis) to suggest meanings acceptable to most readers, even if such meanings had not been sensed before. In the passage from *Ulysses*, on the other hand, there is no such guarantee: the elliptical sentences (no 'I' and no verbs, in most cases) force the reader to try to provide the missing links, to turn this non-discourse into a proper discourse which, clearly, will be more his own discourse than that of the protagonist, or that of the author for that matter. The 'transparent mind' is not, as Dorrit Cohn seems to think, the mind of the character but that of the reader (Cohn 1978). This style (for no matter how discourse-like it may seem, it remains a style) challenges the reader to rewrite the text and predicate the sentences, in order to try to make contact with the author who, as a result, becomes much less accessible. It is only by lending our fantasies to Bloom that we can begin to understand what is happening in his preconscious, and, eventually, what the author intended to say, perhaps, through Bloom's tenuous mediation.

Despite its total absence of punctuation, Molly Bloom's lurid soliloquy, at the end, is far less ambiguous than the passage we have just analysed. It may be 'strong draught' in Justice Woolsey's words (Joyce 1969: 717), but it remains perfectly readable:

> Ive a mind to tell him every scrap and make him do it in front of me serve him right its all his own fault if I am an adulteress as the thing in the gallery said O much about it if thats all the harm ever we did in this vale of tears God knows its not much doesnt everybody only they hide it I suppose thats what a woman is supposed to be there for or He wouldnt have made us the way He did so attractive to men then if he wants to kiss my bottom Ill drag open my drawers
>
> (Joyce 1969: 702)

It is the most censorable part in the novel, as Joyce himself obliquely admitted in a letter to Frank Budgen in 1921: 'Though probably more obscene than any preceding episode it seems to me to be perfectly sane full amoral fertilisable untrustworthy engaging shrewd limited prudent indifferent

*Weib. Ich bin der* [sic] *Fleisch der stets bejaht*' (Ellman 1975: 285). Joyce obviously could not view this woman he had invented dispassionately: his discourse flares into a Bloom-like reverie about her at the end of this letter. Molly's soliloquy has all the characteristics of a discourse, and as such it can easily be censored. It is a discourse through which the author himself clearly wanted to express his love–hatred for women; one does not need Joyce's statement to that effect in this letter to sense that. This text is still largely author-oriented, whereas Bloom's text was clearly reader-oriented. It is censorable because it is insufficiently ambiguous and saturated. The author's obsessions and passions appear too obviously through the fantasies of this nymphomaniac; his 'I' looms too large behind Molly's 'I'.

## FREE INDIRECT SPEECH REVISITED

The distancing of the text reached its peak, perhaps, with so-called free indirect speech. This style, which has been called by different names in the last fifty years, generates an intensely poetic effect in fiction. In her marvellous book *Unspeakable Sentences,* Ann Banfield calls it 'represented speech' and 'represented thought'; she defines it in the following way: 'Represented speech and thought is recognized as a distinct style by its departures from the spoken forms of reported speech and thought' (Banfield 1982: 70). For her, represented speech and thought is a distorted form of reported speech. As we hope to show in the following pages, it is characterized in the main by a mixture of oral and writerly forms.

Though this style began to attract the attention of the critics only towards the end of the nineteenth century, it appeared very early in the history of the novel. Here is a passage from *Tom Jones* in which Tom is begging 'Mr Allworthy, "to have compassion on the poor fellow's family, especially as he himself had been only guilty, and on the other had been very difficultly prevailed on to do what he did. Indeed sir," said he' (Fielding 1980: 132). This is not pure reported speech since the passage is between quotes, and there is a direct address ('sir') which should not appear in reported speech. For reported speech is, by definition, a written and eminently writerly transcription of speech, with no traces of oral discourse. One finds an even clearer case in *Bleak House*, in the transcription of the dialogue between the coroner and Jo after Nemo's death:

> Name, Jo. Nothing else that he knows on. Don't know that everybody has two names. Never heerd of sich a think. Don't know that Jo is short for a longer name. Thinks it long enough for *him*. *He* don't find no fault with it. Spell it? No. *He* can't spell it. No father, no mother, no friends.
> (Dickens 1971: 199)

It is comparatively easy to recover the original utterances of the interlocutors. The coroner's 'you's' have been deleted, Jo's 'I's' and 'me's' have been translated as 'he's' and 'him's'. This passage is not direct speech, since these pronominal transcriptions have been made, nor reported speech, since the traces of oral speech have been retained (faulty pronunciation, faulty grammar, question marks, italics simulating emphasis).

The German critics Frank K. Stanzel in *Die typischen Erzählsituationen im Roman* (1955) and Käte Hamburger in *Die Logik der Dichtung* (1968), were among the first to adopt a purely narratological and linguistic approach to this style which has recently become one of the chief obsessions of the critics. These two critics do not claim to study these forms in terms of psychological realism but in terms of textual semiotics.

This is also what Ann Banfield does in *Unspeakable Sentences*: as she suggests in her excellent title (which unwittingly echoes Barthelme's title, *Unspeakable Practices, Unnatural Acts*): she wants to examine the language and not the 'transparence of the mind' as Dorrit Cohn did. Her book can be called the first true grammar of this kind of discourse; it is the first to scientifically show that represented speech and represented thought share the same grammar and that they are writerly styles far removed from natural language. In her conclusion, entitled 'Narration and Representation', she echoes, in different terms, Lubbock's distinction between telling and showing. Here is the key passage of that conclusion:

> There is thus something essential to fiction in its representation of consciousness. The linguistic cotemporality of PAST and NOW and the coreference of SELF and the third person supply a language for representing what can only be imagined or surmised – the thought of the other. By separating SELF

from SPEAKER, this style reveals the essential fictionality of any representation of consciousness, of any approximation of word to thought, even of our own. Through it, language represents what can exist without it, yet which can scarcely be externalized except through language, but it does it without bringing this externalization to the level of speech.

(Banfield 1982: 260)

This passage summarizes the theory developed throughout her book, namely that represented speech and thought is a style which violates the laws of oral speech in so far as it utterly erases the distinction between *énoncé* and *énonciation*. The narrator, who is the textual 'speaker' (Banfield still writes as if she were dealing with oral communication), seems to withdraw from the writing stage and to lend his voice to his protagonist (the 'self' in Banfield's theory, the 'reflector' in that of Stanzel) who is thinking or speaking through it. This style creates, as it were, an impossible or writerly subject; yet it seems to give a more realistic representation of consciousness than previous literary styles. This paradox takes the form of a double bind in Banfield's last sentence: 'Through it, language represents what can exist without it, yet which can scarcely be externalized except through language'. The 'real' is beyond the reach of language, but it is only through language that it can be explored.

The problem raised so brilliantly by Ann Banfield may be even more complex, as we hope to show through the analysis of a few typical samples, some of them already examined in her book.

One of the earliest samples of genuinely ambiguous 'free indirect style' is the transcription of the first conversation between Emma and Charles in *Madame Bovary*:

On parla d'abord du malade, puis du temps qu'il faisait, des grands froids, des loups qui couraient les champs la nuit. Mlle Rouault ne s'amusait guère à la campagne, maintenant surtout qu'elle était chargée presque à elle seule des soins de la ferme. Comme la salle était fraîche, elle grelottait tout en mangeant, ce qui découvrait un peu ses lèvres charnues, qu'elle avait coutume de mordillonner à ses moments de silence.

(Flaubert 1961: 30)

> First they spoke of the patient, then of the weather, of the great cold, of the wolves that infested the fields at night. Mademoiselle Rouault did not at all like the country, especially now that she had to look after the farm almost alone. As the room was chilly, she shivered as she ate. This showed something of her full lips, that she had a habit of biting when silent.
>
> (Flaubert 1965: 11)

The first sentence cannot be called represented speech; it is simply a summary of the conversation between Charles and Emma after Charles has taken care of M. Rouault. The second sentence contains two words which echo oral speech: the adverb *guère* ('not at all') which is somewhat colloquial, and the deictic adverb *maintenant* ('now') which, in writing, does not normally occur with a past tense. As Banfield shows, the use of colloquialisms and the co-occurrence of *maintenant* with a past tense in French are clear markers of represented speech as opposed to reported speech. We are therefore induced by the text itself to translate this sentence into direct speech: 'Je ne m'amuse guère à campagne, maintenant surtout que je suis chargée presque à moi seule des soins de la ferme' (I do not at all like the country, especially now that I have to look after the farm almost alone).

Grammatically speaking this translation is satisfactory. Yet, there is another notation in the sentence that we have not accounted for, 'Mlle Rouault'. When Charles arrived at the farm, Emma was referred to as '[u]ne jeune femme' ('[a] young woman') a neutral phrase which implies that Charles was not particularly impressed by her at first; then, two paragraphs later, she was called 'Mlle Emma' obviously because of the presence of the maid who was watching her as she was working with her needle. The referential tags are therefore strictly coded and always reflect the observer's point of view. So, to come back to the sentence we rephrased earlier, we must conclude that 'Mlle Rouault' reflects the fact that Charles (the stranger) is the observer, and perhaps even more than that.

Psychology comes to our rescue here: how could Emma, a comparatively reserved girl who has just come out of a convent, be so forthright with a young man the first time she meets him? She is too shy (though she is capable of *hardiesse* too) to beg for help so openly. So, another interpretation must be proposed. Since this sentence is probably not a transcription of Emma's words, what is it? Probably a representation, that is, a writerly transcription, of Charles's thoughts. While he was discussing with Emma the various subjects summarized in the first sentence, Charles gradually understood the girl's frustration and translated it inwardly into a sentence like the following: 'Mlle Rouault ne s'amuse à la campagne, maintenant surtout qu'elle est est chargée presque à elle seule des soins de la ferme' (Mademoiselle Rouault does not at all like the country, especially now that she has to look after the farm almost alone), in which only the tense is different from the original. Presumably, Charles has merely recovered the unsayable (the abject) of Emma's discourse. Emma's frustration had to be manifest for dull-witted Charles to sense it during his first visit. It is as if he had practically overheard the sentence which we thought we had recovered earlier: 'Je ne m'amuse guère à la campagne . . .'

To understand a text like this, the reader must make a number of educated guesses based, first, on a grammar of discourse and, second, on psychology. This apparently straightforward sentence turns out to have at least two word-for-word-transcriptions: Emma's direct speech and Charles's conscious thoughts, plus an embedding: Emma's preconscious thoughts as echoed in Charles's conscious thoughts. These different readings are possible because represented speech and represented thought share exactly the same grammar. This is not a question of realism but of style. Our thoughts and reveries are a jumble of words, images, and affects, as Bloom's soliloquy quoted earlier suggests. They do not constitute a discourse, whereas represented speech and thought is a style which has the grammatical coherence of a discourse.

One of the most skilful manipulators of this style was Henry James. In *The Bostonians*, just a few pages before the conversation we analysed earlier, there is the following report of a conversation between Olive and Mr Pardon, one of the 'young men' Olive disliked so much:

> The truth was, Miss Verena wanted to 'shed' her father altogether; she didn't want him pawing round her that way before she began; it didn't add in the least to the attraction.

> Mr Pardon expressed the conviction that Miss Chancellor agreed with him in this, and it required a great effort of mind on Olive's part, so small was her desire to act in concert with Mr Pardon, to admit to herself that she did.
>
> (James 1981: 111)

It is comparatively easy, in the first sentence, to recover the words uttered by Mr Pardon: 'The truth is, Miss Verena wants to "shed" her father altogether; she doesn't want him pawing round her that way before she begins; it doesn't add in the least to the attraction'. This is a good sample of represented speech in which traces of oral forms ('The truth was', 'shed', 'that way') are easy to identify.

The translation of the second sentence is far more difficult to make: it is not represented speech but reported speech. In represented speech, there are enough echoes of the original utterance to recover the exact wording; this is not the case in reported speech, which is a polished, writerly, transcription spelling out the meaning, rather than the actual wording, of the original utterance. It is often difficult to recover the oral utterance from a reported speech, especially when the speaker speaks in a truly oral style. Pardon probably said something like this: 'I am sure, Miss Chancellor, you agree with me on this.' In reported speech, the illocutionary force of the utterance must be spelt out ('Mr Pardon expressed the conviction'), but not in represented speech where Pardon's words (assuming we recovered them properly) would read: 'Mr Pardon was sure that Miss Chancellor agreed with him on this'. But, as this sentence is clearly focused on Olive, we cannot say for sure what were Pardon's exact words. We only know what Olive's interpretation of them was, and what reaction they induced in her: she hates to agree with a man like him, so she has to answer in such a way as to keep her distance while admitting that he is probably right. Olive's original utterance cannot therefore be fully recovered, only the meaning she intended to load it with, its perlocutionary force, that is; if she did not answer, on the other hand, it is only the content of her thoughts which is provided.

Here again, as in the represented conversation of Charles and Emma, the situation is somewhat circular. Mr Pardon has understood, while talking with Olive, that the latter disapproves of the Tarrants; so, in order to develop a complicity with this reserved, and possibly hostile, woman, he verbalizes what he thinks he overheard through her words. He spells out the abject of her discourse which will become later, in her dialogue with Verena, an open injunction: 'Don't listen to *them*', that is, the young men. Olive is speaking, as it were, through Mr Pardon, but she is doing so perversely, forcing him to apologize for verbalizing her own abject thoughts, as the rhetorical precaution at the beginning, '[t]he truth was', indicates.

To summarize, here are the various levels of discourse in this passage: Mr Pardon's direct address to Olive; Olive's secret thoughts about the Tarrants as 'overheard' by Mr Pardon; Mr Pardon's apologetic verbalization of Olive's secret thoughts.

This extraordinary passage induces the reader to undertake a transcription which is doomed to fail, eventually. The narrative discourse does echo fragments of speech and thought, but the reader cannot positively sort out the various discourses which have been so cleverly interwoven on the page. He minutely analyses the words he is confronted with and tries to decide what voice or what interior monologue they transcribe. As he does so, he becomes more and more entangled in the syntax of the text and loses his confidence, realizing that he will never completely disambiguate the words on the page, that is to say, turn them into plausible fragments of discourse. He is not even sure that it was a discourse to start with.

Another interesting example, which was analysed by Banfield, is the opening of *Mrs Dalloway*:

Mrs Dalloway said she would buy the flowers herself.
    For Lucy had her work cut out for her. The doors would be taken off their hinges; Rumpelmayer's men were coming. And then, thought Clarissa Dalloway, what a morning – fresh as if issued to children on a beach.

(Woolf 1967: 5)

Banfield's investigation of this passage is somewhat scanty. She notices that the first sentence probably contains indirect speech and that the 'sentiments in the passage must be attributed to Mrs Dalloway and not to a narrator', but she does not really manage to account for the extreme complexity of this apparently straightforward passage (Banfield 1982: 66).

The first sentence can tentatively be translated as follows: 'Mrs Dalloway said: "I will buy the flowers myself".' But only Lucy, the servant, would call Clarissa Mrs Dalloway here, as Emma's servant was the only one who could refer to her mistress as 'Mlle Emma' in *Madame Bovary*. This would imply that the introductory phrase ('Mrs Dalloway said') echoes Lucy's thoughts and that the sentence in direct speech must be understood not from the speaker's but from the listener's point of view. This first paragraph, considered from this angle, would therefore be the transcription of Lucy's represented thought ('she says she is going to buy the flowers herself'), rather than that of Mrs Dalloway's direct speech ('I am going to buy the flowers myself').

In the next paragraph, it is clear that Clarissa needs to justify her decision to go and buy the flowers herself; she intimates that Lucy would probably have liked to do it herself, but she overruled her for good reasons: 'Lucy had her work cut out for her.' Apparently, she didn't say that to Lucy but only to herself, otherwise the conjunction 'for' (which suggests that she is trying to justify the decision to herself) would be superfluous. There is a great deal of bad faith involved here: Clarissa senses intuitively that she may have hurt Lucy's feelings, though she probably took every precaution not to. Knowing her as we do after many rereadings of the novel, we doubt very much that she could have so openly snubbed a servant by saying: 'I will buy the flowers myself.' The reflexive pronoun would have been somewhat insulting, implying as it necessarily would have that she did not trust a servant to do it. If this interpretation, which is as linguistically grounded as that of Banfield but relies heavily on psychology and conversational maxims as well, is correct, then we cannot recover Clarissa's exact words but only their perlocutionary effects through Lucy's reflections and thoughts.

The same sentence is therefore liable to have more than one reading, to be supported concurrently by two subjects of enunciation, two speakers, in deep structure. One cannot subscribe, therefore, to the following principle stated by Banfield:

a. 1 E/1SELF. For every node E, there is at most one referent, called the 'subject of consciousness' or SELF, to whom all expressive elements are attributed. That is, all realizations of SELF in an E are coreferential.
b. Priority of SPEAKER. If there is an *I*, *I* is coreferential with the SELF. In the absence of an *I*, a third person pronoun may be interpreted as SELF.
c. If E is related anaphorically to the complement of a consciousness verb, its SELF is coreferential with the subject or the indirect object of this verb.

(Banfield 1983: 93)

If E is the textual expression ('Mrs Dalloway said she would buy the flowers herself', for instance), it is not true, as Banfield claims, that it has only one subject of consciousness. Banfield's concept of SELF and SPEAKER, which is supposed to be linguistically grounded, is in fact extremely ambiguous. The *raison d'être* of this style is precisely that it confuses speaker and self, produces an ambiguous and poetic utterance, and burdens the reader with a very complex task.

It is ultimately impossible to adopt a purely linguistic approach when one wants to study this kind of discourse. Represented speech and thought is a literary style, characterized by the linguistic features identified by Banfield, which violates the traditional principles of enunciation: for one textual sentence, there are two enunciatory processes, one oral, the other writerly, and two selves (and sometimes more when two or more speakers are involved) which constantly switch parts. The deictic parameters are so confused that, ultimately, the reader can never be sure that he has interpreted the text cogently or identified the voices and the selves correctly. This style, which simulates oral discourse, flouts the laws of oral communication: it is unspeakable, because it is claimed by different subjects at one and the same time. It is a writerly style which manages to erase the discursive breaks and to muddle the enunciatory processes.

This style presents us with a difficult challenge. In order to make sense of these complex texts, we have to transcribe the written sentences into oral or pseudo-oral forms; but as we do so, we become more and more entangled in the verbal mesh. We think we are hearing countless voices, but in fact we are merely lending our own voices to the characters, as an actor does when performing a play. We are merely projecting ourselves on to the page, into the words, confusing the textual voices with our own. Such texts are gigantic ego-traps: they induce us to interact with them intensely, but, at the same time, they devour us. They fill us fleetingly with alien egos that need our intervention to exist but which eventually saturate our psyche.

We are not entirely fooled by the game. We have the feeling, while playing like this with the text, of appropriating it, of making it our own. We have the pleasurable impression that whatever we say about it, whatever translation we provide, is nothing but our own contribution to the text, or rather our own text, since the 'true' text, the original utterance, is ultimately unrecoverable for the simple reason that it has never been voiced. Whatever we see through it pleases us immensely, gives us a great deal of narcissistic pleasure, even though, or rather because, our interpretative activity makes the author more inaccessible: the text is not only the author's property any more; it belongs to us to a certain, undefinable, extent.

## CONCLUSION: TELLING AND SHOWING

The modernist novel attained such a high degree of poeticity that it finally lent an artistic legitimacy to the genre as a whole. In his 'Art of Fiction', James insisted on this evolution:

> Only a short time ago it might have been supposed that the English novel was not what the French call *discutable*. It had no air of having a theory, a conviction, a consciousness of itself behind it – of being the expression of an artistic faith, the result of choice and comparison.
>
> (James 1978: 35)

As we hope to have shown in this chapter, it was the gradual recognition of the resources of the medium which led to this development. The author had now become acutely aware of the distance which the printed text, the industry, and the law were imposing between him and his reader. This also implied that he had to exert himself a great deal more if he wanted to interact with his elusive reader and give him the illusion of producing and writing the text, instead of simply consuming it.

This is what the debate on telling and showing, opened by a disciple of James, was all about. In his *Craft of Fiction*, Percy Lubbock writes: 'the art of fiction does not begin until the novelist thinks of his story as a matter to be *shown*, to be so exhibited that it will tell itself' (Lubbock 1957: 62). He was reacting against the many elements of orality which still survived in the nineteenth-century novel, especially in historical or realistic novels where the characters were described and the plots developed in an expository manner. The Balzacian opening, the informative dialogue, and the open interference of the author in a pseudo-Sternian manner, were some of the most conspicuous traces of orality showing that the author was pulling the strings from behind the printed pages.

Lubbock considered Defoe to be the archetypal novelist who told rather than showed:

> in fiction there can be no appeal to any authority outside the book itself. Narrative – like the tales of Defoe, for example – must look elsewhere for support; Defoe produced it by the assertion of the historic truthfulness of his stories. But in a novel, strictly so called, attestation of this kind is, of course, quite irrelevant; the thing has to *look* true, and that is all. It is not made to look true by simple statement.
>
> (62)

The difference between Defoe and, for instance, Fielding is not as clear-cut as Lubbock seems to think. Fielding, too, insisted that the novel is a historical form, that is to say a narrative art which abides by the laws of verisimilitude upon which historians evolve their reconstructions of the past (consensual representations of life and of the cosmos, laws of causality, etc.). Yet it is true that, at its birth, the modern novel was fundamentally a mixed genre: though it was constructed mostly like an oral narrative and foregrounded its 'storicity', it usually exhibited its bookhood in a preface or pseudo-preface and through its typographical games. Lubbock inveighs against such practices, and he decides, somewhat arbitrarily, that Defoe's stories do not deserve to be called novels because their historicity is openly asserted by the author in his prefaces rather than exhibited in the texts themselves. As far as *Moll*

*Flanders* is concerned, this criticism is unwarranted, as we explained earlier: the preface is already part of the book itself, and the author is not Defoe but a fiction in which author and narrator become curiously entangled.

The most revealing statement in Lubbock's passage is the one concerning 'the book itself'. Lubbock claims that the author must completely absent himself from his novel, that he must let his book speak for itself. Here lies the root of the opposition between telling and showing: the line of communication between author and reader must be radically cut by the text. The discourse must not be that of the author but of a textual subject. This confirms our theory that the novelhood of a novel depends first of all on the recognition of its bookhood, that is to say of its non-orality. A novel stops being a novel from the moment one realizes that its author has failed to extricate himself from the text. In the eighteenth century, such a novel as *Remembrance of Things Past* would never have been accepted as a novel because of its flaunted autobiographicality. And yet, one of the first major autobiographical novels was written during that period: it is *Tristram Shandy*. None of the reviews written at the time, as far as I know, question the fictionality of the book. Sterne had cleverly managed to promote the bookhood and printhood of his novel, while parodying the oral discourse. The difference, therefore, is that in the eighteenth century the bookhood of the novel had to be foregrounded, whereas in the modernist era, when this bookhood was taken for granted, it had to be undermined so that the reader might have the illusion of stumbling upon an *objet trouvé*.

Lubbock acknowledges the fact that his own principles are somewhat shaky: 'And yet the novelist must state, must tell, must narrate – what else can he do?' (63). He seems to be caught in a double bind; he is saying: 'I don't want to hear the voice of the author in a novel, but on the other hand I know that whatever I hear, I read, must necessarily come from him.' A little earlier, he had written: 'The reader of a novel – by which I mean the critical reader – is himself a novelist; he is the maker of a book which may or may not please his taste when it is finished, but of a book for which he must take his own share of the responsibility' (17). According to this principle, which echoes Tristram's promise to 'halve the matter amicably' with the reader, the novelhood of a novel comes largely from the fact that there are numberless gaps, breaks, and ambiguities in the text that encourage the reader to exert his talents. A novel should not be univocal, like a linear oral narrative, but intrinsically paradoxical and even undecidable. Whenever we have the feeling of hearing the identifiable voice of the author designating us as his target, as in didactic novels for instance, a large share of this undecidability vanishes. This univocity, or phonocentricity as Derrida would call it, produces a kind of promiscuity: the reader feels too dangerously close to the author.

Reading a novel is a very narcissistic form of behaviour. The reader projects himself into the book, uses it more or less as a mirror. Whenever he catches a glimpse, however fleeting, of the author, as in straightforward commentaries for example, he suddenly discovers with a shock that the mirror is in fact a two-way mirror and realizes that someone has been watching him. He becomes terribly restless, his blissful solitude having irremediably been shattered. Hence the novelist's effort during the modernist era to create a text which does not seem to be the expression of his own ego and fantasies, but which echoes the ultimate Other under whose law the reader must fall. The only way for the reader not to be intimidated by that law is to transcribe the text, to submit it to his own analysis, as if his desk had suddenly become the psychoanalyst's divan.

# Chapter 5

# The postmodernist novel

The communication explosion in the last fifty years has had a decisive impact on the evolution of the book trade. The cinema, television, and computers have not supplanted the printed book, as McLuhan rashly prophesied in 1962, but they have helped redefine its role and its place in our culture.

In the present chapter, we will look at how the communication explosion and the development of the paperback have radically changed the structure of the fiction market as well as the narrative strategies used in the novel. With the development of mass culture, more innovative writers find it more difficult than ever to make a living with their pens and must find other sources of income, in universities, for instance. In return, the popular media have largely diverted the attention of the censors away from the novel, not only in the US but also in France and in Britain. Faced with this unprecedented freedom and with the fact that his readers are often his colleagues on campus, the novelist has become more self-conscious and been forced to develop more sophisticated devices to beat his self-consciousness.

The postmodernist novel is even more international than the modernist one from which it gradually developed, from Joyce and Kafka to Nabokov and Beckett, in the last fifty years. We take it to include not only the American school of innovative fiction which has been labelled postmodernist by Ihab Hassan, but also the French New Novel and some of the South American, South African, and Indian schools of fiction-writing. The postmodernist novel constitutes a specific response to the communication explosion, as well as to many other political and economic phenomena. As we will show, it has radically changed the respective roles of author and reader and promoted a more sophisticated form of textual communication between two real through two ideal subjects.

## THE ENVIRONMENT

### The market

In the last fifty years, the book trade has gone through an extraordinary expansion in most countries. Here are the figures for Britain as they appear in *Mumby's Publishing and Bookselling in the Twentieth Century* (Mumby 1982: 220–2):

| Year | New books | Total incl. reprints | New novels | New + reprinted novels |
|------|-----------|----------------------|------------|------------------------|
| 1937 | 11,327 | 17,137 | 2,153 | 5,097 |
| 1943 | 5,504 | 6,705 | | |
| 1950 | 11,638 | 17,072 | | |
| 1955 | | | 2,249 | 3,702 |
| 1960 | 17,794 | 23,783 | | |
| 1965 | | | 2,244 | 3,877 |
| 1970 | 23,512 | 33,489 | | |
| 1981 | 33,651 | 43,083 | 2,910 | 4,747 |

These figures do not take into account imported books. They clearly show that fiction represents a much smaller share of the market now than it did fifty years ago. This phenomenon is even more striking if one takes into account the print orders. In 1975, Anthony Burgess wrote: 'A novel which sells 2,000 copies on publication in hardback is virtually a bestseller today: the average sale for a novel of literary merit by an unknown author is 200 to 300 copies' (Sutherland 1978: 40).

In France, the expansion of the book market was slow until 1952, but after that date a boom occurred. In 1958, 11,879 titles were published for 141 million volumes sold; in 1980, 26,635 titles were published for 379 million volumes sold (Vessillier-Ressi 1982: 84). Though the book market has grown since 1900 in money value, its share has regularly been diminishing in the communication trade. The total amount of copyrights in 1900 was 398.17 million francs, 89.16 per cent of which went to authors of books, and the rest to playwrights or musical composers. By 1980, when the copyrights had reached the 2,023.40 million francs mark, only 46.45 per cent went to authors of books, the rest going to playwrights, film directors, musical composers, and authors writing for radio and television. Literature, which represented 29.64 of the total in 1900, had come down to 9.3 per cent in 1980 (Vessillier-Ressi 1982: 69).

For the US, the figures, as given in *Publishers' Weekly* ( 20 January 1945, 20 January 1951, 16 January 1961, 8 February 1971, 13 March 1981, and 10 March 1989), show that here too the book trade has expanded steadily since the war:

| Year | New books | Total incl. reprints | New books of fiction | New + reprinted books of fiction |
|---|---|---|---|---|
| 1943 | 6,764 | 8,325 | 933 | 1,478 |
| 1950 | 8,634 | 11,022 | 1,211 | 1,907 |
| 1960 | 12,069 | 15,012 | 1,642 | 2,440 |
| 1970 | 24,288 | 36,071 | 1,998 | 3,137 |
| 1979 | 36,112 | 45,182 | 2,313 | 3,264 |
| 1987 | 44,638 | 56,027 | 3,264 | 6,298 |

Here again, fiction's share of the book market has been steadily diminishing. Naturally, these figures do not take into account the numbers of copies sold which, for fiction especially, have increased considerably with the development of the paperback. After Allen Lane started Penguin Books in 1935, the formula became a huge success, providing the novel with a brand new market; in the 1960s, just a little less than half of the volumes published by Penguin Books were fiction. In all, forty million paperbacks were sold in the United Kingdom in 1961, and 135 million ten years later (Johannot 1978: 77). In 1960, 5,886 titles were listed in *Whitaker's Paperbacks in Print*; by 1968, there were six times as many (Bradbury 1972: 221).

In the United States, Robert de Graff started the Pocket Books series in 1939 after sending thousands of letters to test the market. The first ten titles were: *Lost Horizon* by James Hilton, *Bambi* by Felix Salten, *The Murder of Roger Ackroyd* by Agatha Christie, *Wuthering Heights* by Emily Brontë,

*Enough Rope* by Dorothy Parker, *Wake Up and Live* (a self-help book) by Dorothea Brande, *Topper* by Thorne Smith, *The Way of All Flesh* by Samuel Butler, *Five Shakespeare Tragedies*, and *The Bridge of San Luis Rey* by Thornton Wilder (Sutherland 1978: 180). The collection was already selling ten million volumes a year by 1941 and twenty million the following year. Other publishers soon joined the market; Bantam was publishing more than 5,000 new titles every year in the 1970s (Johannot 1977: 78).

Print orders for paperbacks have been steadily increasing. In 1975, the print order for William Golding's *Marathon Man* was for 900,000 copies, and for Sidney Sheldon's *The Other Side of Midnight*, it was for 800,000, plus 200,000 two days later (Tebbel 1981: 352). Never had the successful novelists sold so many copies of their books. By 1979, Mario Puzo's *The Godfather* (1969) had sold 292,765 copies in hardcover and 13,225,000 in paperback; by the same date, William P. Blatty's *The Exorcist* (1971) had sold 205,265 copies in hardcover and 11,948,000 in paperback (Walters 1985: 125–6). Even such a difficult and innovative novel as Pynchon's *Gravity's Rainbow* (1973) was a success in paperback. Viking brought out 9,000 copies in hardcover at $10, and 75,000 in softcover at $4.75. It sold so well that in the same year Bantam gave $369,000 for the paperback rights and published a true paperback at $2.50; 290,000 copies were in print by 1975 (Sutherland 1978: 169). The paperback rights for this novel were still comparatively low; in 1965, Fawcett had given $700,000 for James A. Michener's *The Source*, and, in 1975, Bantam paid $2 million for the paperback rights of Doctorow's *Ragtime* (Tebbel 1981: 349–50).

In France, the Livre de Poche series started only in 1953, but it was selling nine million volumes a year by 1959, twenty-two million by 1963, and had brought out a total of 100 million by 1964. It reached its peak in 1969 with thirty million volumes sold that year (Johannot 1978: 82). All the bestsellers published by Livre de Poche were novels, except Anne Frank's *Journal*, as the list on page 197, showing the number of copies sold by 1970, indicates (Johannot 1978:160).

The formula gave an unprecedented public to popular novels whose copyrights were owned by the big publishing firms like Gallimard, Calman-Lévy, Laffont, Grasset, and le Seuil.

| Title | Number of volumes published |
|---|---|
| *La Peste* (Camus) | 1,700,000 |
| *Journal* (Anne Frank) | 1,100,000 |
| *Vol de nuit* (Saint-Exupéry) | 1,100,000 |
| *La Condition humaine* (Malraux) | 1,000,000 |
| *Le Mur* (Sartre) | 1,000,000 |
| *Thérèse Desqueyroux* (Mauriac) | 966,000 |
| *Vipère au poing* (Hervé-Bazin) | 890,000 |

The development of the paperback often made it more difficult to get new and more innovative books published. Most of the so-called New Novelists in France were first published by comparatively unknown publishers: Pinget by La Tour de Feu, Nathalie Sarraute by Robert Marin, Claude Simon by Sagittaire, Butor and Robbe-Grillet by Editions de Minuit. When *La Jalousie* came out in 1957, it sold only a few hundred copies during the first few months (Ricardou 1973: 22); now, Robbe-Grillet claims that he has sold more than two million copies of that novel in different languages around the world.

The paperback more or less took over that part of the market that the chapbook or *bibliothèque bleue* abandoned in the late nineteenth century. Naturally, the reading public has changed enormously with the development of public education and the greater amount of leisure which has accompanied economic affluence in the western world. The readers of paperbacks are infinitely more educated than were the readers of chapbooks, but, in many cases, they belong to the same category of people who are not ready to spend too much money on books or who would not buy them if they had to go into proper bookshops. The paperback is a commodity which is often sold in supermarkets, just as the chapbooks were sold with other goods by the chapmen. It is not really meant to be kept in libraries or on bookshelves, but to be carried around, like the railway books of the nineteenth century.

The fact that the paperback is so cheap, and all too often cheap-looking, encourages a different kind of reading and appropriation. It is a product to be consumed here and now and to be thrown away afterwards. The reader is aware that the book he is reading is already very well known and comparatively well accepted by a large public of not necessarily fastidious readers. This induces him to read it through if only to become a member of the reading community.

The development of the paperback and the greater sophistication of the market in general have totally changed the economics of the book trade. Now the printing cost of a book represents only a small share of its selling price. In 1977, Curtis G. Benjamin estimated that the fixed costs, when publishing a book were the following:

| | |
|---|---:|
| Editing, design, proofing | $ 1,900 |
| Plant costs: | |
|    composition | $ 5,600 |
|    artwork for illustrations | $ 800 |
|    photo plate preparation | $ 1,500 |
|    miscellanenous | $ 200 |
| Total fixed costs | $10,000 |

This represents $10 per copy for 1,000 copies, but $0.10 for 100,000 copies. The variable costs per copy (printing, paper, binding) were $1.30 if one printed only 1,000 copies and $0.67 if one printed 100,000 copies. In other words, the total costs for 1,000 are $11.30 per copy as against $0.77 for 100,000 (Benjamin 1977: 48). It is essentially the cheapness of paper, along with the increasing cost of distribution and publicity, which has changed the structure of the publishing economy.

The transformation of the trade has led to a greater and greater concentration within the publishing and distribution industry. In France, thirteen publishers, that is 3.28 per cent of the total, have a turnover of over 100 million francs every year, representing 46.7 per cent of the total market. This concentration is also geographical: 311 publishers have their headquarters in Paris, that is, 78.53 per cent of the total, and 101 of them are in the 6th *arrondissement*. In addition to this, four distributors handle three quarters of all the books sold on the French market (Vessillier-Ressi 1982: 85).

In the United States, the dominant role of New York City is acknowledged by everyone, but the concentration there of the publishing trade is less extreme than in France. Of the 812 publishers listed in the *Directory of Publishers* published by the National Association of College Stores (1988), only 158 are stationed in the state of New York. Yet many of the novels published in the United States are brought out by New York publishers. Most of the American novelists presented in volumes 2 and 6 of the *Dictionary of Literary Biography* (1978 and 1980) which cover the period since the Second World War, have been published by New York publishers almost from the start.

This is true also of the more experimental novels presented in Larry McCaffery's book *Postmodern Fiction* (McCaffery 1986). Of the thirty-two best-known writers listed in the book (Abish, Barth, Barthelme, Brautigan, Carver, Coover, Davenport, DeLillo, Dick, Elkin, Federman, Gaddis, Gass, Hawkes, Hoban, Irving, Katz, Kennedy, Kosinski, LeGuin, McElroy, Matthews, Millhauser, Phillips, Pirsig, Pynchon, Reed, Sorrentino, Sukenick, A. Theroux, Vonnegut, T. Wolfe), sixteen have been exclusively published in New York or distributed by a New York publisher (like the Fiction Collective authors); fourteen brought out their first works with other than New York publishers but were published later in New York when they became recognized. Only one, Guy Davenport, has never been published in New York.

The greater concentration and affluence of the book trade as revealed by Tebbel (1981) and Shatzkin (1982) for the US, by Sutherland (1978) for Britain, and by Vessillier-Ressi (1982) for France, has often left the average writer in dire straits. As the 1980 Columbia survey of 2,241 authors, ordered by the Authors' Guild and presented in *The Wages of Writing* (Kingston and Cole 1986), indicates, the 'representative (i.e. median) author . . . earned a total $4,755 from writing . . . A quarter of the authors earned less than $1,000 from their writing; 10 percent of the authors had a writing income of more than $45,000; 5 percent, more than $80,000' (Kingston and Cole 1986: 5).

As a result, almost half (46 per cent) of the authors held a regular paid position in professional occupations (7). Of these, 36 per cent were university teachers and 11 per cent worked as editors or publishers (49). Writers have long since been welcomed by colleges and universities in the US. William Faulkner taught at the University of Virginia, Vladimir Nabokov continued to teach at Cornell until *Lolita* made him a rich man again. Of the thirty-two postmodernists mentioned earlier, twelve are (or were) full-time professors, like Barth, Coover, Elkin, and Gass; Hawkes retired from Brown University in 1988. Four started as journalists, eight worked as editors, rewriters, or translators; only five were full-time writers from the start. Even among the nineteen who did not start as professors, most have been visiting professors or poets in residence in American universities at some time or other. Richard Brautigan, who is the only one on the list never to have studied in college, was poet in residence at the California Institute of Technology in 1967; Barthelme, though not a professor, taught creative writing in a number of institutions. The only major postmodernist never to have been professionally associated with a university, as far as I know, is William Gaddis.

The postmodernist writer, therefore, often lives on or close to a campus; he usually has the opportunity to give poetry readings and to comment upon his works in the presence of professors and students. He often reads from his works in progress before they are processed and distributed by the publishing industry. In one case, at least, this closeness may have prevented the completion of the work itself. William Gass has read excerpts from his long-promised *Tunnel* on many occasions, and he has published long sections of it in *Salmagundi*; yet there is no evidence that the novel will ever be finished. This is probably a case where academic closeness killed the work in progress.

In 1974, some novelists who were also university teachers undertook to bypass the publishing industry. Jonathan Baumbach, Ronald Sukenick, Clarence Major and a number of others, who were all teaching in universities at the time, founded the 'Fiction Collective', a cooperative of writers which proposed to publish innovative works without having to clear all the hurdles imposed by the market-minded industry. Each writer would finance the printing of his books some way or other; then he would get back not only the usual copyrights but also the publisher's share. The 'Fiction Collective' still had to use the services of a New York publisher, George Braziller, to distribute the books, but at least the writers were the only ones collectively to decide what books would get published. Sukenick and Major claim that most of the writers got their money back and even made some profit. Many of the better-known postmodernists, like Barthelme, Coover, Elkin, Gass, were interested in the enterprise at the start but never published any book through it (Sutherland 1978: 201–2).

The market still reigns supreme, though writers often struggle to gain their independence, either by holding full-time jobs, with universities mainly, or by starting their own publishing firms (other collectives have been created, especially for poetry). In 1981, James Lincoln Collier published an article entitled 'Can Writers *Afford* to Write Books?' in which he claimed that the industry was actually being subsidized by the writers. Here is his conclusion: 'The writer, after all, is the person on whom all else depends; and at present writers are little more than sweated labor. It seems to me simply cruel to ask them to take their belts in one more notch so that nobody else gets hurt' (Collier 1981: 24).

### The law

In the meantime, the law had gradually loosened its grip on the industry. Though the British Copyright Act of 1956 and the American Copyright Act of 1976 further extended the term of protection of authors' rights, they did little to counter the growing power of the profession (Wittenberg 1978: 37; McFarlane 1982: 5). In both countries, the law has virtually stopped censoring books, and especially novels, since the late fifties.

The publication of *Lolita* in 1955 marked an important date in that respect. Nabokov had sent his manuscript to four American publishers who had all turned it down, until his French agent, Madame Ergaz, submitted it to Maurice Girodias of the Olympia Press. Girodias was the son of Jack Kahane, who had founded the Obelisk Press in Paris in 1931, and published Wallace Smith's *Bessie Cotter*, Frank Harris's *My Life and Loves*, and Henry Miller's *Tropic of Cancer*. Girodias had started the Olympia Press and the Ophelia Press in 1953. The Ophelia Press specialized in pornography (it published Count Palmiro Vicarion's *Lust* and Pierre Louÿs's *The She-*

*Devils*); the Olympia Press, on the other hand, published unconventional 'classics', such as Jean Genet's *Our Lady of the Flowers* and *The Thief's Journal*, Beckett's *Watt, Molloy, Malone Dies,* and *The Unnamable*, Queneau's *Zazie dans le Métro*, and Burroughs's *The Naked Lunch* (Thomas 1969: 306–7). When *Watt* came out (under the joint imprint of Collection Merlin-Olympia Press), a vice squad raided the offices of the Olympia Press, in the hope of getting evidence for a pornography suit (Bair 1978: 434). The Olympia Press books were usually green-backed, which made it easy for the US customs to stop them.

After Girodias successfully brought out *Lolita*, Nabokov started to tussle with him in order to regain his rights and prepare an American edition of the novel. He suggested in an article that Girodias wanted to use the *succès de scandale* of *Lolita* to save the reputation of his publishing house and to promote the sales of his other titles (Nabokov 1973: 268–83). There was no trial either in France or elsewhere, and the novel was finally published by Putnam's in the US in 1958 after the *Anchor Review* had published a long section of it in 1957.

In England, the publication of the novel by Weidenfeld and Nicolson almost became a political issue. Nicolson was a Member of Parliament; the Attorney-General, Mannigham-Buller, and Prime Minister Macmillan told Weidenfeld and Nicolson that they risked prosecution if they published the book. When the novel came out, however, the government immediately informed them that there would be no prosecution after all (Field 1986: 309–10).

This skirmish played an important part in the introduction and the passing of the Obscene Publications Act of 1959; the principal innovation of this Act is to be found in Section 4, which provides that a person shall not be convicted 'if it is proved that publication of the article in question is justified as being for the public good on the ground that it is in the interests of science, literature, art or learning, or of other objects of general concern' (Tribe 1973: 85). Despite this innovation, the Penguin edition of *Lady Chatterley's Lover*, published in 1960, was immediately prosecuted under the same Obscene Publications Act. On 2 November 1960, at the end of the trial, the Old Bailey returned a verdict of 'Not

Guilty', thus making 'D. H. Lawrence's last novel available for the first time to the public in the United Kingdom' (Lawrence 1965: 1). The publishers dedicated the book to the twelve jurors who had returned this verdict, just as Flaubert had dedicated his *Madame Bovary* to Marie-Antoine-Jules Senard. The paperback edition of *Fanny Hill* in 1964 did not meet with a similar success: copies were seized from a shop and a magistrate confirmed the seizure, though the book continued to be sold under the counter (Tribe 1973: 94).

Penguin Books were not always as tolerant with sexually explicit fiction, however. When, in 1961, they brought out Faulkner's *The Wild Palms* (1939), they bowdlerized it heavily. Here are two interesting passages (the deleted words are given in square brackets; the italics are, of course, in Faulkner's text):

> – *males and females but without their sex* [instead of: '*without their pricks and cunts*']
> (Faulkner 1939: 52; Faulkner 1961: 39)

> the abrupt [stallion-like] surge . . . the woman's [panting] moans, [and at times a series of pure screams tumbling over one another,] though such was not for them . . . there would come the ruthless impact [stallion crash] with no word spoken, as if they had been drawn violently and savagely to one another out of pure slumber like steel and magnet, [the fierce breathing, the panting and shuddering woman-moans, and Charlotte saying, 'Can't you all do that without pulling the covers loose?']
> (Faulkner 1939: 192–3; Faulkner 1961:136)

The current Penguin retains all these deletions. The publisher practically rewrote Faulkner's text in some cases, removing all the passages which are too sexually explicit. Faulkner partly lost the battle of the book, in this case; he had not saturated his text sufficiently, in terms of information, and failed to impose his authority on his book, so that his publisher easily appropriated it.

In the US, censorship against sexually explicit fiction slowly disappeared after the mid-fifties. The last major restrictive ruling occurred in 1957 when the Supreme Court confirmed the indictment of Samuel Roth, a poet, publisher, and dealer in erotic books, who had sent various materials (books, periodicals, photographs) through the mails. The Court stated that 'obscenity is not within the area of constitutionally protected speech or press' and confirmed the rights of the Postmaster General to confiscate obscene publications (Lewis 1976: 187).

In the following years, the federal courts grew gradually more permissive. When, in 1959, Grove Press brought out the first unexpurgated edition of *Lady Chatterley's Lover*, the Postmaster General invoked the Comstock Act and intercepted the book. The publisher brought a suit to restrain the Postmaster and a New York District Court judge, leaning on the reputation of Lawrence and using the *Ulysses* precedent, cleared the book which, in his opinion, had no intention 'to appeal to prurient interest' (Lewis 1976: 201). The 1961 Grove Press edition of *Tropic of Cancer* was similarly cleared by the Supreme Court in 1964.

The last important case concerned the 1963 Putnam edition of *Fanny Hill*. The Corporation Counsel of New York and five district attorneys immediately tried to suppress the book. There was a two-day trial at the end of which Supreme Court Justice Arthur G. Klein stated that the publication of the book was protected by the First Amendment to the Constitution. In his statement, he explained that four tests had been applied to the book: the 'social value' test, the 'prurient interest' test, the 'patently offensive' test, and the 'hard core pornography' test, and that it passed them all with success. The court also accepted Untermeyer's argument that the novel contained at least three attributes of a good novel: '(1) treatment of the subject matter with grace and beauty; (2) skillful and eloquent charm of writing; and (3) characters coming to life' (Quennell 1963: xxv). The Supreme Court finally cleared the book in 1966.

After this last victory, Charles Rembar, the lawyer who had defended most of these books in the courts, wrote with confidence:

> So far as writing is concerned, I have said there is no longer any law of obscenity. I would go farther and add, so far as writing is concerned, that not only in our law but in our culture, obscenity will soon be gone.
>
> (Rembar 1968: 493)

His claim that institutional censorship had come to an end was too optimistic. All these US courts' decisions had created some unrest amont the 'silent majority'. At the instigation of Congress, President Johnson finally appointed a Federal Commission on Obscenity and Pornography which, in 1970, issued its report. It recommended that 'federal, state and local legislation should not seek to interfere with the rights of adults who wish to do so to read, obtain, or view explicit sexual material' (Lewis 1976: 226).

Johnson was then replaced by Nixon, who objected strongly to the permissive attitude of the courts in the following terms:

> So long as I am in the White House there will be no relaxation of the national effort to control and eliminate smut from our national life... Pornography is to freedom of expression what anarchy is to liberty.
>
> (Tribe 1973: 200)

The Supreme Court, whose composition had partly been changed by his appointees, brought in a decision in 1973 which reflected the new mood. This ruling, which dealt with five cases, one of them concerning a fictional paperback, *Suite 69*, supported the view that 'censorship of hard-core pornography was constitutional when obscenity statutes were properly specific', and it suggested how the states could formulate legislation that would pass the test of constitutionality (Lewis 1976: 226). This decision meant that the federal courts were divesting themselves of their censoring power and passing it on to the state courts.

Since then, school authorities have banned novels such as *The Catcher in the Rye*, *God's Little Acre*, and *The Wild Palms* from school curricula, but no court has imposed an outright ban on so-called obscene novels. This does not mean that censorship has totally disappeared, of course. In 1966, on the same day as it cleared *Fanny Hill*, the Supreme Court upheld the conviction of Edward Mishkin for publishing sado-masochistic material, and Ralph Ginzburg for publishing a pornographic magazine, *Eros* (Lewis 1976: 202). The law has always censored the more popular media, and fiction has now been supplanted by magazines or television in that respect.

This evolution, for which novelists have pleaded for more than two centuries, has perhaps been a mixed blessing. The novel is now deprived of the chief obstacle which, paradoxically, encouraged the development of many of its most elaborate strategies. As we will see in this chapter, this single event largely helps to account for some of the most important characteristics of the postmodernist novel as well as for the myth of the death of the novel.

This evolution gave a free hand not only to authors who could now deal with almost any subject they liked, but to the industry, which did not have to bargain with the law any more. The diagram we proposed in our first chapter must now be revised:

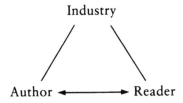

The law, which had kept the industry under its control since the seventeenth century, has finally surrendered its power over the book trade. Now, the industry is in a position to impose its tastes and choices without any other consideration than the market which, through appropriate means, can be made to buy the product.

## VOICELESS OPENINGS

The fact that author and reader brush shoulders on campuses, together with the greater awareness of the psychological phenomena involved in writing and reading novels, has induced postmodernist fiction-writers to resort to more sophisticated devices to break the line of communication with their audience. The modernist writers did insist on absenting themselves from their works, as the debate about telling and showing testified, but, on the whole, they did so by simulating real discourses or by creating discourse-like styles. As the following study of a few typical openings, all written in the present tense, will show, the postmodernists have struggled to create non-discursive and intensely writerly styles which echo no 'natural' discourses. We cannot, this time, separate first- from third-person narratives, a fact which already suggests that we are dealing with non-discourses.

The opening of Robbe-Grillet's *La Jalousie* reads at first like a straightforward description:

> Now the shadow of the column – the column which supports the southwest corner of the roof – divides the corresponding corner of the veranda into two equal parts. This veranda is a wide, covered gallery surrounding the house on three sides.
> (Robbe-Grillet 1965a: 39)

There is here the same attempt to erase the predicative process as in *Bleak House*. But there are two deictics which betray the presence of an observer: the adverb 'now' and the demonstrative adjective 'this'. Here, too, the reader is being shown an object of fascination, the house, which is metonymically related to the woman who is soon going to be introduced. The narrative act seems to be simultaneous with the narrated events, which was not the case in the so-called stream of consciousness. It is as if the jealous husband's thoughts were written even before they materialize. This narrative 'now' has little to do with Virginia Woolf's 'now' which co-occurred with a past tense and was a marker of the oral discourse; it is more writerly and points to the moment and to the process of writing rather than to the moment and process of speaking or thinking of one of the characters.

The second paragraph also begins with a 'now', and contains a clearer reference to the jealous husband:

> Now, A . . . has come into the bedroom by the inside door opening onto the central passage. She does not look at the wide open window through which – from the door – she would see this corner of the terrace. Now she has turned back toward the door to close it behind her. She still has on the light-colored, close-fitting dress with the high collar that she was wearing at lunch when Christiane reminded her again that loose-fitting clothes make the heat easier to bear. But A . . . merely smiled.
> (39)

This is a sample of the filmic style made popular by Robbe-Grillet: the reader is being turned into a voyeur until he realizes that there is somebody else present who is not only watching the scene with him but projecting it for his benefit. That other person designates himself through the deictic 'this' in 'this corner of the terrace'. The reader now begins to understand that the chief story-line in this book concerns the husband's re-presentation or projection of the events, rather than the telling of the events themselves. This representation is turned into a kind of performance through the use of 'objective correlatives' like the dress, which is 'close-fitting' and elicits Christiane's comment. Since Christiane is the wife of the man who is having an affair with A – the narrator's wife – the reader understands that this comment, though probably meant as a candid piece of advice, is in fact an index pointing towards A's promiscuousness.

But who is pointing at what, and when? The husband never designates himself as the narrator: he never says 'I'. Apparently, Christiane is not aware that the dress could be an index of her friend's promiscuousness, though, unconsciously perhaps, she senses that it may be the case since she keeps telling A that she should dress differently. Perhaps A's husband had not yet understood what the close-fitting dress might suggest about his wife until Christiane unwittingly drew his attention to it. One cannot tell what the right interpretation is: we are confronted with a text which never interprets things but merely shows and describes them, a voiceless and indexical text, as it were, which presents the scenes before our eyes and lets us interpret them.

Robbe-Grillet did not quite understand what he was doing in such descriptions. In *For a New Novel* he wrote: 'The entire interest of the descriptive pages – that is, man's place in these pages – is therefore no longer in the thing described, but in the very movement of the description' (Robbe-Grillet 1965b: 148). His indexical descriptions have little in common with Flaubert's focused descriptions, such as the portrait of Emma Rouault through the eyes of Charles; since they are repeated, and slightly altered each time, the reader has no way of either projecting a comprehensive view of the thing described, or identifying with the reflector, that is, the jealous husband.

There is, of course, nothing the novelist can do to prevent

the reader from semanticizing the text and turning it into a proper discourse, as Barthes explains in reference to Robbe-Grillet:

> However, these empty forms irresistibly beg for a content, and one can see increasingly in the criticism, in the very work of the author, a yearning for feelings, a rebirth of archetypes, fragments of symbols, in brief all the elements that belong to the reign of the adjective slip back into the superb 'being-there' of things.
>
> (Barthes 1964: 205; my translation)

The novel is a narrative genre which is both time-bound and language-bound. Its sheer size makes it impossible for us to 'picture' it in one sweeping glance; we must read it in time. We cannot allow the sequences to remain floating; we must try to organize them in order to make sense of the whole. For instance, we cannot help trying to decide whether all the passages about the crushing of the centipede refer to one and the same scene, or whether Frank and A went to town only once. The reader must take his chances, knowing all the time that he will never reach a satisfactory interpretation.

In *La Modification* (*A Change of Heart*), Michel Butor experimented with another kind of non-discourse which is also very disturbing. The protagonist apparently belongs to our own world: he has a name, Léon Delmont; he is assigned a hereness in geographical space, from Paris to Rome, and a nowness in historical time, from 1938 until 15 November, 1955. Yet he does not belong to our universe of discourse because he is designated and addressed throughout the novel as '*vous*' by no identifiable narrator. Here is the opening:

> You have put your left foot on the copper groove, and, with your right shoulder you are vainly trying to shove the sliding panel a little further.
>
> You slip through the narrow opening, brushing against its edges, then, your suitcase covered with dark and granulous leather the colour of a thick bottle, your comparatively small suitcase of a man who is used to long journeys, you pull it up by its sticky handle, with your fingers chafing, despite its light weight, from having carried it this far, you lift it and you feel your muscles and your sinews tensing up

not only in your phalanxes, in your palm, your wrist and your arm, but also in your shoulder, in the upper part of your back and in your vertebrae from the neck all the way down to your loins.

(Butor 1971: 9; my translation)

In the first paragraph, the narrator seems to be an observer, like the jealous husband in Robbe-Grillet's novel, who addresses – inwardly perhaps – the protagonist. But this interpretation does not hold in the second paragraph, which evokes the protagonist's sensations from inside.

The combination of *vous* (you) with the present tense reads like a transformation of the 'now + preterite' formula favoured by the modernists. It is a writerly form which has no equivalent in real life, in real discourses. Yet it institutes an authority, not the godlike Other whose presence could acutely be felt in *L'Immoraliste*, but a diffuse Other, constituted by the protagonist and the text itself, who/which guarantees the reality of the character and the significance of the text. Through this *vous*, Delmont does not only apostrophize himself as a protagonist, he also tests his behaviour according to the law of the Other.

Our incapacity to think up a plausible subject for this discourse creates the fiction effect and designates the text as a literary construct. Somehow, we have the feeling of being summoned as the 'I-origin' of this *vous*, to borrow Hambürger's terminology, as if we were instructed to make this narrative discourse our own. Yet we know all the time that it is nobody's discourse. The line of communication between the author and us has been broken by this *vous*. We have no choice but to settle in the poetic present of the text, though the latter is constantly luring us away from that here-and-now – back to the pre-war honeymoon trip to Rome with Henriette, back to that other trip to Rome, two years ago, when he met Cécile, and to other meetings with her until a week ago; forward to his return from Rome the following Monday. The train is like Zeno's arrow, both moving and motionless. The only real 'now' of the book is not that of the journey but that of a style, of a writing characterized by the grammatical formula, '*vous* + present'. Through this unprecedented formula, Butor managed to make writing time, story time, and reading time overlap completely, and to foreground the writing-here-for-me-on-the-page, what the Russian Formalists called 'literarity', and which is the opposite of a discourse.

Whereas in *La Jalousie* and *La Modification*, one can still sense the author's compulsion to silence the Other and to burden the reader with a large share of the interpretative work, or of the guilt, in Beckett's *Comment c'est* and in Barthelme's *Snow White* there is no trace of such a compulsion, as if neither author really cared to know how their texts were going to be read.

In his first English novels, from *More Pricks than Kicks* to *Watt*, Beckett wrote in the past tense and in the third person. But as soon as he started to write in French, he turned to the present tense (with many passages in the past tense, of course, as in *Molloy*) and to the first person, the syntax becoming looser and looser in *L'Innommable* until it completely collapses in *Comment c'est*. This novel has no real plot, so that one cannot easily summarize it. One can only describe it. It has three parts, the first one evoking mostly, though not only, the protagonist's difficult progress, fifteen metres at most at a time, through the mud, like a larva, in search of a brother; the second introducing at last the brother, Pim, whom the protagonist bullies and robs of his bag and even of his memories; and the third simulating rather than describing the protagonist waiting for the executioner who will torture him as he himself tortured Pim.

Like Robbe-Grillet, Beckett telescopes story and discourse from the start: 'comment c'était je cite avant Pim avec Pim après Pim comment c'est trois parties je le dis comme je l'entends' ('how it was I quote before Pim with Pim after Pim how it is three parts I say it as I understand it, Beckett 1961: 9; my translation). There is not a single punctuation mark here or elsewhere in the novel to guide our reading; one stumbles from word to word, one stops, one goes back a few words and starts again in order to isolate identifiable sentences. The 'protagonist' in the second verse (these linguistic aggregates do not really deserve to be called paragraphs) begs the voice to narrate him, to support the words he is putting together, and to give them a coherence. Yet the words remain unvoiced, unintoned, and we must read them slowly, spacing them out evenly more or less, in the hope that they will fall back in place as we read on.

However, no plausible syntax materializes. In the first verse, as in most of the other verses in the novel, we can provide a plausible punctuation, but the resulting text does not make much sense all the same: 'Comment c'était avant Pim avec Pim après Pim. Comment c'est. Cela fait trois parties. Je le dis comme je l'entends'. The phrase 'comment c'est' ('how it is'), which is reminiscent of the sentence Walter Cronkite used to utter at the end of his news bulletin, 'And that's the way it is', seems to be a present transformation of 'comment c'était' ('how it was') at the beginning which itself seemed to designate a pre-textual story. But, in this case, there is no pre-textual story, no succession of events but a body of words, either written ('je cite', 'I quote') or spoken ('comme je l'entends', 'as I hear it'), we don't know which. The story is nothing but a verbal construct here-now, and the 'I' remains referentless, designating a succession of roles: a speaker, a writer, a character, and a narrator, we suppose.

In *La Jalousie* and *La Modification*, there was at least a story, however confused; not here. We are confronted with a succession of unlikely scenes and details obliquely referred to but never fully described. The predicative process is never completed. The reader must do more than his normal share of the rewriting of the text; the semantic and pragmatic links are not easily recoverable, and the world described or alluded to is manifestly different from our own. *Comment c'est* reads like the interior monologue of a creature even more alien to us than Kafka's beetle-hero. How can we be sure that his psychology is the same as ours, that in his world the language functions the way it does in our own? This is not an indexical text, therefore, since it does not even point towards a story or world out there; it is more like a text kit, which lends itself to endless combinations for which the author will not be held responsible. It is a fragmented body of words which gets born at the beginning and which dies ('crève', 'dies') at the end; a body which is intensely real to the reader because it is clearly beyond the pale of consensual reality.

*Comment c'est* still remains too tortured and demented for the Other not to be exerting his power somehow, somewhere, as it did in the disrupted texts produced by the Surrealists.

Barthelme's *Snow White*, though more clearly surrealistic, bears considerably less the imprint of a racking Other. It is based on a pre-textual story which is itself a text, the Grimms' 'Snow White', but that pre-text is never felt as the Other's time-honoured utterance, as was Homer's text in Joyce's *Ulysses*.

Here is the opening of the novel:

> She is a tall dark beauty containing a great many beauty spots: one above the breast, one above the belly, one above the knee, one above the ankle, one above the buttock, one on the back of the neck. All of these are on the left side, more or less in a row, as you go up and down:
> •
> •
> •
> •
> •
> •
> The hair is black as ebony, the skin white as snow.
>
> (Barthelme 1972: 3)

This passage reads at first like an indexical portrait *à la* Robbe-Grillet. Yet the dots, representing the 'beauty spots', totally erase the referent and even the pre-textual story (quoted in the last line), turning Snow White into a snow-white page on which the dwarfs are projecting their fantasies.

In the next sequence, which introduces all the dwarfs, a narratorial 'we' appears for the first time:

> Bill is tired of Snow White now. But he cannot tell her. No, that would not be the way. Bill can't bear to be touched. That is new too. To have anyone touch him is unbearable. Not just Snow White but also Kevin, Edward, Hubert, Henry, Clem or Dan. That is a peculiar aspect of Bill, the leader. We speculate that he doesn't want to be involved in human situations any more. A withdrawal.
>
> (4)

This is not a new version of Flaubert's *'nous'* at the beginning of Madame Bovary, which designated the narrator as one of the pupils. This 'we', which reappears throughout the novel, never points to any identifiable 'I'; the narrator is not an individual speaker or writer, but a collective entity, the six dwarfs (Bill is apparently excluded; he will be executed at the end). This impossible situation marks this style as a non-discourse.

Barth experimented with this formula in *The Tidewater Tales*, which is narrated concurrently by both husband and wife: 'That won't be easy from our coupled point of view–P's promptings, K's cadenzas–but she'll draw a great breath; we'll try. Here's the woman of us, in her man's opinion' (Barth 1987: 29). There are some awkward moments when Peter and Katherine are not together, but, on the whole, the formula works, lending to the couple a kind of enunciative unity and to the text a discursive coherence.

There is no such discursive coherence in *Snow White*. The narratorial 'we' appears arbitrarily, even when all the dwarfs are not present; this does not create any particular awkwardness because the text is mistreated in so many other ways. For instance, one finds 'moth-eaten' passages like the following:

> Those men     hulking     hulk in closets and outside gestures eventuating against a white screen difficulties intelligence     I only wanted one plain hero of incredible size and soft, flexible manners     parts     thought dissembling     limb     add up the thumbprints on my shoulders.
> (Barthelme 1972: 31)

Part of the text is missing; the reader is induced to do his share of the writing. Elsewhere the text is merely a stack of titles or phrases printed in block letters:

**THE HORSEWIFE IN HISTORY**
**FAMOUS HORSEWIVES**
**THE HORSEWIFE: A SPIRITUAL PORTRAIT**
**THE HORSEWIFE: A CRITICAL STUDY**
**FIRST MOP, 4000 BC**
**VIEWS OF ST. AUGUSTINE**

(61)

Are these book titles, simple jottings, or what? There is no way to find out, the exact status of these expressions being undecidable (Couturier and Durand 1983: 66–9).

In *Snow White*, the writing is anchored to no reliable totality, be it an author, a discourse, or a consistent world. This novel reads like an allegory about the oft-announced death of the novel. There is no Other (be it the language or a literary convention) exerting its law, so that the reader is only concerned about his relationship with the elusive author and about his own mental sanity (or unity). In a metafictional novel like this, the content of the act of communication, which was still very important until Joyce and Woolf, is supplanted by the problem of the relationship between author and reader. The reification of the text and of the book encouraged by the development of printing is almost complete.

## THE BLACK BOX

The model set by Beckett and Barthelme has been followed by many writers, such as Sukenick, Federman, and McElroy, who have all experimented with elaborate textual games, as if they wanted to deprive the language of that phonocentricity denounced by Derrida in *De la grammatologie*, and to lend it a kind of spatiality. This fetishization of the text has often been counterproductive, however. A body of printed words will never be like a set of lines or colours on a canvas: the self always adheres to the words, somehow. The only compelling way for an author to beat the self is to saturate the reader and lure him into the black box of the book. This is what Nabokov and Pynchon have done by promoting the poeticity of their texts and composing complex intratextual games.

In Nabokov's *Pale Fire*, which contains four different texts (Kinbote's 'Foreword', Shade's poem 'Pale Fire', Kinbote's 'Commentary' on the poem, and his 'Index'), Kinbote invites the reader, right from the start, to break the book apart or buy another copy of it: 'I find it wise in such cases as this to eliminate the bother of back-and-forth leafings by either cutting out and clipping together the pages with the text of the thing, or, even more simply, purchasing two copies of the same work' (Nabokov 1962: 28). Here again, one senses, on the part of the author, a kind of sadistic desire to destroy the book as it was manufactured by the industry.

A strange conflict develops between the two writers, Kinbote the commentator and Shade the poet, and between their respective texts. Kinbote rashly claims towards the end of his foreword that without his notes 'Shade's text simply has no human reality at all'; then he flippantly concludes: 'for better or worse, it is the commentator who has the last word' (28–9).

Yet Kinbote gradually gets caught in the black box of the book, and with him the reader. His commentary on Shade's autobiographical poem begins with an annotation about the heraldic creatures of his own country, Zembla, and about the departure from there of the terrorist who, Kinbote intends to prove, has killed the poet 'accidentally'. In the second note concerning 'that crystal land' in line 12 of the poem, Kinbote quotes a 'half-obliterated draft' which he claims to have found in the poet's manuscript:

Ah, I must not forget to say something
That my friend told me of a certain king.
(74)

At the time when Shade was composing his poem, Kinbote, who was then his next-door neighbour, was telling him the story of the King of Zembla who had been removed from the throne by the revolutionaries and imprisoned, before escaping to western Europe and North America. Kinbote was convinced that the poet was turning his narrative into a poem; when he started to read the manuscript, he was terribly disappointed to find out that it never openly referred to his story, except perhaps in variants like this. Availing himself of such tenuous details, however, he starts deciphering the poem as if it obliquely reflected the story of the King. This allows him to smuggle his own story into his commentary apropos some more or less plausible comments concerning the poet and his daily life.

His commentary gradually turns into a novel. It is many times longer than Shade's poem (a clear case of self-parody: Nabokov was then writing endless annotations on *Eugene Onegin*) which appears now more and more as a pre-text for Kinbote. In the course of his commentary, however, the erudite scholar becomes highly confused and loses his confidence.

Finally, he confesses that he has not always been as honest with us as he originally claimed to be:

> I wish to say something about an earlier note (to line 12). Conscience and scholarship have debated the question, and I now think that the two lines given in that note are distorted and tainted by wistful thinking. It is the *only* time in the course of the writing of these difficult comments, that I have tarried, in my distress and disappointment, on the brink of falsification. I must ask the reader to ignore those two lines (which, I am afraid, do not even scan properly). I could strike them out before publication but that would mean reworking the entire note, or at least a considerable part of it, and I have no time for such stupidities.
>
> (227-8)

Kinbote is needlessly exposing himself to charges of unscholarly practice near the end of his commentary. Why does he have to ridicule himself before his readers and his jealous colleagues? He alleges mental disorders to allay our scholarly wrath but he refuses to strike out the contrived lines. It is likely that most of the trusting readers did not bother to check the note to line 12, considering no doubt that such a confession completely exonerates Kinbote and confirms his reliability. In fact, Kinbote behaves like a judge who advises the members of the jury to disregard an uncalled-for testimony, knowing all the time that they will not be able to do so.

With this note, it becomes clear that Kinbote is not only presenting his friend's poem but borrowing it to smuggle his own story into a publishable book. He is not a conscientious scholar but a madman and a megalomaniac who wants to prove, as it appears more and more clearly towards the end, that he is that same King of Zembla whose story he has been telling in so many details.

This accounts for his own version of Shade's death. The poet's colleagues at the university had claimed that the man who had shot Shade on the doorstep of Kinbote's house was a lunatic, Jack Grey, who had been sent to prison by Kinbote's landlord, Judge Goldsworth, and had escaped to take his revenge. He killed Shade accidentally because the latter looked like the Judge. Kinbote's version is naturally different: he explains that the killer is one Jakob Gradus (a name which looks strangely like that of Jack Grey), a terrorist sent by the new government of Zembla to execute the fugitive King, and who 'accidentally' killed Shade because he was an awful bungler. In the index, which constitutes the fourth text in the novel, Jack Grey is not mentioned of course, but Jakob Gradus (elsewhere referred to as 'Sudarg de Bokay'!) is. This index, which again resembles that of Nabokov at the end of his annotated *Eugene Onegin*, refers only to the Zemblan version of the novel (Couturier 1979: 100–12).

This extraordinary novel taxes the reader's intelligence and sanity. The intratextual games devised by Richardson, Choderlos de Laclos, and their followers are here totally eclipsed. Two narrators, using two different sets of conventions, are addressing us in the first person. Their respective stories mirror each other: most of the important anecdotes and images mentioned in the poem reappear, somewhat displaced and metaphorized, in the commentary. Eventually, we cannot help asking ourselves which of the two texts is the original, and which is the metatext. In many respects, the story of the King of Zembla as told by Kinbote is more interesting, and better written, than the story of Shade's life as mirrored in the poem. The poet obviously took it for granted that he was a better man than his pathetic neighbour who was constantly spying on him from an upstairs window while he was composing his poem. Kinbote gives evidence that he may be a better writer than the poet, despite his mental confusion.

In this novel, the chief question always is: Which is to be master? The aesthetic judgement of the reader is constantly being tested: since neither Shade nor Kinbote can be considered reliable, being both judges and judged, we must conscientiously work on the text, appropriate it, and construct our own story. In other words, we are compelled, no matter how scrupulous we are, to behave like Kinbote and run away with the text of the novel, purloining it just as the Minister D. purloined the Queen's letter in Poe's famous story (Couturier 1976: 55–69).

In the meantime, Nabokov has completely absconded from his novel: he has burdened us with such an impossible task that he can stand back and watch us getting more and more entangled in the verbal mesh of the text. The intratextual game works as a very elaborate snare from which the reader cannot hope to extricate himself. If he did, say by reconstructing a satisfactory narrative, he would immediately know that he had been manipulated by the text, by Nabokov, and become a helpless character in the fiction which he wanted to objectify. He is therefore caught in a double bind: if he suceeds, he automatically knows that he has failed, having become one of the naïve subjects that Nabokov wanted to catch with his story. And yet, he must try to make the two writers and the four texts interact, otherwise he can never hope to break out of the black box of the book. In the process, he probably interacts in some way or another with the inaccessible author who hides in this magic hall of mirrors, but he never knows exactly when or how well. Sometimes, he has the illusion of catching a glimpse of the magician, but he refrains from apostrophizing him for fear that it might be yet another of his impersonators.

*Pale Fire* constitutes perhaps the final stage in the history of the intratextual novel which started with *Don Quixote* or the epistolary novels of Richardson. The diagram we drew to represent the communication process in *Pamela* cannot be used here, for the reader is not outside the black box and on the same footing as the editor/commentator; he is inside it, doing his best to arbitrate between the two writers:

Shade ◄──────► Reader ◄──────► Kinbote

The line of communication between the author and the reader, which Richardson had started to sever through his epistolary devices, is here definitively cut: the text, though it looks as discursive as Pamela's letters, is not a proper discourse; it is a restive object which strains our intelligence, our imagination, and even our sanity. There is nobody to tell us whether we have played the game correctly.

John Shade tells an anecdote which makes the reader terribly restless: he explains that during one of his heart attacks he caught a glimpse of a white fountain, and that immediately after that he read an article reporting that an old lady had seen the same white fountain in similar circumstances. To compare notes with the old lady, he decides to call on her with the journalist who reported the event, but somehow he never manages to raise the subject during his visit; on the way back, the journalist 'accidentally' mentions that there was a misprint in the article, that a fumbling compositor had printed 'fountain' instead of 'mountain'. Shade lamely comments: 'Life Everlasting – based on misprint!' (Nabokov 1962: 62). The reader of this novel, who is trying to find out not only whether there is a world beyond, but whether there is an author behind this book, has every reason to think that if he does find either one or the other, he may be mistaken and may have grossly misread the text.

In *The Crying of Lot 49* (1966), Thomas Pynchon – a former student of Nabokov at Cornell – achieved another kind of *tour de force*: he managed to catch his reader in the black box of the book without multiplying the narrators and the texts. This novel appeared only four years after the publication of McLuhan's *The Gutenberg Galaxy* (1962), a book which proclaimed the impending, but fortunately still remote, demise of scriptural and typographical communication. Pynchon seems to react against McLuhan's hasty prophesy, and he insists on the marvellous ambiguity of textual communication against the other types of communication. He jettisons his protagonist, Œdipa, into a monumental text which entraps her and the reader, and breeds a tragic paranoia in both.

In *The Crying of Lot 49*, reality insidiously becomes a text, namely the novel we are reading. The process begins with Inverarity's will which named Œdipa executrix of her former lover in a codicil. The codicil does not properly duplicate the will, but it adds a second executor, since Metzger has been named chief executor. Inverarity has entrusted her and Metzger with the difficult job of 'sorting . . . out' his property, of checking that its referent, the wealth he has collected and which is to be distributed, conforms with the description given in the will (Pynchon 1974: 5).

Œdipa, who expects the items listed in the will to correspond exactly with the reality of the estate, gets terribly confused when she finds out that the text and the referent do not match each other, either because Inverarity deliberately fooled her, or because something has 'slipped through' in spite of Inverarity (136).

The chief item on the list is a city, San Narciso, whose name apparently points to the fact that Inverarity founded the city and developed it in his own image. San Narciso is not a 'real' city born of people's need to find shelter, warmth, happiness together, but a 'grouping of concepts', as Œdipa finds out when she arrives: 'Like many named places in California it was less an identifiable city than a grouping of concepts – census tracts, special purpose bond-issue districts, shopping nuclei, all overlaid with access roads to its own freeway' (15). The city is not real, it is textual: everything has meticulously been planned and projected in advance. It existed on paper before it found its way on to an actual tract of land and on a map of California.

Spontaneously, Œdipa senses that there is something wrong with this city which is too meticulously ordered:

> and she thought of the time she'd opened a transistor radio to replace a battery and seen her first printed circuit. The ordered swirl of houses and streets, from this high angle, sprung at her now with the same unexpected, astonishing clarity as the circuit card had. Though she knew even less about radio than about Southern Californians, there were to both outward patterns a hieroglyphic sense of concealed meaning, of an intent to communicate.
>
> (15–16)

As this passage reveals, Gutenberg's vocabulary has contaminated the technological world: one speaks of 'printed' circuits, of 'circuit card'. Œdipa vaguely senses the pervading presence of a text behind or underneath the city, a text authored by her narcissistic lover and showing as hieroglyphics in the streets and houses.

The new housing development, called Fangoso Lagoons, is a model text, a miniature of San Narciso as it were:

> It was to be laced by canals with private landings for powerboats, a floating social hall in the middle of an artificial lake, at the bottom of which lay restored galleons, imported from the Bahamas; Atlantean fragments of columns and friezes from the Canaries; real human skeletons from Italy; giant clamshells from Indonesia – all for the entertainment of Scuba enthusiasts.
>
> (21)

The model for this project is first Little Venice in Los Angeles, and eventually Venice, Italy. Everything is borrowed from another place, the Bahamas, the Canaries, Italy, Indonesia, etc. Each item is meant to contribute to the exoticism of the place. Fangoso Lagoons is an intertextual place, each item pointing towards an idealized representation of another country, towards another text. Like Disneyland, Enchanted Village, or Marine World in Los Angeles, it is not a real place inhabited by real people but, to paraphrase Baudrillard, an imaginary power station which generates 'de l'imaginaire' and whose chief function is to bolster the shaky reality of the world outside (Baudrillard 1981: 26).

It is the sad story of the skeletons salvaged from Lago di Pieta which triggers the proliferation of texts in the novel. The Paranoids, who have been listening to Manny di Presso's story about how Inverarity got the bones, mention that a similar slaughter is evoked in a Jacobean play, *The Courier's Tragedy*: 'Bones of lost battalion in lake, fished up, turned into charcoal – ' (46). Œdipa starts seeing patterns everywhere; she takes the hint and goes to see the play with Metzger. The theatre is 'framed' between two firms involved in information gathering and broadcasting, 'a traffic analysis firm and a wildcat transistor outfit' (47). We gather that all three institutions fulfil complementary tasks in that information-crazy society.

The play itself is crammed with references to Inverarity's California: Faggio sounds like Fangoso; Saint Narcissus, Bishop of Jerusalem, is the namesake of Inverarity's city; and there is the tale of the lost Guard, 'everyone massacred by Angelo and thrown in the lake. Later on their bones were fished up again and made into charcoal, and the charcoal into ink' (54). This ink will be used by Angelo in his subsequent communications with Faggio. With this anecdote, Pynchon makes palpable the link between death and writing: the writers draw their ink from their mortality.

It is immediately after this incident that Trystero (or Tristero) is mentioned for the first time in the story proper. Pynchon obviously exploits the time-honoured technique of *mise en abyme* used by Shakespeare in *Hamlet*'s play-within-the-play. *The Courier's Tragedy* is to this novel what 'The Mousetrap' is to Shakespeare's tragedy: it reflects the main plot and helps quicken its pace.

It also marks the true beginning of Œdipa's investigation. After the performance, she goes to speak to Randolph

## The postmodernist novel 223

Driblette, the director and actor, and asks him if she can have a look at the script and the original text from which the copies were made. Driblette says the original, a paperback he bought at Zapf's Used Books 'over by the freeway', has been stolen; but there is another copy at the bookstore. He is somewhat unnerved, however, by this interrogation, and he asks: 'Why... is everybody so interested in texts?' (58). He does not care about texts, only about the life that he can inflate them with through his own performance. His system is aesthetically correct: he is not a text fetishist, as Œdipa is; he believes that a text is merely an object through which some form of symbolic exchange between author and reader, actor and audience, can develop.

Œdipa is only interested in what Barthes called 'l'œuvre' (the work), the typographical materiality of the book, since she only wants to trace the reference to Trystero. Later, she visits Zapf's Used Books to buy the paperback; then she goes all the way to San Francisco to get the hardcover edition right from the publisher. She had good reasons to doubt the authenticity of the reference since Trystero is not mentioned in the hardcover. In the meantime, however, her quest has developed into all-out paranoia.

Her next stop is at Professor Bortz's place. Bortz, the editor of the book, now lives in San Narciso; he briefly alludes to another edition of the play, a pornographic version kept in, of all places, the Vatican library. There are, therefore, five different versions of the same play: Driblette's theatrical performance; the script he used; the paperback copy; the hardcover copy examined by Œdipa in San Francisco; and the pornographic version mentioned by Bortz.

Bortz also shows Œdipa a book about one Dr Diocletian Blobb in which the massacre at the Lake of Piety is described, and he tells her about the history of Trystero and its age-old struggle against Thurn and Taxis (a real company which created the first postal system in Europe) present throughout the novel in the graffiti and the phoney stamps. Œdipa senses that he is making things up as he goes, and she begins to realize that history is nothing but a text, after all. She will never know the truth about Trystero but will pursue her demented investigation, discovering new texts referring directly or obliquely to it or him. The Real Text becomes ever more elusive and the reality which started the process of textual inflation, death, the death of Inverarity and that of the GIs, fades into oblivion, being supplanted by paranoia, itself a prefiguration of Œdipa's own death.

When she finds the WASTE symbol (the muted horn) for the first time in the watermark of one of Inverarity's stamps she is scared by the discovery of this shadow world which shows in filigree through her own world, by the emergence of this other text described or pointed at in the underground letters travelling through WASTE. She never gets a chance to read those letters, not even the one handed to her by the dying sailor, but begins to picture that other world thanks to her growing familiarity with the postal system which carries those letters. With the help of Genghis Cohen, in chapter 6, she learns to read some of the signs, and particularly the word WASTE which is supposed to stand for 'WE AWAIT SILENT TRISTERO'S EMPIRE'. This annotation does not allay her fears in the least. It only makes her more acutely text-conscious.

Whenever she thinks she is getting closer to the Real Text, it immediately eludes her, as if the perverse puppeteer, Tristero (Tristram?) or Inverarity, were teasing her to distraction. Her last hope is that the book bidder who wants to buy the 'Lot 49' of the estate – it contains the collections of phoney stamps – could be a representative of Tristero and might want to 'keep evidence that Tristero exists out of unauthorized hands' (134). Having failed to make sense of the proliferating text, she now hopes to make contact with the keeper of the word through the book bidder! In the last scene, she reverently waits for the revelation, in the company of the other bidders, like the Apostles at the Pentecost waiting for the descent of the Holy Spirit (Couturier 1987).

This extraordinary little novel is composed of a multiplicity of overlapping and conflicting texts which are like the relics left by the dead; it proclaims the advent of ultimate death and the collapse of reality as a lofty edifice of stable representations. Œdipa belongs to the post-Saussurian and the post-Freudian world: her experience of reality has been marred by the daily application of grids, books, intellectual formulae. She is assailed by numberless representations which, far from allowing her access to the real, make her utterly obsessed with its inaccessibility.

Our paranoia similarly has its roots in the proliferation of texts and doubles. It assumes a tragic dimension with the discovery, at the end, that there is no denouement, no closure. The text is stubbornly opaque and does not lend itself to the convenient cleavage between discourse and story (*énonciation* and *énoncé*) which allowed the structuralists to develop their elaborate theories. It baffles the reader and leads him to emulate Œdipa's quest: he tries to make contact with the author, just as Œdipa was trying to make contact with Inverarity. The situation can be represented in the following way:

Reader ⟶ [Œdipa ⟶ (Inverarity/Tristero)] ⟶ // ⟶ Author

The reader must first crack the Œdipa secret, that is to say, witness how she herself cracks the Inverarity/Tristero secret, before he can begin to make contact with the author. Since the secret cannot be cracked, partly because of the absence of closure, the reader will never communicate directly with the author but only indirectly with reflections of him, like inaccessible Inverarity.

## CONCLUSION: TEXTUAL COMMUNICATION

Reading writerly novels like those we have studied in this chapter is a highly narcissistic enterprise. In his solitary reading, the reader deciphers the signs as conscientiously as he can, constantly investing them with his unconscious which tends to contaminate everything it touches. His author is not the real author but a figment of his imagination; it is the persona he recreates through his reading and which is supposed to have written the text as he understands it. Since that persona gradually emerges in his imagination in the course of his reading and analysis of the novel, it inevitably bears many of his own features. That specular or ideal author is the better, the artistic part of himself which has come to life during his exploration of that particular novel.

The communication diagram, from the reader's angle, is therefore the following:

Real reader ⟶ [TEXT] ⟶ Ideal author

The text is a medium, like the telephone used so frequently in *The Crying of Lot 49*, through which the real reader tries to make contact with the ideal author. Somehow, the real reader can see in this ideal author, born of his interpretation of the text and of his conversion of the medium into a message, features which do not belong to himself but which must reflect the desire, the unconscious, of the real author who wrote the book and addressed it to the reader from a distant past. The reader is constantly afraid, of course, that this ideal author may have little in common with the real one who is either dead, like Nabokov, or inaccessible, like Pynchon; he always wonders whether he meets the expectations of the real author who is/was to all appearances a very intelligent and imaginative word-handler.

Nabokov, though he claimed not to be concerned about how his novels were read, realized at the end of his career that his many readers had, in a way, reinvented him and taken something from him in the process. In his last novel, *Look at the Harlequins!*, the narrator-protagonist, whose first name is Vadim but whose last name will never be known, though it is said to begin with an N ('Mr. N., a Russian nobleman'; Nabokov 1974: 15), has many things in common with the real author, including a literary work. Like Nabokov, whose career was comparatively well known at the time this last novel was published in 1974, Vadim McNab, as his future brother-in-law humorously calls him, was born in Russia, studied in Cambridge, and wrote novels both in Russian and in English. Their titles are often reminiscent of Nabokov's own titles: *Pawn Takes Queen*, 1927, seems to be the mirror-image of Nabokov's *King, Queen, Knave*, 1928, *Camera Lucida (Slaughter in the Sun)*, 1931, that of *Camera Obscura (Laughter in the Dark)*, 1932, and *Ardis*, 1970, that of *Ada*, 1969. Vadim is acutely aware of these similarities; and he is deeply affected when people confuse him with that other, better-known, writer who, we gather, is none other than Nabokov himself.

Nabokov's other texts, which are mirrored through Vadim's narrative, constitute the chief intertext in the novel. The reader is teased to reconstruct Vadim's novels from what he remembers of Nabokov's own novels. Of course, the newcomer who has not read the author's previous novels is bound to miss many references and little jokes. The Nabokov aficionado, on the other hand, constantly exchanges friendly smiles with the jovial author at the expense of the befuddled narrator whose world and work are undermined by the existence of that other author; at the expense also of the reader who has not read Nabokov's other novels mirrored or twisted in this one. This restricted intertext seems to generate an unprecedented sense of complicity with the author, who turns up constantly on the stage of his own novel, like Hitchcock in his films.

The technique is very deceptive, though. Nabokov's histrionics insidiously build up a dramatic distance between the reader and the author. Vadim is not simply a pale replica of Nabokov. As we follow his bumpy career through three or four marriages, twelve novels, and numberless mental breakdowns, we begin to believe in his existence outside the author who all the time insists on reminding us that he has invented him. Vadim's mental confusion and his incapacity to retrace his steps in imagination, may well be a reflection of the aging author's own embarrassment. He is a replica of the author who is about to die and who realizes that, no matter what he does, he cannot go back, he cannot retrieve his past or rewrite his novels, which will continue to live and be read after him. This last attempt to retake everything has failed since a new layer of writing has been added. His name will continue to be associated in the centuries to come with those of his own inventions because he has allowed his inventions to circulate in thousands, nay millions, of printed books. The author has turned himself into a fiction, as it were, into what Barthes used to call 'un être de papier', and he painfully realizes that he cannot regain his pre-literary self.

In this novel, which prefigures *LETTERS* or *If on a Winter's Night a Traveler*, in which Barth and Calvino indulge in similar histrionics, Nabokov is not only fighting his little battle against the ideal Nabokov we have invented, he is also trying to snub us and to say that he had a much better reader in mind while writing this and his former novels. This better reader is someone like the 'model reader' described by Umberto Eco:

> To make his text communicative, the author has to assume that the ensemble of codes he relies upon is the same as that shared by his possible reader. The author has thus to foresee a model of the possible reader (hereafter Model Reader) supposedly able to deal interpretatively with the expressions in the same way as the author deals generatively with them.
> 
> (Eco 1981: 7)

The real author wants his model reader to be a replica of himself, a projection of his ideal self with which he wants to communicate without any interference from outside. Nabokov once said: 'He [the author] clashes with readerdom because he is his own ideal reader and those other readers are so very often mere lip-moving ghosts and amnesiacs' (Nabokov 1973: 183). He obliquely defined this ideal reader in an interview in which he was talking about the artist's audience:

> His best audience is the person he sees in his shaving mirror every morning. I think that the audience an artist imagines, when he imagines that kind of thing, is a room filled with people wearing his own mask.
> 
> (Nabokov 1973: 18)

The aristocrat in him did not readily accept the idea that the artist could care much about his real audience; he recognized the need, on the other hand, for an ideal reader, that is someone who looked like himself and was infinitely more perceptive and imaginative than any real reader. This ideal reader is not a person but a persona or a function: it is the mirror-image of the author trying to imagine how his text will be deciphered by readers as clever and imaginative as himself.

If we now consider the novelistic text from the author's angle, we have the following diagram:

Real author ⟶ [TEXT] ⟶ Ideal reader

The real author develops an elaborate medium, the text, to communicate with his ideal reader. He wants to ex-press himself, to get things out of himself, so that he may know and respect himself better, love himself better. The problem, of course, is that the ideal reader, whose mirage boosts the real author's ego, cannot exist as a persona unless real readers appropriate the book and voice their aesthetic pleasure and their admiration for the real author. In other words, the text and the ideal self (ideal reader) will be lovable only if the author can get somebody else to love them, that is to say, if he can communicate them to his reader. The tragic alternative is madness.

There is an obvious symmetry between the two diagrams. The text is not a message addressed by a speaker to a listener; it is a medium which brings together but also keeps apart the real author and the real reader, the only real subjects involved. It allows the two masked and distant interlocutors to interact with each other in obscure ways. Yet no matter how brilliant the real author is, how well he has saturated his text, he cannot fully programme its reading. To the author's passionate and compulsive effort to produce the book, an effort which is often sustained for years and sometimes is never completed, the reader, who also wants to love himself through the text, responds by making a sustained effort to gather all the information deposited in the text, in the hope of making contact with the real author.

These complementary efforts are represented in the following diagram which brings together the two diagrams:

$$\begin{matrix} \text{Real author} \longrightarrow \\ \text{Ideal author} \longleftarrow \end{matrix} \Bigg[ \text{ TEXT } \Bigg] \begin{matrix} \longrightarrow \text{Ideal reader} \\ \longleftarrow \text{Real reader} \end{matrix}$$

The two interlocutors communicate tangentially with each other, that is, through ideal projections, or masks, of themselves.

Textual communication is not totally different from oral interaction, though it cannot be equated to conversation as Tristram claimed it could. We cannot communicate with another person unless we wear a mask, the mask of our so-called identity, which tends to change a little with each new conversation. When we are interacting with somebody we do not particularly like, we try to address his unmasked self which shows through the cracks of his armour, and our interlocutor does the same with us, hoping thereby to boost his own identity. When, on the other hand, we are interacting with someone we love, we address the other's masked and ideal self, and the loved one does the same with us, hence the feeling, when being in love, of being lovable, of loving oneself.

The novelist does want to be loved but he also wants to show that he is the master. He intends to remain in the one-up position. The medium he is using, the printed novel, allows him to love himself through the ideal reader reflected by the mirror-like book, while remaining the master of the real reader whom he keeps at a safe distance and sometimes snubs with a haughty 'Do I know you?' This distancing is achieved both through his own narrative strategies, which break the line of communication between himself and the real reader, and through the intervention of the printing and publishing industry, which not only acts as a medium but also as a screen.

The reader acutely senses, on the other hand, that the author's haughtiness is a mask, the mask of the seducer. As Baudrillard explained in his marvellous book on seduction, the 'seducer is he who allows the signs to float, knowing all the time that only their suspense matters and points towards fate' (Baudrillard 1979: 149; my translation). The author does not only want to be loved by the real reader; he wants to seduce him and keep him under his authority, and he does so by letting the 'signs float' and by keeping his text undecidable.

The industry plays a very important part in this communication process. Though it has lost the aura that its complicity with the legislator once gave it, it remains a powerful force, which the author does his best to challenge by saturating his texts and by making them more difficult either to censor or to print accurately, just as Sterne did more than two centuries ago.

# Epilogue
# Is the author really dead?

Since the modernist era, many critics, from Joseph Warren Beach to Roland Barthes, have claimed with Nietzschean accents that the author is dead. In an essay originally published in 1968, Barthes wrote: 'the text is henceforth made and read in such a way that at all its levels the author is absent' (Barthes 1977: 145). This statement made some sense in the wake of the *Nouveau Roman*; it basically implied that such novels as those of Robbe-Grillet have no discursive status and that, therefore, the line of communication between author and reader has been broken. For the illusion of the absence or death of the author derives from the latter's refusal to structure his text as a discourse and, therefore, to submit himself to the law of the Other.

As many critics have realized since, the postmodernist writer, while toying with this idea of the death of the author, which also suggests that the novel may be in the process of dying, does his utmost to impose his authority on his book. One of the most recent statements of the paradox is that of Brian McHale:

> Fully aware that the author has been declared dead, the postmodernist text nevertheless insists on authorial presence, although not consistently. The author flickers in and out of existence at different levels of the ontological structure and at different points in the unfolding text. Neither fully present nor completely absent, s/he plays hide-and-seek with us throughout the text, which projects an illusion of authorial presence only to withdraw it abruptly, filling the void left by this

withdrawal with surrogate subjectivity once again.

(McHale 1987: 202)

The paradox is real, but McHale does little to dissipate it; he puts it in terms which practically apply to most of the major novels written since *Pamela*.

One of the most seminal texts about the status and function of the author is that of Michel Foucault, 'What is an Author?' originally published in 1969. After his introduction on the status of the work, Foucault goes on to discuss the function of the author's name: 'The author's name manifests the appearance of a certain discursive set and indicates the status of this discourse within a society and a culture' (Foucault 1980: 147). This is an important point considering the fact that for a long time the author's name did not appear on the title-page. The modern novel began as an *objet trouvé* which had all the characteristics of a real discourse. The author considered that this discursiveness would have been shattered if he had signed his works since he would have proclaimed himself the ultimate source of his characters' discourses; and the industry alleged that it was better all around to publish the books anonymously in order to protect the author from censorship. Censorship and self-censorship therefore helped promote authorhood considerably, and Foucault explains why: 'Texts, books, and discourses really began to have authors . . . to the extent that authors became subject to punishment, that is, to the extent that discourses could be transgressed' (148). The law of the Other, in spite or because of its perverseness, guaranteed the discursiveness of the novel, and therefore its unity.

Meanwhile, the industry, which manufactured and marketed the product, and claimed to be protecting the author, was supplanting him and appropriating the text. But, very rapidly, it was compelled to surrender some of its prerogatives and to promote what Foucault calls the 'author-function' necessary to the success of the book: 'literary discourses came to be accepted only when endowed with the author-function' (149). In our present era, the author's name (and his portrait, occasionally) is exhibited on the cover and looms larger, sometimes, than the title. Foucault argues that this author-function 'is linked to the juridical and institutional system', that 'it does not affect all discourses in the same way at all times and in all types of civilization', that 'it is not defined by the spontaneous attribution of a discourse to its producer, but rather by a series of specific and complex operations', and finally that 'it does not refer purely and simply to a real individual' (153). Though the author can never be identified absolutely in the course of one's reading, his existence, as a principle of unity of the work, is always posited and recognized. It guarantees that there must be an end to interpretation: 'The author allows a limitation of the cancerous and dangerous proliferation of significations' (158–9). This limitation may not be felt when we are reading an individual novel, but we know at least that it exists as a principle.

This leads Foucault to suggest that the author counts less as a person than as a persona or social figure: 'The author is therefore the ideological figure by which one marks the manner in which we fear the proliferation of meaning' (159). The author-function appeared at a specific moment when western man really started to put the world and its mysteries into print. This function was therefore as much developed by readers and society at large as by writers themselves. Foucault prophesies that, 'as our society changes', this function may 'disappear, and in such a manner that fiction and its polysemic texts will once again function according to another mode, but still with a system of constraint' (160).

Foucault's essay, which offers one of the most perceptive theories of authorhood, fits our theory of textual communication only up to a point. It gives precedence to the social dimension of the phenomenon but fails to take into account the single most important change that gave birth to the 'author-function', that is, the invention of print. The social and ideological environment and the industrial revolution played a very important part, no doubt, in this development, but they would have been totally unable to bring about the rise of the author without Gutenberg's invention, which not only created a new medium but also gave birth to a new industry intimately associated with the law.

Foucault does not sufficiently view the problem from the author's angle. The amount of information actually programmed by a novelist and picked up by the reader remains extraordinary. William Gass used this argument to show that the author is still very much in control:

Yet, when readers read as if the words on the page were only fleeting visual events, and not signs to be sung inside themselves – so that the author's voice is stilled – the author's hand must reach out into the space of the page and put a print upon it that will be unmistakable, uneradicable. With lipstick, perhaps. And if, in their new-found yet unearned annoyance, the critics ululate at the death of the author – one more god gone – we shall merely remind them that we were never myths, rode our lovers to death long since, and before they drew breath, and shall henceforth create texts so intelligent they will read themselves.

(Gass 1983: 41)

There are two important ideas in this passage: first, that the printed page is crammed with signs that the author has done his best to organize in such a way as to suggest a multiplicity of intended significations. Second, that the author is not only trying to serve a function, be it Foucault's author-function, but is fighting his own private war against his readers to boost his ego.

That is where the postmodernist novelist differs from the modernist one. Flaubert, James, or Joyce obliquely acknowledged in the body of their works that they accepted (however reluctantly) the law of the Other. They insisted on simulating plausible discourses, that is, discourses whose unity was guaranteed by the Other; this led them to compose represented discourses which were not proper discourses but poetic styles. Yet, the compulsion remained the same: to ridicule and beat the Other while paying tribute to it. The postmodernist novelists, on the other hand, refuse the authority of that law and want only to impose the private law of their own racked egos. They even refuse to submit to the law of the market which the publishing industry wants them to abide by. Like Gass, they try to promote their own selves and damn the rest of the world. The only evidence that their self-consciousness is not sterile is that it induces a similar self-consciousness in the reader.

With postmodernism, the logic of the medium, print, has reached its ultimate development: the page, which is now technically perfect and never draws the reader's attention to the process of its fabrication through some technical defects, is like a twin-faced mirror reflecting the fantasies and egos of the two protagonists. The industry, while apparently trying to promote the author-function and to please the reader, remains none the less in control, hence the postmodernist demented struggle to defeat it. The postmodernist's self-consciousness, which has been denounced on ideological grounds by Graff (1979) and praised on poetic grounds by Linda Hutcheon (1984) and Brian Stonehill (1988), may be as much an effect of as a reaction to the medium whose law is perhaps more arbitrary than ever.

# Bibliography

This bibliography lists only the works cited or mentioned in the text.

Allott, Miriam, ed. (1980) *Novelists on the Novel* (1959), London: Routledge.
Altman, Janet G. (1982) *Epistolarity: Approaches to a Form*, Columbus: Ohio State University Press.
*Amadis de Gaul* (1974) trans. Edwin B. Place and Herbert C. Behm, Lexington: University Press of Kentucky.
Anon (1762) *A Vindication of the Exclusive Right of Authors to Their Own Works: A Subject Now Under Consideration Before Twelve Judges of England*, London: R. Griffiths.
Aristotle (1958) *Poetics*, trans. G. M. Grube, Indianapolis: Bobbs-Merrill.
Bair, Deirdre (1978) *Samuel Beckett: A Biography*, New York: Harcourt Brace Jovanovich.
Bakhtin, Mikhail (1968) *Rabelais and His World*, trans. Helene Iswolsky, Cambridge: MIT Press.
Balzac, Honoré de (1967) *Le Père Goriot* (1833), Lausanne: Rencontres.
Banfield, Ann (1982) *Unspeakable Sentences*, Boston: Routledge and Kegan Paul.
Barth, John (1985) *The Floating Opera* (1956), London: Granada.
——(1987) *The Tidewater Tales*, New York: Fawcett Columbine.
Barthelme, Donald (1972) *Snow White* (1967), New York: Atheneum.
——(1976) *Unspeakable Practices, Unnatural Acts* (1968), New York: Pocket Book.
Barthes, Roland (1964) *Essais critiques*, Paris: Seuil.
——(1968) 'L'effet de réel', *Communications* 11: 84–9.
——(1973a) *Le Plaisir du texte*, Paris: Seuil.
——(1973b) 'Théorie du texte', *Encyclopaedia Universalis*.
——(1977) 'The death of the author', *Image-Music-Text*, trans. Stephen Heath, New York: Hill and Wang.
Bataille, Georges (1988) 'Interview avec Pierre Dumayet', *Nouvel Observateur*, 7–13 October, 128.
Baudrillard, Jean (1979) *De la séduction*, Paris: Galilée.

——(1981) *Simulacres et simulation*, Paris: Galilée.
Beckett, Samuel (1961) *Comment c'est*, Paris: Minuit.
Behn, Aphra (1987) *Love Letters Between a Nobleman and His Sister* (1684–7) ed. Maureen Duffy, Harmondsworth: Penguin Books.
Belanger, T. (1982) 'Publishers and writers in eighteenth-century England', in Isabel Rivers, (ed.) (1982) *Books and their Readers in Eighteenth-Century England*, New York: St Martin's Press.
Benjamin, Curtis G. (1977) *A Candid Critique of Book Publishing*, New York: R. R. Bowker.
Bennett, H. S. (1970) *English Books and Readers 1603 to 1640*, Cambridge: Cambridge University Press.
Bjornson, Richard (1977) *The Picaresque Hero in European Fiction*, Madison: University of Wisconsin Press.
Booth, Wayne C. (1961) *The Rhetoric of Fiction*, Chicago: University of Chicago Press.
Bradbury, Malcolm (1972) *The Social Context of Modern English Literature*, Oxford: Basil Blackwell.
Bray, Bernard (1983) 'Introduction', *Lettres portugaises* (1669), Paris: Garnier Flammarion.
Brown, Mary Elizabeth (1913) *Dedications: An Anthology of the Forms Used From the Earliest Days of Book-Making to the Present Time*, New York: Burt Franklin.
Butor, Michel (1971) *La modification* (1957), Paris: UGE, 10–18.
Carroll, Lewis (1970) *The Annotated Alice* (1865 and 1871), ed. Martin Gardner, Harmondsworth: Penguin Books.
Cervantes, Miguel de (1949) *Don Quixote* (1605 and 1615), trans. Samuel Putnam, New York: The Modern Library.
Chartier, Roger (1987) *Lectures et lecteurs dans la France de l'Ancien Régime*, Paris: Seuil.
Clanchy, M. T. (1988) 'Hearing and seeing *and* trusting writing', in Eugene R. Kintgen et al. (eds), *Perspectives on Literacy*, Carbondale: Southern Illinois University Press.
Cohen, Murray (1977) *Sensible Words: Linguistic Practice in England 1640-1785*, Baltimore: Johns Hopkins University Press.
Cohn, Dorrit (1978) *Transparent Minds: Narrative Modes for Presenting Consciousness in Fiction*, Princeton: Princeton University Press.
Collier, James Lincoln (1981) 'Can writers *afford* to write books?' *Publishers' Weekly*, 31 July, 1981, 21–4.
Collins, A. S. (1973) *Authorship in the Days of Johnson* (1927), Clifton: Augustus M. Kelley.
Couturier, Maurice (1976) 'Nabokov's *Pale Fire*, or The Purloined Poem', *Revue Française d'Etudes Américaines*, 1 (April 1976), 55–69.
——(1979) *Nabokov*, Lausanne: L'Age d'Homme.
——(1987) 'The death of the real in *The Crying Lot 49*', *Pynchon Notes*, 20–21 (Spring–Fall 1987), 5–30.
——and Durand, Régis (1982) *Barthelme*, London: Methuen.
Day, Geoffrey (1987) *From Fiction to the Novel*, London: Routledge and Kegan Paul.

Defoe, Daniel (1966) *Moll Flanders* (1722), London: Dent, Everyman.
——(1970) *Moll Flanders* (1722), ed. Paul Hunter, New York: Thomas Y. Crowell.
Delany, Paul (1969) *British Autobiography in the Seventeenth Century*, London: Routledge and Kegan Paul.
Derrida, Jacques (1967) *De la grammatologie*, Paris: Minuit.
Dickens, Charles (1971) *Bleak House* (1852–3), Harmondsworth: Penguin Books.
*Dictionary of Literary Biography*, vol. 2: *American Novelists Since World War II* (1978), Detroit: Gale Research Co.
——, Vol. 6: *American Novelists Since World War II, 2nd Series* (1980), Detroit: Gale Research Co.
*Dictionnaire des œuvres* (1984) Paris: Laffont.
Diderot, Denis (1962) *La Religieuse* (1796), Paris: 10–18.
Donaldson, William (1975) *The Life and Adventures of Sir Bartholomew Sapskull* (1768), New York: Garland Publishing (facsimile of 1st edn).
Dreyfus, John and Richaudeau, François (1985) *La chose imprimée*, Paris: Editions Retz.
Dudden, F. Homes (1966) *Henry Fielding: His Life, Works and Times*, Hamden, Conn.: Archon Books.
Dupriez, Bernard (1984) *Gradus*, Paris: UGE.
Eaves, T. C. Duncan and Kimpel, Ben D. (1971) *Samuel Richardson: A Biography*, Oxford: Clarendon Press.
Eco, Umberto (1981) *The Role of the Reader*, London: Hutchinson.
Eisenstein, Elizabeth L. (1979) *The Printing Press as an Agent of Change*, Cambridge: Cambridge University Press.
Ellman, Richard (1959) *James Joyce*, New York: Oxford University Press.
——(1975) *Selected Joyce Letters*, New York: Viking Press.
*Encyclopédie* (1778), 3e édition, Genève: J. L. Pellet.
Farrell, William (1963) 'The style and the action in *Clarissa*', *Studies in English Literature* 3, 3: 365–75.
Faulkner, William (1939) *The Wild Palms*, New York: Random House.
——(1961) *The Wild Palms*, Harmondsworth: Penguin Books.
Febvre, Lucien and Martin, Henri-Jean (1971) *L'Apparition du livre* (1958), Paris: Albin Michel.
Field, Andrew (1986) *The Life of Vladimir Nabokov*, New York: Crown Publishers.
Fielding, Henry (1742) *The History of the Adventures of Joseph Andrews*, 2 vols, London: A. Millar.
——(1749)*The History of Tom Jones*, 6 vols, London: A. Millar.
——(1754) *The Life of Jonathan Wild*, 2nd edn, London: A. Millar.
——(1980) *Tom Jones* (1749), Harmondsworth: Penguin Books.
——(1987) *Joseph Andrews* (1742), ed. Homer Goldberg, New York: Norton.
Flaubert, Gustave (1961) *Madame Bovary* (1857), Paris: Livre de Poche.

——(1965) *Madame Bovary* (1857), trans. Paul de Man, New York: Norton.
Fothergill, Robert A. (1974) *Private Chronicles: A Study of English Diaries*, London: Oxford University Press.
Foucault, Michel (1980) 'What is an author?' (1969), in Josué V. Harrari (ed.) *Textual Strategies*, London: Methuen.
——(1976) *La volonté de savoir*, Paris: Gallimard.
Friedman, Melvin (1955) *Stream of Consciousness: A Study in Literary Method*, New Haven: Yale University Press.
Furet, F. and Sachs, W. (1974) 'La croissance de l'alphabétisation en France, XVIIIe–XIXe siècle', *Annales. Economies, sociétés, civilisation* 29: 714–37.
Gass, William (1983) 'Tropes of the text', in Maurice Couturier (ed.) *Representation and Performance in Postmodern Fiction*, Montpellier: Delta.
Genette, Gérard (1972) *Figures III*, Paris: Seuil.
——(1986) 'Introduction à l'architexte', *Théorie des genres*, Paris: Seuil-Points.
Gide, André (1958) *L'Immoraliste* (1902), in *Romans*, Paris: Gallimard-Pléiade.
Gifford, Don and Seidman, Robert J. (1974) *Notes for Joyce: An Annotation of James Joyce's Ulysses*, New York: E. P. Dutton.
Glaister, Geoffrey Ashall (1960) *Glossary of the Book*, London: George Allen and Unwin.
Gopnik, Irwin (1970) *A Theory of Style and Richardon's Pamela*, The Hague: Mouton.
Graff, Gerald (1979) *Literature Against Itself: Literary Ideas in Modern Society*, Chicago: University of Chicago Press.
Guenot, Jean (1982) *Ecrire*, St Cloud: chez Jean Guenot.
Hamburger, Käte (1986) *Logique des genres littéraires* (1977), trans. Pierre Cadiot, Paris: Seuil.
Hawthorne, Nathaniel (1902) *The Scarlet Letter* (1850), ed. Sculley Bradley et al., New York: Norton.
Head, Richard (1961) *The English Rogue* (1665), ed. Michael Shinagel, Boston: New Frontiers Press.
Howell, Wilbur S. (1971) *Eighteenth-Century British Logic and Rhetoric*, Princeton: Princeton University Press.
Humphrey, Robert (1954) *Stream of Consciousness in the Modern Novel*, Berkeley: University of California Press.
Hutcheon, Linda (1984) *Narcissistic Narrative*, New York: Methuen.
James, Henry (1934) *The Art of the Novel*, ed. Richard P. Blackmur, New York: Charles Scribner's Sons.
——(1954) *What Maisie Knew* (1897), New York: Doubleday Anchor Books.
——(1966) *The Turn of the Screw* (1898), ed. Robert Kimbrough, New York: Norton.
——(1978) 'The art of fiction' (1884), *The English Novel*, ed. Stephen Hazell, London: Macmillan.
——(1981) *The Bostonians* (1885), Harmondsworth: Penguin Books.

Jennett, Seán (1973) *The Making of Books*, London: Faber and Faber.
Johannot, Yvonne (1978) *Quand le livre devient de poche*, Grenoble: Presses Universitaires de Grenoble.
Johnson, Samuel (1755) *A Dictionary of the English Language*, 2 vols, London: Printed by W. Strahan, for J. and P. Knapton *et al.*
Joyce, James (1964) *A Portrait of the Artist as a Young Man* (1916), London: Heinemann.
——(1969) *Ulysses* (1922), Harmondsworth: Penguin Books.
Kennedy, George A. (1980) *Classical Rhetoric and Its Christian and Secular Tradition*, Chapel Hill: University of North Carolina Press.
Kingston, Paul William and Cole, Jonathan R. (1986) *The Wages of Writing: Per Word, Per Piece, or Perhaps*, New York: Columbia University Press.
Krupp, Lewis Mansfield (1963) *Tobias Smollett, Doctor of Man and Manners* (1949), New York: Russell and Russell.
Laclos, Choderlos de (1924) *Dangerous Acquaintances* (1782), trans. Richard Aldington, London: Routledge.
Lane, Michael (1982) *Books and Publishers: Commerce Against Culture in Postwar Britain*, Toronto: Lexington Books.
Laugaa, Maurice (1986) *La Pensée du pseudonyme*, Paris: PUF.
Lawrence, D. H. (1965) *Lady Chatterley's Lover* (1928), Harmondsworth: Penguin Books.
Lennox, Charlotte (1974) *Female Quixote* (1752), New York: Garland Publishing (facsimile of 1st edn).
Lewis, Felice Flanery (1976) *Literature, Obscenity, and Law*, Carbondale, Ill: Southern Illinois University Press.
Lhomeau, Franck and Coelho, Alain (1988) *Marcel Proust à la recherche d'un éditeur*, Paris: Olivier Orban.
*(The) Life of Lazarillo de Tormes and His Fortunes and Adventures* (1917), trans. Louis How, New York: Mitchell Kennerley.
Lough, John (1978) *Writer and Public in France from the Middle Ages to the Present Day*, Oxford: Clarendon Press.
Lubbock, Percy (1957) *The Craft of Fiction* (1921), New York: Viking Press.
Lukacs, Georg (1971) *The Theory of the Novel* (1920), trans. Anna Bostock, London: Merlin Press.
Lyons, Martyn (1987) *Le Triomphe du livre: Une histoire sociologique de la lecture dans la France du XIXe siècle*, Paris: Promodis, Editions du Cercle de la Librairie.
McCaffery, Larry, ed. (1986) *Postmodern Fiction*, New York: Greenwood Press.
McFarlane, Gavin (1982) *A Practical Introduction to Copyright*, London: McGraw-Hill.
McHale, Brian (1987) *Postmodernist Fiction*, New York: Methuen.
McKenni, D. F. (1976) *The London Book Trade in the Later Seventeenth Century*, printed privately.
McKeon, Michael (1987) *The Origins of the English Novel*, Baltimore: Johns Hopkins University Press.

Mackinnon, Frank (1988) 'Notes on the history of English copyright', in Margaret Drabble (ed.) *The Oxford Companion to English Literature*, Oxford: Clarendon Press.
McLuhan, Marshall (1962) *The Gutenberg Galaxy*, Toronto: University of Toronto Press.
McMurtrie, Douglas C. (1941) *The Gutenberg Documents*, New York: Oxford University Press.
Martens, Lorna (1985) *The Diary Novel*, Cambridge: Cambridge University Press.
Martin, H.J. (1988) *Histoire et pouvoirs de l'écrit*, Paris: Librairie Académique Perrin.
Melville, Herman (1987) *Moby Dick* (1851), Harmondsworth: Penguin Books.
Mumby, Frank A. (1967) *The Romance of Book Selling: A History from the Earliest Times to the Twentieth Century*, Metuchen, NJ: Scarecrow Reprint Corporation.
——(1982), ed. Ian Norrie, *Publishing and Bookselling in the Twentieth Century*, London: Bell and Hyman.
Nabokov, Vladimir (1962) *Pale Fire*, London: Weidenfeld and Nicolson.
——(1969) *Ada*, London: Weidenfeld and Nicolson.
——(1970) *The Annotated Lolita*, New York: McGraw-Hill.
——(1973) *Strong Opinions*, London: Weidenfeld and Nicolson.
——(1974) *Look at the Harlequins!*, New York: McGraw-Hill.
Newton, A. Edward (1971) *The Format of the English Novel* (1928), New York: Burt Franklin.
Ong, Walter J. (1982) *Orality and Literacy*, London: Methuen.
*(Le) Petit Robert* (1988) Paris: Le Robert.
Plant, Marjorie (1965) *The English Book Trade*, 2nd edn, London: G. Allen and Unwin.
Pottinger, David T. (1958) *The French Book Trade in the Ancien Régime 1500–1791*, Cambridge, MA: Harvard University Press.
Prince, Gerald (1973) 'Introduction à l'étude du narrataire', *Poétique* 14: 178–96.
Proust, Marcel (1934) *Remembrance of Things Past*, vol. I, trans. C. K. Scott Moncrieff, New York: Random House.
——(1954) *A la recherche du temps perdu*, 3 vols (1913–27), Paris: Gallimard-Pléiade.
Pynchon, Thomas (1974) *The Crying of Lot 49* (1966), Harmondsworth: Penguin Books.
——(1975) *Gravity's Rainbow* (1973), London: Picador.
Quennell, Peter (1963) 'Introduction to *Memoirs of a Woman of Pleasure*', *Fanny Hill*, New York: P. Putnam's Sons.
Quirk, Randolph et al. (1972) *A Grammar of Contemporary English*, London: Longman.
Rabelais, François (1973) *Œuvres complètes*, ed. Guy Demerson, Paris: Seuil.
Rembar, Charles (1968) *The End of Obscenity: The Trials of Lady*

*Chatterley, Tropic of Cancer* and *Fanny Hill*, New York: Random House.
Ricardou, Jean (1973) *Le Nouveau roman*, Paris: Seuil.
Richardson, Samuel (1741a) *Pamela; or Virtue Rewarded*, 2 vols, London: C. Rivington and J. Osborn.
—— (1741b) *Pamela*, 2nd edn, London: C. Rivington and J. Osborn.
—— (1742) *Pamela: or Virtue Rewarded*, second part, 2 vols, London: C. Rivington and J. Osborn.
—— (1748) *Clarissa; or, the History of a Young Lady*, 8 vols, London: Printed for S. Richardson and sold by A. Millar *et al.*
—— (1980) *Pamela*, Harmondsworth: Penguin Books.
—— (1985) *Clarissa*, Harmondsworth: Penguin Books.
Robbe-Grillet, Alain (1965a) *Jealousy* (1957), trans. Richard Howard, New York: Grove Press.
—— (1965b) *For a New Novel* (1963), trans. Richard Howard, New York: Grove Press.
Ross, C. L. (1979) *The Composition of the Rainbow and Women in Love*, Charlottesville: University Press of Virginia.
Rosset, Clément (1979) *L'Objet singulier*, Paris: Minuit.
Rousseau, Jean-Jacques (1964) *Lettres de deux amans (La Nouvelle Héloïse*, 1761) in *Œuvres complètes*, vol 2, Paris: Pléiade-Gallimard.
Sartre, J. P. (1948) 'Qu'est-ce que la littérature?', in *Situations II*, Paris: Gallimard.
Shatzkin, Leonard (1982) *In Cold Type: Overcoming the Book Crisis*, Boston: Houghton Mifflin.
Shebbeare, John (1974) *Lydia* (1755), New York: Garland Publishing.
Souchu, Laurent, alias Maurice Couturier (1984) 'Le texte à trous: *The Bostonians*', *Revue Française d'Etudes Américains*, 20 (May 1984), 195–207.
Spufford, Margaret (1981) *Small Books and Pleasant Memories: Popular Fiction and Its Readership in Seventeenth-Century England*, Athens, Ga.: University of Georgia Press.
Stanzel, F. K. (1984) *A Theory of Narrative* (1979), trans. Charlotte Goedsche, Cambridge: Cambridge University Press.
Sterne, Laurence (1761) *The Life and Opinions of Tristram Shandy*, vol. IV, London: R. and J. Dodsley.
—— (1965) *The Life and Opinions of Tristram Shandy*, ed. Ian Watt, Boston: Houghton Mifflin.
—— (1980) *The Life and Opinions of Tristram Shandy*, ed. Howard Anderson, New York: Norton.
—— (n.d.) *A Sentimental Journey* (1769), London: Thomas Nelson and Sons.
Stonehill, Brian (1988) *The Self-Conscious Novel*, Philadelphia: University of Pennsylvania Press.
Sutherland, John (1976) *Victorian Novelists and Publishers*, London: Athlone Press.
—— (1978) *Fiction and the Fiction Industry*, London: Athlone Press.
Tebbel, John (1981) *A History of Book Publishing in the United States*, vol. IV, 1940–80, New York: R. R. Bowker.

Thomas, Donald (1969) *A Long Time Burning: The History of Literary Censorship in England*, New York: Frederick A. Praeger.
Tribe, David (1973) *Questions of Censorship*, New York: St Martin's Press.
Versini, Laurent (1979) *Le Roman épistolaire*, Paris: PUF.
Vessillier-Ressi, Michèle (1982) *Le Métier d'auteur*, Paris: Dunod.
Viala, Alain (1985) *Naissance de l'écrivain*, Paris: Minuit.
Wagner, Peter (1985) 'Introduction to *Fanny Hill*,' in John Cleland, *Fanny Hill*, Harmondsworth: Penguin Books.
Walters, Ray (1985) *Paperback Talk*, Chicago: Academy Chicago Publishers.
Warburton, William (1747) *A Letter from an Author to a Member of Parliament, concerning Literary Property*, London: Printed for J. and P. Knapton.
——(1762) *An Enquiry into the Nature and Origin of Literary Property*, London: Printed for William Flexney.
Watt, Ian (1965) 'Introduction to *Tristram Shandy*', in Laurence Sterne, *Tristram Shandy*, Boston: Houghton Mifflin.
——(1967) *The Rise of the Novel* (1957), Berkeley: University of California Press.
Watzlawick, Paul et al. (1967) *Pragmatics of Human Communication*, New York: Norton.
Williams, Ioan (1970) *Novel and Romance, 1700–1800*, New York: Barnes and Noble.
——(1979) *The Idea of the Novel in Europe, 1600–1800*, London: Macmillan.
Wittenberg, Philip (1978) *The Protection of Literary Property*, Boston: The Writer, Inc.
Woolf, Virginia (1967) *Mrs Dalloway* (1925), Harmondsworth: Penguin Books.
——(1978) *A Writer's Diary* (1953), ed. Leonard Woolf, St Albans: Panther.

# Index

Abish, Walter 199
Addison, Joseph 37
Altman, Janet G. 134, 138
*Amadis de Gaul* 3-4, 11, 98
Amboise, Michel d' 125
Amyot, Jacques 4
Anonymity 60-6
*Antonius and Aurelia* 11
Apuleius *The Golden Ass* 110-11
Aristotle 97-8
Arnauld, Antoine 94
*Aucassin et Nicolette* 3
Austin, J. L. x

Bacon, Francis 94
Baïf, J. A. 4
Baillet, Adrien 61
Bakhtin, Mikhail 120
Balzac, Guez de 126
Balzac, Honoré de 48, 150, 151, 160-1
Balzac, Jean 34
Banfield, Ann xi, 180-2, 187-8
Barbauld, Anna L. 96, 109, 138
Barrin, Jean *Venus in the Cloister* 30, 31, 43
Barronso, Christophe de 125
Barth, John 81, 114-15, 199, 200, 214, 227
Barthelme, Donald xi, 70, 181, 199, 200, 201; *Snow White* 211, 213-15
Barthes, Roland 46, 51, 93, 168, 174, 209, 223, 227, 231
Bataille, Georges 64

Bateson, Gregory x
Baudrillard, Jean 222, 230
Baumbach, Jonathan 200
Beach, Joseph Warren 231
Beach, Sylvia 152
Beckett, Samuel 193, 202, 215; *Comment c'est* 211-12
Behn, Aphra *Love Letters Between a Nobleman and His Sister* 126-9
Belanger, Terry 17, 22
Bellay, Joachim du 4
Benjamin, Curtis G. 198
Bennett, Arnold 150
Bentley, Thomas 147, 148, 150
*Beowulf* 97
Besant, Walter 147
*Bibliographia Gallicana* 19
*Bibliographia Parisiana* 19
*Bibliothèque bleue* 9-15, 46, 197
Bjornson, Richard 112, 120
Blair, Hugh 141
Blatty, William P. 196
Boccacio, Giovanni 6, 154
Booth, Wayne C. viii, 106-8
Borges, J. L. 111
*(The) Boudoir* 154
Bradbury and Evans 150
Bradbury, Malcolm 146
Brahm, Alcanter de 56
Brande, Dorothea 196
Brautigan, Richard 199, 200
Bray, Bernard
Breton, Nicholas 126
Brontë, Emily 195

Brown, Mary Elizabeth 70
Budgen, Frank 179
Buffon, G. L. 40
Bullock, William 147–8
Burgess, Anthony 194
Burroughs, William 202
Butler, Samuel 196
Butor, Michel 197; *La Modification* 209–11, 212

Cabell, J. B. *Jurgen* 157
*Cabinets de lecture* 20
Caldwell, Erskine 205
Calmette, Gaston 150
Calvino, Italo 227
Campbell, George 94–5
Campbell, Lord 153
Camus, Albert 197
*Canard* 9–10
Carroll, Lewis *Alice in Wonderland* 78–9
Carver, Raymond 199
Caxton, William 98
Censorship (seventeenth and eighteenth centuries) 24–36 (late nineteenth and early twentieth centuries) 153–8 (since World War II) 201–6
Cervantes, Miguel de *Don Quixote* 3, 7–8, 57, 66, 96, 98–105, 108, 219
*(La) Chanson de Roland* 3
Chapbooks 9–15
Chapman and Hall 149, 150
Chariton 126
Chartier, Roger 9–12, 45
*(La) Châtelaine de Vergi* 3
Chaucer, Geoffrey 4
Chesterfield, Philip 139
Chorier, Nicholas *L'Académie des dames* 34
Chrétien de Troyes 97
Christie, Agatha 195
Circulating libraries 20
Clanchy, M. T. 1
Cleland, John *Memoirs of a Woman of Pleasure (Fanny Hill)* 30–1, 57, 58, 113, 120, 124, 154, 203, 204, 205

Cockburn, Alexander 153
*Code Michaux* 33
Cohen, Murray 43, 55, 94
Cohn, Dorrit 179, 181
Collier, James Lincoln 201
Collins, A. S. 20, 22, 42, 43
Collins, Benjamin 19
Commission on Obscenity and Pornography 205
Comstock Law 154, 204
Conger and New Conger 22
Congreve, William 37, 139–40
Constable, Archibald 148
Cooper, James Fenimore 46
Coover, Robert 199, 200, 201
Copeau, Jacques 150
Copyright (seventeenth and eighteenth centuries) 24–36, 50; (nineteenth and twentieth centuries) 152–3 (since World War II) 201
Corneille, Pierre 40
*Cremone* 154
*Critical Review* 19
Cronkite, Walter 212
Cunningham, John 9
Curll, Edmund 30

D'Alembert, Jean 40
Daudet, Lucien 150
Davenant, William 98
Davenport, Guy 199
Day, Geoffrey 138
Dedications 5–6, 8, 67–70
Defoe, Daniel 20, 27, 147, 190; *Moll Flanders* 58, 59, 60, 67, 71–4, 77–9, 83–4, 110, 119, 120, 121, 124, 129, 191
Delany, Paul 111
De Lillo, Don 199
Derrida, Jacques 47, 215
Descartes, René 34
Dick, Philip K. 199
Dickens, Charles 46, 148, 149, 150; *Bleak House* 159–63, 165, 169, 173–4, 181, 207
Diderot, Denis 34, 35–6, 40, 41, 120, 143; *La Religieuse* 113, 121

## Index

Doctorow, E. L. 196
Dodsley, Robert 20, 39
Dolet, Etienne 33
*Don Bellianis of Greece* 11
Donaldson, William *The Life and Adventures of Sir Bartholomew Sapskull* 55, 64–5
Dos Passos, John *Manhattan Transfer* 157
Double bind 78–9
Dreiser, Theodore *Sister Carrie* 156; *An American Tragedy* 157
Dryden, John 37, 98
Du Camp, Maxime 154
Duclos, Charles 37
Dujardin, Edouard 177
Dumas, Alexander 147, 150, 151
Durand, Etienne 33
Dürer, Albrecht 111

Eco, Umberto 227–8
Eisenstein, Elizabeth L. 23, 42, 49
Elkin, Stanley 199, 200, 201
*Encyclopédie* 35–6, 62
English Society of Authors 151
Estival, Robert 146

*(La) Farce de Maître Pathelin* 3
Farrell, William 136
Faulkner, William 200; *The Sound and the Fury* 142; *Mosquitoes* 157; *The Wild Palms* 203, 205
Febvre, Lucien and Martin, H. J. 1–3, 17, 40
Federman, Raymond 199, 215
Fénelon, François 147
Fiction Collective 38, 199, 200–1
Fielding, Henry 20, 31, 39, 67, 124, 141, 190; *Shamela* 31, 59; *Joseph Andrews* 16, 53, 58, 65, 96, 104–6, 140; *The Life of Mr Jonathan Wild* 54, 66; *Tom Jones* 30, 37, 43, 52, 53, 58, 60, 65, 67–9, 95, 96, 106–10, 154, 172, 180–1; *Amelia* 20–1
Fielding, Sarah 124; *The Adventures of David Simple* 67
*Fierabras* 14
*Flamenca* 3
Flaubert, Gustave 87, 203, 234; *Madame Bovary* 154–6, 158–9, 163–4, 169, 173, 182–4, 187, 208, 213
Fleury, Claude 147
Fontenelle, Bernard Le Bovier de 34
Format of books 52–3
Fothergill, Robert A. 111
Foucault, Michel ix, xi, 119–20, 232–4
Frank, Anne 196, 197
Free indirect style 180–9
Friedman, Melvin 177
Froissart, Jean 3
Fulwood, William 125
Furet, François 44
Furetière, Antoine 3

Gaddis, William 199
Gallimard, Editions 196
Garnier, Etienne 11
Garth, Samuel 136
Gass, William 52, 199, 200, 201, 233–4
Gay, John 37
Geneste, de La 13
Genet, Jean 202
Genette, Gérard viii, 73, 96, 169–71
Gent, I.-W. 126
Gent, Thomas 21
Gerald of Wales 1, 8
Gibbon, Edward 98
Gide, André 172; *L'Immoraliste* 119, 165–8, 210–11
Gifford, Don and Seidman, Robert J. 178
Gildon, Charles 126
Ginzburg, Ralph 205
Girodias, Maurice 201–2

Gissing, George 150, 151
Goffman, Erving x
Golding, William 196
Goldsmith, Oliver 20, 38, 39
Goody, Jack 49
Gopnik, Irwin 136
Graff, Gerald 235
Graff, Robert de 195
Grasset, Bernard 150-1, 196
Gray, Thomas 20
Gréban, Arnoul 5
Greene, Robert *Dorastus and Fawnia* 11
Greenwood, James 55-6
Grice, H. P. x
Griffiths, Ralph 30
Guenot, Jean 65
Guillerages, Gabriel de Lavergne 62; *Lettres portugaises* 126, 128
Guilleri, Philippe and Mathurin 12-14
Gusdorf, Georges 111
Gutenberg, Johann 1, 48, 95, 111, 121, 143, 145, 147, 221, 233

Halkett and Laing 61
Hamburger, Käte 96, 181
Hardy, Thomas 150
Harris, Frank 201
Hassan, Ihab 193
Hawkes, John 199, 200
Hawkesworth, John 31
Hawthorne, Nathaniel *The Scarlet Letter* 80-2
Head, Richard *The English Rogue* 58, 115-20, 127
Héroët, Antoine 4
Hervé-Bazin 197
Hilliard, Nicholas 111
Hilton, James 195
Hinxman, John 21
Hitchcock, Alfred 227
Hoban, Russell 199
Hobbes, Thomas 98
Holcroft, Thomas 141
Howell, Wilbur S. 93
Hugo, Victor 118, 150, 151

Hume, David 21
Humphrey, Robert 177
Hutcheon, Linda 235
Hutton, William 21

Ideal author 225-7
Ideal reader 227-9
Implied author 108-10
Interior monologue 177-80
Irving, John 199

James, Henry 151, 189, 234; *The Bostonians* 174-7, 184-6; *What Maisie Knew* 165; *The Turn of the Screw* 82-3; *The Ambassadors* 120
Johnson, Marmaduke 154
Johnson, Samuel 4, 18, 20, 31, 38, 70, 98, 139, 140
Johnston, William 19
*Journal des savants* 19
Joyce, James 151-2, 193, 215, 234; *A Portrait of the Artist as a Young Man* 73-4, 100; *Ulysses* 141, 154, 157, 158, 177-80, 204; *Finnegans Wake* 48

Kafka, Franz 193
Kahane, Jack 201
Kames, Lord 98
Katz, Steve 199
Kennedy, George A. 93
Kit-Kat Club 38
Klein, Justice Arthur G. 204
Knox, Vicesimus 31-2
Kosinski, Jerzy 199

La Calprénède, G. de Costes 39
Lacan, Jacques x, 171
Laclos, Choderlos de 218; *Les Liaisons dangereuses* 71, 76-7, 79, 135
La Fayette, Mme de *La Princesse de Clèves* 139, 143
Laffont, Robert 196
La Fontaine, Jean de 36, 147
La Harpe, J. F. 40
Lane, Alan 195

Lane, John 156
Lawrence, D. H. *Women in Love* 156–8; *Lady Chatterley's Lover* 157, 202–4
Le Guin, Ursula 199
Lennox, Charlotte *Female Quixote* 69
Léon, Manuel de 124
Le Petit, Claude *Bordel des muses* 34
Lesage, Alain-René *Gil Blas* 116, 120
L'Estrange, Roger 22, 25–7
Lévy, Michel 154
Lewis, Sinclair 157
Licensing Acts (1662) 25–7; (1709) 27–8
*(The) Life of Lazarillo de Tormes and His Fortunes and Adventures* 96, 112–15
Lintot, Bernard 20
Livre de Poche 196–7
Locke, John 27, 94
Lough, John 5, 40
Louys, Pierre 202
Lubbock, Percy *The Craft of Fiction* 181, 190–1
Lukacs, Georg *The Theory of the Novel* 142
Lyons, Martyn 147
Lyttleton, George 67–8

McCaffery, Larry 199
McElroy, Joseph 199, 215
McFarlane, Gavin
McHale, Brian 231–2
Machaut, Guillaume de 5, 125
McKeon, Michael 99
McLuhan, Marshall *The Gutenberg Galaxy* vii–x, 48, 95, 126, 142, 193, 220
Macmillan 150
Maittaire, Michael 56
Major, Clarence 200–1
Malesherbes, C. G. de Lamoignon 36, 41
Mallarmé, Stéphane 87
Malory, Thomas 98
Malraux, André 197

Manton, Justice Martin T. 158
Marivaux, Pierre 40
Martens, Lorna 111
Martin, H. J. 1
Matthews, Harry 199
Mauriac, François 197
Melville, Herman *Moby Dick* 79–80
Michener, James A. 196
Millar, Andrew 20–1, 28, 67, 68
Miller, Henry 201, 204
Milleran *Secrétaire des courtisans* 125
Millhauser, Steven 199
Millot, Michel *(L') Escole des filles* 26
Milton, John 25; *Paradise Lost* 16, 39, 97
Mishkin, Edward 205
Model reader 110, 227–8
Molière 33, 40
Montagu, Charles 37
Montaigne, Michel Eyquem de 112
Montalvo, Garcia Rodriguez de 3–4, 98
Montesquieu, Charles de Segondat 34
*Monthly Review* 19
Morellet, André 40
Morin, A. 11
Mudie, Charles Edward 149
Munday, Anthony *Paladine of England* 11
Murphy, Arthur 141

Nabokov, Vladimir xi, 193, 200, 201–2, 228; *Lolita* 65, 83–6, 117, 119; *Pale Fire* 142, 215–20; *Ada* 48, 89, 128, 131; *Look at the Harlequins* 226–7
Nadeau, Maurice 167–8
Net Book Agreement 148
Neville, Henry 154
New Rhetoric 93–7
Newbery, John 18
Newnes, George 148
Newton, A. Edward 64

Newton, Isaac 37

Obscene Publications Act (1857) 153 (1959) 30, 202–3
Occasionnels 12
Ong, Walter J. vii, 7, 47–50, 93, 111–12, 120, 121, 140, 141–3
Ordonnance de Moulins 33
Osborne, John 60, 66
Otway, Thomas 136
Oudot, Jean 12, 14
Oudot, Nicolas 11
Oudot, Nicolas II 13

Palmerin in England 11
Paperback 195–8
Parker, Dorothy 196
Parry, Milman 119
Patient Griselda 11
(The) Pearl 154
Penguin Books 195, 202–3
Pepys, Samuel 10–11, 26
Phillips, Jayne Anne 199
Philosophical Transactions 19
Pierre de Provence 14
Pinard, Ernest 154–5, 157, 164
Pinget, Robert 197
Pinker, J. B. 150
Piracy 23, 28–9
Pirsig, Robert 199
Plant, Marjorie 15–17
Plato 94, 168
Poe, E. A. 142, 218
Pope, Alexander 20, 37, 98
Preambles 6–8, 66–86
Prefaces (eighteenth-century) 70–9; (nineteenth and twentieth centuries) 79–86
Prévost, Antoine (Abbé) 34
Price, Richard Observations on the Nature of Civil Liberty 16
Prince, Gerald 90
Privileges 6–8, 14, 23, 35
Proclamation Society 153
Proust, Marcel viii, 172; Remembrance of Things Past 61, 119, 150–1, 162, 168–71, 191
Prynne, William 24

Publishing (until the seventeenth century) 1–15; (eighteenth century) 15–41; (late nineteenth and early twentieth centuries) 145–52; (since World War II) 194–201
Puzo, Mario 196
Pye, Henry 43
Pynchon, Thomas 2, 49, 199, 215; The Crying of Lot 49 220–6; Gravity's Rainbow 48, 196

Quarles, Francis Argalus and Parthenia 11
(Les) Quatre fils d'Aymon 14
Queneau, Raymond 202
Quevedo Villegas, Francisco de 124; Historia de la vida del Buscón 13–14

Rabelais, François 6–7, 14, 113, 118, 154
Racine, Jean 40
Ralph, J. 38
Reed, Ishmael 199
Rembar, Charles 204–5
Rembrandt 111
Richards, I. A. viii
Richardson, Samuel 28–9, 31, 56, 62–4, 67, 79, 96, 125, 218; Pamela 31, 43, 53, 54, 58, 60, 64, 66, 71, 74–7, 95, 104, 105, 110, 124, 126, 128–35, 138, 219; Clarissa 44, 53, 54, 55, 58, 59, 60, 86, 135–8; Sir Charles Grandison 16, 44
Rivington, Charles 60, 66
Robbe-Grillet, Alain 168, 231; Jealousy 197, 207–9, 211, 212
Robertson, William 21
Ronsard, Pierre de 4, 5
Ross, C. L. 156
Rosset, Clément 121
Roth, Samuel 204
Rousseau, Jean-Jacques 34–5, 40–1, 45, 52, 53, 61, 143, 146

## 250 Index

Rousset, Jean 168
Rudel, Jaufre 1
Ruffhead, Owen 141
Russian Formalism viii

Sainte-Beuve, C. A. 151, 168
Saint-Exupéry, Antoine de 197
Salinger, J. D. 205
Salten, Felix 195
Sarraute, Nathalie 197
Sartre, J. P. 41, 197
Saussure, Ferdinand de 47, 224
Scarron, Paul 39, 139, 143
Scott, Walter 145-6
Scott-Moncrieff, C. K. 169
Searle, J. R. x
Secker, Martin 156
Sellon, Edward 154
Sénard, Marie-Antoine-Jules 155, 164, 203
Serre, Puget de la 125
Seuil, Editions du 196
Shatzkin, Leonard 199
Shebbeare, John *Lydia* 58, 69
Sheldon, Sidney 196
Sherlock, Thomas (Bishop) *Letter from the Lord Bishop of London* 16
Simon, Claude 197
Smith, Adam 94
Smith, Thorne 196
Smith, W. H. 150
Smith, Wallace 201
Smollett, Tobias 18-19, 39, 53, 120, 141, 142
*Société des Gens de Lettres* 151
Society for the Encouragement of Learning 38, 67
Society for the Reformation of Manners 27
*Sodom: or, The Quintessence of Debauchery* 26-7
Sorrentino, Gilbert 199
Soulié, Frédéric 151
Spufford, Margaret 9-10
Stanzel, F. K. 96, 105, 181, 182
Stationers' Company 21-2, 24-5, 27-8, 152
Sterne, Laurence 20, 39, 64, 141, 230; *Tristram Shandy* xi, 55, 56, 60, 63-4, 69-70, 87-92, 96, 120, 121-3, 142, 191, 229; *A Sentimental Journey* 92
Stonehill, Brian 235
Strawson, P. F. x
Stream of consciousness 177
Sue, Eugène 150
Sukenick, Ronald 199, 200-1, 215
Sutherland, J. A. 30, 199
Swift, Jonathan 16, 31, 39

Taylor, William 20, 28
Tebbel, John 199
*Term Catalogue* 26
Thackeray, William M. 31
Theroux, Alexander 199
Thomas, Donald 26
Thomson, James 20, 28, 37
*(The) Thousand and One Nights* 147
Tindal, Matthew 27
Title-pages 56-66
Tonson, Jacob 20, 37
*(A) Treatise of the Use of Flogging in Venereal Affairs* 30
Trollope, Anthony 149
Twyn, John 26
Tyard, Pontus de 4

Untermeyer, Louis 204
Urfé, Honoré d' 39, 128

Vendryes, Joseph 170
Versini, Laurent 125, 126
Vessillier-Ressi, Michèle 199
Viau, Théophile de 34
Vicarion, Palmiro 202
Vice Society 153
Voiture, Vincent 126
Voltaire 35, 40
Vonnegut, Kurt 199
*Voyage de Jean de Mandeville* 3

Walpole, Horace 38
Warburton, William 29, 50

Warton, Thomas 98
Watt, A. P. 150
Watt, Ian vii, ix, 16, 46, 56, 133, 140
Watzlawick, Paul x
Weaver, Harriet Shaw 152
Wechel, Christian 6
Weidenfeld and Nicolson 202
Wharton, Edith 151
Whitehead, Paul 38
*(The) Whore's Rhetorick* 26
Wilberforce, William 153
Wickens, John 26
Wilder, Thornton 196

Williams, Ioan 138
Wittenberg, Philip 37
Wolfe, Tom 199
Woolf, Virginia 43, 141, 151, 215; *Mrs Dalloway* 186–7
Woolsey, Justice John M. 157–8, 178–9
Worde, Wynkyn de 23
Wythorne, Thomas 111

Xenophon Ephesius 125

Young, Edward 20, 37